Start Your Own

SELF-PUBLISHING
BUSINESS

Additional titles in *Entrepreneur's* **Startup Series**

Start Your Own

Bar or Club

Bed & Breakfast

Business on eBay

Business Support Service

Car Wash

Child Care Service

Cleaning Service

Clothing Store

Coin-Operated Laundry

Consulting

Crafts Business

e-Business

e-Learning Business

Event Planning Business

Executive Recruiting Service

Freight Brokerage Business

Gift Basket Service

Growing and Selling Herbs and Herbal
   Products

Home Inspection Service

Import/Export Business

Information Consultant Business

Law Practice

Lawn Care or Landscaping Business

Mail Order Business

Medical Claims Billing Service

Personal Concierge Service

Personal Training Business

Pet-Sitting Business

Restaurant and Five Other Food Businesses

Retail Business and More

Seminar Production Business

Staffing Service

Travel Business

Vending Business

Wedding Consultant Business

Wholesale Distribution Business

startup

Start Your Own

2ND EDITION

SELF-PUBLISHING BUSINESS

Your Step-by-Step Guide to Success

Entrepreneur Press and Jennifer Dorsey

EP
Entrepreneur.
Press

Editorial Director: Jere L. Calmes
Managing Editor: Marla Markman
Cover Design: Beth Hansen-Winter
Production and Composition: Eliot House Productions

This publication is designed to provide accurate and authoritative information in regard to
the subject matter covered. It is sold with the understanding that the publisher is not
engaged in rendering legal, accounting or other professional services. If legal advice or other
expert assistance is required, the services of a competent professional person should be
sought.

Library of Congress Cataloging-in-Publication Data
   Dorsey, Jennifer.
      Start your own self-publishing business/by Entrepreneur Press and Jennifer Dorsey.—
2nd ed.
         p.   cm.
      Includes index.
      ISBN-13: 978-1-59918-103-5 (alk. paper)
      ISBN-10: 1-59918-103-7 (alk. paper)
         1. Self-publishing. 2. New business enterprises—Management. I. Entrepreneur
Press. II. Title.

Z285.5.A33 2007
070.5'93—dc22   2007022371

Printed in Canada
12 11 10 09 08   10 9 8 7 6 5 4 3 2

Contents

Preface xv

Chapter 1
The Write Stuff 1
    Tradition, Tradition 2
    Travails of a Novice 3
    The Star-Maker. 4
  The Reasons Why. 5
    No One Else Will 5
    Control Issue 5
    Money, Honey. 6
    Career Springboard 6
    Make a Difference 7
    Do It for Love. 8
  Profits from Pages 8
  Starter Fuel 9
  Personality Plus 10
    To Boldly Go. 11
    All Walks of Life 11
    Caring for Your Own 12
    Horrors! 12
    Machine Guns and Memoirs 13

       Baby Hearts and Books 13

   Seeing into the Future 17

Chapter 2

Self-Publishing 101 . . . . **19**

   Ah, Vanity. 20

   The Three Graces 20

       All Fired Up 21

       Books by Mail 21

   Anatomy of a Bestseller 21

       Fib or Fact 22

   The Nonfiction Edge 22

       Constants with Clout 23

       The Format 24

   Back to the Fiction 25

       Fictional Formats 26

   Outsourcing Options 27

   The Potential of e-Publishing. 28

       e Is for Internet 28

       The e-Advantage 29

       Too Good 29

Chapter 3

Plotting Your Bestseller: Market Research **31**

   The First Task 32

   Your Target Market 33

       Nudging into Your Niche 33

   Researching Your Reader Base 34

       Send Me a Letter. 34

       Hello Central 35

   Statistics on Tap 36

       Library Look-Up. 38

       Get on the Net 38

       Try the Target 38

   Check Out the Competition 38

Chapter 4

Your Publishing House:

Office and Business Structure **41**

   Creating an Image 42

The Name Game 42
Name Fiction 42
Of Logos and Letterhead 44
Laying Your Foundation 45
The Soul of Your Proprietorship 45
A Taxing Affair 46
Expert Advice 46
On Location 47
The Home Office 47
The Big Write-Off 48
Organized and Efficient 48
The Storage Space 50
The Commercial Office 51
Outfitting Your Space 51

Chapter 5
Your Start-Up Finances **53**
Computer Caveats 54
Soft on Software 55
Go ISP! 56
Web Weaving 56
Doing It Digitally 57
Photo Finish 57
Printer Mania 58
Fax Facts 59
Phone Fanatic 59
Misery. 60
Electronic Money 61
Domain Décor 61
Pen and Paper 63
Get Professional 64
Spanning the Industry. 65
PMA Pals. 67
Read All About It 67
Are You Insured? 68
Tally It Up 68
Romancing the Bank 72
Friends and Family 72
Going Plastic 72

▲

Chapter 6
More Bookkeeping: Production Costs 73
Pre-Production Basics 74
   A Book by Its Cover 74
   Designer Search 75
   Drawing the Line 75
   Copy Quality 76
   Proof Positive 77
By the Numbers 77
   Lucky Number 13 78
   Name, Rank, and Serial Number 78
   Bar Codes in Bookland 79
   Advanced Information 79
   Getting Carded 80
   The CIP on Your Shoulder 81
Print Talk 82
   Vital Statistics 83
   Front Line Wisdom 84
   Covering the Spectrum 84
   Proof Is in the Pudding 88
   Printing Price Tag 89
   Overs, Unders, and Other Quirks 90
   The POD Effect 90
More Bang for Your Book 93
   Easy Listening 93
   Lights, Action, Camera! 94
   Merchandise Madness 96
   Going e! 96
   The Do-It-Yourself Site 97
   e-Book Publishers 98
   e-Book Reader 98

Chapter 7
Writing and Designing Your Book 99
Exhilaration and Panic 100
   Writing 101 100
   Ghosts and Other Writers 101
Layout and Design Decisions 101
   The Signature 102

Page Primer 103
    Front Matter 103
    The Body 106
    Back Matter 106
    Fit and Trim 107
    Paper Stock 108
    More Color 108
    Fantastic Fonts 109
    Point Taken 109
    Take the Lead 110
    Going Marginal 110
    Running Ahead 110
    Head of the Chapter 110
Got It Covered 112
    Front Cover Story 112
    Back Cover Sensation 113
    Growing a Spine 114
    Cover Stock 115
    Taking Stock 115
In a Bind 116
    Perfectly Bound 117

Chapter 8
Pricing and Selling **119**
The Sticker Price 120
Divvying Up Discounts 120
    Distributor/Wholesaler Dance 120
    Distributor Dating Game 121
    Wholesaler Heaven 123
    The Bottom Line Revisited 124
Ship Shape 125
    Return to Sender 125
    Storage Story 127
Trade Sales and Alternative Venues 127
    Bookstore Bonanza 127
    Appearance Is Everything 128
    Libraries and Educational Markets 129
    The Amazon of Bookstores 130
    Premium Grade 130

The Catalog Game 131
Specialty of the House 131
Museum-Quality 132

Chapter 9
Stepping into the Spotlight: Publicity **133**
Pre-Publication Pow 134
Setting the Date 134
Bound for the Galleys 134
Announcements and Accompaniments 135
The Pre-Pub Revue 136
Trade Reviewers 136
General Interest Reviewers 138
Significant Others 138
The Post-Pub Revue 139
Reviewing the Package 139
Traveling Man 141
Guest Spot 141
Adventures in Autographing 144

Chapter 10
Advertising and Marketing **147**
The Golden Word 148
Headline Fever 149
My Fair Book Fair 150
Take-Along Kit 150
Mail Order Magic 151
Winged Success 151
The Hook 152
Prospecting for Attention 153
Winning Ways 153
The List 155
The Response, Please 155
Going for Broke 156
The Rules 156
Seminar Time 157
Net-Etiquette 158
Web Relations 159
No Shouting, Please 159

Chapter 11
Controlling Your Finances **161**
   Operating Expenses 162
      Phone Facts 162
      Access to the Net 163
      Web Host 163
      Getting Carded 163
      Paper Tiger 163
      Paying the Piper 164
   Making a Statement 164
      Adding It All Up 165
   Getting a Grip 166
      Raising Cain 166
   Uncle Sam Speaks 171
      Driving Yourself Crazy 171
      Let Me Entertain You 172
      Planes, Trains, and Automobiles 172

Chapter 12
Looking Ahead: Small Press to Publishing Giant **173**
   Let's Make a Deal 174
      Selling Out 174
      The Acquisition 174
      Demanding More 175
   Selling Subsidiary 176
      Hot Serial 177
      Join the Club 178
      Foreign Affairs 178
      The Reel Story 178
   The Adventure Continues 179
      Launch Pad 179
      Somebody Else's Baby 180

Chapter 13
Bestseller or Bomb **181**
   Words of Wisdom 182
      Helping Thousands 182
      Ever Erratic 182
      Swing Low 183

▲

Love What You Do 184
The Happiness Factor 184
Success and Failure 185
Stress! 185
Springboard to Success 186
Goose Bumps! 186
Honors 187
A Job Well-Done 187

Appendix A
One Day at a Time: Basics of the Publishing Process 189

Appendix B
The Grass Is Greener: Tips and Tricks
for Great Grassroots Marketing 193

Appendix C
Self-Publishing Business Resources 197
ABI Forms 198
Associations 198
Bookland Bar Codes 199
Book Clubs. 199
Book Designers and Cover Artists 199
Book Expos and Fairs 199
Book Printers. 200
Books 200
Consultants 201
Copy Editors and Proofreaders. 201
Distributors 201
e-Publishers 201
Helpful Government Agencies 202
ISBN and SAN Provider. 202
Magazines and Publications 202
Mailing Lists 203
Merchant Card Services 203
Print On Demand 203
Shipping Supplies 203
Software for Publishers 204
Successful Self-Publishers 204

Wholesalers 204
Workshops and Seminars 204

Glossary 207

Index 213

For Michael

Preface

You've chosen this book for a very special reason: You're planning on starting your own business—and not just any business, but one as a self-publisher. You'll be treading ground that most people only fantasize about. You will be writing your own book and then seeing it through production and promotion to success on bookstore shelves.

You're stepping into exhilarating territory, which can also be frightening. Owning your own business means you're the boss; you make the rules and lay down the law. It also means you cannot let somebody else worry about making enough to

▲

cover expenses, and you can't pass that intimidating distributor or pesky printer on to a higher authority. You're it. Add to all these normal new-business anxieties the very natural fear of putting your writing project—your creative heart and soul—out in public where you risk failure and rejection. These are all valid concerns. But concern is not the same as can't, so don't worry. Instead, keep reading.

You're probably contemplating becoming a self-publisher for one or more of the following reasons:

- You've been an author for years and have collected enough rejection slips from conventional publishers to pave the Florida Turnpike.
- You've written books that have been produced by conventional publishers, but now you want to take creative, editorial, and financial control of your own work.
- You want to establish yourself as an authority in your field—be it medicine, law, golf, culinary arts, or whatever—and you believe your own book on the subject will be a smart promotional tool.
- You have a message that's important and can help people, and you believe your own book on the subject will be an effective tool for getting the word out.
- You believe the self-publishing industry is booming, and you're eager to share in the excitement and willing to take a chance on success.

Which did you choose? It doesn't matter because there is no wrong answer. Any of these responses is entirely correct so long as you realize they all involve a lot of learning and a lot of hard work. They can also involve a heck of a lot of fun, as well as a tremendous amount of personal and professional satisfaction.

Our goal in this book is to tell you everything you need to know to:

- Decide whether self-publishing is the right business for you
- Get your book written and your business started
- Successfully promote your book

We have interviewed many people out there on the front lines of the industry—all around the country—to learn the nitty-gritty, hands-on tasks, tips, and tricks to successful self-publishing. We've set aside places for them to tell their own stories and give their own hard-won advice—a sort of virtual round-table discussion group with you placed right in the thick of things. (For a listing of these successful business owners, see the Appendix at the back of this book.) We've broken our chapters into manageable sections on every aspect of start-up, production, and promotion. And we've left some space for your creativity to soar.

We've packed our pages with helpful tips so that you can get up and running as quickly as possible complete with contacts and sources in the Appendix to jumpstart your research. So pour a giant mug of java, take a deep breath, turn down the phones, turn off the TV, set your brain to learning mode, and let's go!

The Write
Stuff

Self-publishing is a hot industry today and growing hotter all the time. New publishers as well as new services for self-publishers and authors are springing up all over the country. Everybody, from writing stars like Stephen King to publishing powerhouses like Random House, is rushing to join the new generation of independent publishers.

▲

Despite the proliferation of movies, TV programs, and videos with which we find ourselves surrounded, Americans read books—a lot of books. According to the National Education Association (NEA), 93 million adults read fiction novels each year and 25 million people choose poetry. People who regularly read literature spend 2.7 hours in front of the television a day. Fans of cold turkey TV (gasp!) read between 12 and 49 books per year and are 48 percent more likely to read frequently. Book consumers eagerly gobble up everything from nonfiction recipes for improving health, wealth, and spirituality, to sci-fi. Cruise the aisles of any book emporium and you will find cookbooks, travel tomes, car repair manuals, mysteries, Westerns, advice for the lovelorn, astrology, Christian ethics, kids' tales, business guides, biographies, and much, much more. "We are a nation hungry for information," says Marilyn Ross, an early proponent of self-publishing and co-founder of SPAN, the Small Publishers Association of North America.

"People have more leisure time with which they may choose to entertain, educate, or motivate themselves," explains Jan Nathan, executive director of PMA, the Publishers Marketing Association. "Also, people have developed niche interest areas and want to read all they can on a specific area. Schools have been stressing reading for some time now, not to mention the variety of products available for any age group to read and/or listen to."

Fueled by this voracious appetite for reading material, the publishing industry has soared. More than 83,000 U.S. publishers currently spew forth over 172,000 titles per year, earning sales of more than $25.1 billion annually, according to R.R. Bowker.

The aspect of all this that's particularly exciting for the prospective self-publisher is that there are only a handful of big-league players left in the entire country. Where once there were dozens of "name" New York publishing firms like Simon & Schuster and Warner Books, a mere handful now fills the roster. This means there is now plenty of elbow room for self-publishers to make their own mark on the world. A 2005 survey, aptly titled "Under the Radar," from the Book Industry Study shows that 63,000 small presses generate around $14.2 billion in sales each year.

Tradition, Tradition

So, just what is a self-publisher? As you have probably figured out, it's a person who writes a book, sees it through each step of production—from the artwork for the front cover to typesetting and design to printing—and then goes out and sells and markets it on his or her own.

Fun Fact

Self-publishing isn't new. Famous self-published authors include Mark Twain, Walt Whitman, D.H. Lawrence of the infamous *Lady Chatterley's Lover*, and Edgar Rice Burroughs, creator of the original jungle hunk *Tarzan*.

Stat Fact

According to *Publishers Weekly,* the average book in the United States sells around 500 copies. Only ten books sold more than a million copies last year, so get a dose of reality before you ask for the 50,000 copy print run. Focus on your niche markets and create your own definition of success.

In the traditional world of book publishing, an author pens a work—novel, nonfiction, or a collection of poetry—and then goes out shopping for a publisher. Usually this is on a par with trying for a million-dollar home loan with bad credit, no job, and no fixed address. In other words, it's not easy.

The major publishing houses (as well as many of the midsize houses) are fixated on the bottom line to the point where they cannot and will not take a chance on any project that does not come with an automatic success guarantee. Tell-all biographies of fallen royalty and rock stars, and ghostwritten autobiographies of movie stars and megafinanciers are shoe-ins. So, too, are novels by proven winners like Stephen King and Danielle Steele, and pop-psychology pages by professional speakers who already command thousands of dollars per engagement. The unknown writer with a new story to tell or a new idea to present faces an uphill battle.

This is not to say it can't be done. New voices are heard all the time. J.K. Rowling, author of the celebrated *Harry Potter* series, for instance, was a first-time writer and welfare mum when her first book was bought by a British publisher, Bloomsbury Children's Books. But like the thousands of aspiring actors who haunt Hollywood hoping for a break, there are far more hopeful authors than published ones.

Travails of a Novice

The novice author's travails don't end when the sale is made. Let's say you're clever as well as lucky—you've written a top-notch book, and you've managed to sell it to a bona fide publishing house. Your work is done, you think. You can sit back and wait for the money and the fame to pour in. Well, not quite.

True, you don't need to worry about the production aspects of the book, but you don't get any input either. If the publisher chooses to cut half your golden prose, or print the text in a murky, barely legible typeface—or plaster a photo of the state penitentiary at Gila Bend by night on the cover of your *100 Fun Things for Families to Do in Arizona* book—that's too bad. The publisher holds all the cards, and even though you're the author, you get little or no say in how your baby rolls off the press.

Then, as the final shocks for the newbie writer, after all the blood, sweat, and tears you (and presumably the publisher) have poured into its birth, your book may be released and then abandoned. Most publishing houses spend little time, effort, or money on promoting new books. Yes, you have seen all those celebs touting their books on *Good Morning America* and *Larry King Live*, but those are the rare few deemed splashy enough by the publisher to spend promotional dollars on.

The vast majority of published authors discover, to their dismay, that the publisher makes no promotional efforts whatsoever. All those autograph parties, book signings, media appearances, author tours, bookstore displays, print advertisements, and newspaper and magazine articles turn out to exist only in the writers' fantasies. And with no promotions to help pave the way to bestsellerdom, all those published books die a quick and untimely death. They don't even have time to languish on the shelves. If they don't some-

Stat Fact
According to *Publishers Weekly*, a 2006 report by private equity firm Veronis Suhler Stevenson says that total spending on media products is projected to increase at a 4.5 percent annual rate in the 2006–2010 period, to $231.2 billion. Book sales are expected to grow at a compounded annual rate of 3.2 percent over the next five years, time spent reading books annually will increase, and money spent on books per person will rise slightly.

how sell themselves in a matter of four months to a year, they're yanked out of the stores and the distributor's warehouses, and consigned to book limbo for the rest of eternity.

The Star-Maker

If all this sounds like unrelenting doom and gloom, take heart. There is an upside alternative—you can take the self-publishing route! As a self-publisher, you maintain total creative control of your work. You get to choose how it will look—everything from the size and style of the type to the size of the margins to the dimensions of the book itself. You choose the graphics, line art, or photos that decorate it inside and out. You decide on hardcover or softcover. You choose the layout—whether you'll have *sidebars* (those mini-articles that fit beside the running text), tip boxes or *pull quotes* (oversized quotes pulled from the text). You decide on the cover price, which is a major factor in how well the book will sell. You also decide on how you'll sell it: through distributors, by direct mail, through specialty retailers, or through catalogs.

Perhaps most important of all, you handle the sales and promotions. You become a star-maker. You conceive and carry out a campaign of press releases, media appearances, author tours, internet exposure, media articles—whatever you decide it will take and whatever you want to do—to make your written baby a success.

The Reasons Why

Like just about everything in life, there are some cons that go with the pros of becoming a self-publisher. One is expense. You, not the New York (or New Jersey or wherever) publisher, pay all the costs of production and printing. Another is effort. You have to be willing to expend the energy to plan and then carry out a marketing campaign, for which you will incur more costs. A third potential negative is that you have to have moxie. You must be ready, willing, and able to blow your own horn. This is true for any small-business owner, but even more so for the self-publisher. If you are a shrinking violet, you won't get far. Despite these cons, there are a host of good reasons that lead bright, creative people down the self-publishing lane.

Fun Fact

Publishers of romance novels are notorious for insisting that each book contain at least one of the following as characters: a baby, a bride, a cowboy, or a cop.

No One Else Will

Some writers take the self-publisher route because no one else will publish their work. Traditional publishers send rejection slips for many reasons other than bad prose. Often manuscripts don't fit the publisher's mold because they're too long or too short, the target market is too narrow, the subject matter is too obscure, the characters or setting don't fit a predetermined matrix, or they "don't quite fit our current guidelines" for any of a dozen elusive factors.

Once upon a time, editors who detected a spark of genius (or just plain mass-market saleability) worked with writers, nurturing and guiding them to the development of a terrific book. Now, with the fierce concentration on the bottom line, editors have become minions of the marketing department instead of shepherds of creativity. So even when they spot a new writer with budding talent, they can't offer a contract unless the book fits the marketing department's "blockbuster" mold to a tee.

Smart Tip

Tip...

What's the difference between a *self-publisher,* an *independent publisher,* and a *small press*? A self-publisher produces her own work, while the latter two can also publish the works of other authors.

Control Issue

Authors who have been published by traditional houses, only to find their work hopelessly mangled, sometimes turn self-publisher for their next books to maintain creative control. We have already talked about some of the ways publishers can tamper with the integrity of your book. And there are more. With the proper (often standard) contract, they can obtain the rights to your book but fail to publish it—and then neither can you. Or they can demand first-refusal options on your next book or two, even though they ill-treated the previous one. As a self-publisher, you don't have any of these worries.

Money, Honey

Writers often become self-publishers to keep the lion's share of the profits. In traditional publishing, the author is paid on a *royalty* basis. This has nothing to do with being crowned king or princess, or even being handed a minor dukedom, but instead refers to the percentage of profits from the book. It can get as complex as quantum physics, but basically it works like this: The writer is paid an *advance against royalties*, or a sum of money that represents the minimum royalties the publisher expects the book to earn.

Authors usually get half the advance when they sign the contract and begin writing the book, and the other half when the book is completed to the publisher's satisfaction. After the book hits the stores, the writer generally receives 3 percent to 7.5 percent of the book's net sales, which are paid on a quarterly basis. These are the royalties. If the book never earns more than the advance, the author never sees another dime, which is what happens in most cases. And advances can be shockingly small. As little as $3,000 for a 50,000-word book is not uncommon.

Notice we said the royalties are paid on net sales, not gross. A book that retails for $14.95 on the bookstore shelf is usually discounted about 60 percent to the store chain, which pays only $8.97 to the publisher. The author's 7.5 percent royalty from this tallies in at 67 cents. Kind of scary, huh?

This means the publisher, which isn't exactly knocking itself out to promote the book, must sell a fraction over 4,477 books for the author to earn back the advance on her royalties. When you factor in that many publishers only print 5,000 books on an initial (and probably final) run, you can see that the author is not going to get rich, or even keep body and soul together, on the books' proceeds.

But as a self-publisher, you get to keep everything your book earns over and above the actual expenses involved with production and promotion. Instead of cents on the dollar, you'll earn the dollars themselves. Self-publishing is not a get-rich-quick operation by any stretch, but it can definitely be more financially rewarding than going the traditional route.

Career Springboard

Many self-publishers use their books as career jump-starters. If you're planning to segue from your current position into a new life as a professional speaker or consultant, a book can open a lot of doors. It gives you instant credibility. People think that since you're a published author who's written a book on web site marketing or financial planning (or whatever your subject is), then you must be an expert. It never occurs to them that you and your publisher are one and the same entity.

It goes without saying, of course, that you do need to know your stuff when you write nonfiction. If you offer people information, it's up to you to deliver the real thing. But it is also true that a book—whether traditionally or self-published—is the sort of validation you can't get from anything else.

Make a Difference

Still other authors self-publish to make a difference in the lives of the people around them. They see a need and a way to fill it through their writing, and they feel compelled to put the two together. Anna J. of Temple, Texas, wrote and published her first book after her infant son was diagnosed with a serious heart defect in 1994.

"I immediately asked for information about the heart defect," Anna says. "When the doctors wouldn't give me anything, I started to seek information myself. The only information I could find was dated and very discouraging. I wanted something inspirational and informative. I decided to put together a booklet of helpful information because I was afraid I would not be able to remember everything I needed to know. I wanted a 'reference' book—something I could refer back to when we were having surgery or complications."

Anna soon began sharing her research and inspiration with the parents of other children with the same problem. "I had started a rudimentary support group when my son was in the hospital," she explains. "Even though our children had the fourth most common heart defect (and heart defects are the number one birth defect in the country), we couldn't find anything in print. In 1996, I decided to publish the booklet I had started writing. I called or sent letters to the parents I had shared information with and asked them for feedback. They requested more information on certain topics that I researched and wrote up. Then I added my son's story at the beginning of the book. My booklet grew to the size of a book!"

Anna knew she had a product that could help people who desperately wanted information. But convincing a publisher was another story. "I queried every appropriate publisher I could find, and all of them sent me back nice rejection letters stating that my intended audience was

> **Fun Fact**
> Self-published success stories aren't limited to those that happened a century or two ago. Two hits are *The Celestine Prophecy* by James Redfield and *The Christmas Box* by Richard Paul Evans. These titles were self-published, then picked up by major publishers—Warner Books and Simon & Schuster, respectively.

too small," she recalls. "My husband and I decided that even if we only sold one book, and it helped one family, it would be worth our time and trouble. Now I have three books in print, and my first book is in its third printing (and second edition)."

Do It for Love

A final—but oh-so important—reason for becoming a self-publisher is for the joy of it. This is a business that is going to take up a great deal of your time, effort, energy, creativity, and wallet. So if you're going to do it, you must do it for love. That's how the majority of self-publishers feel. They love writing, reading, and publishing. They have a story inside themselves that's bursting to be told, and they feel they have to get it down on paper and out in print. There's no choice. Even when the actual writing process seems painful (as it does to just about every author at times), they wouldn't have it any other way. Answering the call of the creative muse is fulfilling, addictive, and just plain fun.

Profits from Pages

How much can you expect to earn as a self-publisher? It really depends on how hard you choose to work at it, what your vision is for your company and your products, and your books' market appeal. You may pen the definitive tome on the mating habits of the earthworm, featuring deathless prose and four-color photos, but you're unlikely to find yourself with a runaway mass-market bestseller on your hands. If, on the other hand, you plan and produce books that appeal to a significant market, you have the potential to do well. (We'll explore market research secrets later on in Chapter 3.)

Industry experts are loath to quote potential annual earnings because they can vary radically from publisher to publisher. Gross annual incomes among the publishers we interviewed for this book ranged from under $10,000 for a newbie, to an anticipated $500,000 for a 15-year veteran. "Marketing is the key," says Ross of SPAN. "You can make a living, you can make a comfortable living, or you can starve on the vine." Self-publishing is a business venture and not just an artistic one.

Mary Embree, former executive director of SPAWN (Small Publishers, Artists, and Writers Network) and a literary consultant, agrees with this line of thought. "I know one author who wrote and self-published a book aimed at the

Stat Fact
According to a recent news release from the Small Publishers Association of North America, the number of small publishers has mushroomed more than 200 percent in the last decade.

home-schooling industry and sold 5,000 copies the first year," Embree says. "I know a lot of self-publishers who ordered a printing of 1,000 books and still have 950 gathering dust in the garage after three or four years. That's the norm. Self-publishing may be disappointing unless the author has a workable plan to sell the books."

The financial picture doesn't have to reflect doom and gloom. "Books are fairly inexpensive to produce, and the markup is high," advises Dan Poynter, a self-publishing guru and author of best-selling titles on the subject. "You can produce one for $2 and sell it for $20." There are many expenses that will bridge the gap between these two figures considerably. But, according to Poynter, your gross does not have to be as high as in other industries because, with lower overhead costs, your net is higher.

Poynter makes another positive point for entering into self-publishing. "You do not have to make a lot of money as a self-publisher if your book contributes to your ability to sell other goods and services." If you're a chiropractor, for example, and you write and promote a book on back care, you position yourself to become a sought-after expert in your field—one with a higher-earning potential.

Starter Fuel

As the old adage goes, "You need money to make money." In other words, you need start-up funds. As a self-publisher, you've got it better than many new business owners, like those who decide to open a coffee house or hardware store. You can start out homebased, which means you won't need to worry about leasing office space. You won't need employees right off the bat—or at all—and you don't need to plunk down funds for specialized equipment and sales inventory.

All you really need is a computer, software, a printer, a fax machine and/or scanner, and internet access—and you may already have some of these items. Your other major expenses will be for book printing and for sales and promotions.

So what's the bottom line? "It can be minimal: a DBA ["doing business as"] license, letterhead, phone, answering service, fax, and e-mail access," says Nathan of PMA. "You can work out of your home to start and grow into a company, as many successful self-publishers have. However, many of these publishers have moved from self-publishers to niche publishers, who publish other people's works in a specific genre. These are the successful ones."

"Start-up costs are another question for which there is no clear answer," advises Embree, of SPAWN. "It depends on how many copies you are going to order from the printer, how it is printed (hardcover or paperback), how much you can do for yourself, and how much you will have to hire out (such as editing and typesetting)."

Start-up costs are also extremely dependent on the size of your book—page count as well as outside dimensions—how much artwork is involved, how much

▲

The Risk Factor

Besides earnings and start-up costs, two other important aspects to consider are risk and stability. There's no point in throwing yourself and your money into a new business only to discover that it's about as risk-free as a first-class ticket on the original Titanic, or that it's a fad whose time has already passed. You want a business that has staying power.

Self-publishing is likely to be around for the long haul. People are reading now more than ever—especially nonfiction—and seem poised to continue the trend. We live in the Information Age, and despite the wealth of materials available on the internet, people are eager for books that teach them how to lead smarter, happier, healthier, and wealthier lives.

Readers are also always in the market for entertainment—from mysteries to romances. If you can produce a book that fulfills this need, and follow it up with another volume geared toward the same interested readers, you've got a winning ticket to a successful business.

The self-publisher's risk factor is moderate. You can't guarantee the success of a book unless you're adept with a crystal ball. But if you choose your market wisely, target it closely, and work diligently at sales and promotions, you've got a fair chance at success.

equipment (such as computer and printer) you'll need to buy, and how creative you'll get with your promotional budget. As a ballpark figure, you can expect to spend $10,000 to $29,000 to get up and running, and to print and start promoting your first book.

"Our first book cost us about $11,000 to print the first 5,000 copies," says Steve C., a self-publisher in Hinesburg, Vermont, who we interviewed for this book. "Fortunately, they sold out quite quickly and we went on to a second printing. The business has always paid for itself, although there were lean times in the early years when we didn't make enough to give ourselves decent paychecks."

Personality Plus

Besides earnings, start-up costs, and risk and stability factors, there's one more important element to consider when deciding if self-publishing is the business for you: personality. Not everybody has the makings of a self-publishing pro. This is a career

Stat Fact

According to *Publishers Weekly* magazine, Amazon media (which includes books, magazines, music, DVD, and software) reported sales of $815 million for the first quarter of 2006.

that calls for lots of time spent one-on-one with your computer and nobody else. If you're the type who thrives in the hustle and bustle corporate world, with lots of other bodies and brains sharing your work space, then you may want to think twice.

Self-publishing also requires that you have a strong sense of what your target market wants to read. You don't have to have your finger on the pulse of the entire nation, but you do—like Anna J. in Temple, Texas—need an unerring instinct for the topics that will strike a chord in your particular audience.

You will also need megadoses of talent and creativity. You can get all sorts of assistance with grammar, punctuation, and spelling, but if you can't tell a riveting story that will keep your reader spellbound (and this counts for nonfiction as well!), you definitely need to reconsider. This doesn't mean that only Pulitzer Prize winners or those who won every creative writing contest in high school need apply. One of the most important aspects of writing is that you know your subject, that you're passionate about it, and that your passion shines through. The rest you can learn.

To Boldly Go

To accompany the talent and creativity, you must have follow-through. If you're a dabbler, who thinks writing and then publishing a book might be fun, but you have a penchant for dropping projects before they're half-finished, you won't get far as a self-publisher. Lots of people would like to write a book, but they never get past the wishful thinking stage. As a self-publisher, you'll have to be able to write that book in a timely manner and then see it through all the stages of publishing.

As a final, but terrifically important character trait, you'll need the chutzpah to get out there and promote your books. You can boldly go on TV and radio, or stay discreetly behind the scenes sending out press releases and news articles, but if you really want to succeed, you'll do both. Sales and promotions are the lifeblood of the self-published book, so you'll have to be gutsy at selling a product you truly believe in—your own books.

All Walks of Life

Self-publishers come from all walks of life. The ones we interviewed for this book had a variety of alternate careers including educator, congressional assistant, and branch manager of a state environmental protection agency.

The tip here is that all these entrepreneurs figured out how to make their interests and their backgrounds work for them in their new careers. They have taken the skills and enthusiasm they had already acquired and applied them to the self-publishing business.

Stat Fact
According to *Publishers Weekly,* bookstore sales totaled $2.12 billion in January 2007.

Caring for Your Own

Steve C. in Hinesburg, Vermont, has been a successful independent publisher for 15 years, with over 20 titles under his belt. "We describe our niche as nonfiction to improve the quality of life," Steve says. "That's a much broader niche than most small presses take on. However, I'd rather publish any book I like than stay with a specific narrow niche. (Several of our titles have been on death and dying, but there's no way I'd want to spend full time on those issues.) That's a personal enjoyment decision, not a sound business decision.

"I started in 1986," Steve recalls. "I had left my job as a congressional assistant at that time to care for my mother, who was dying of AIDS. My wife, Lisa, was also tiring of her job as a teacher. She had researched how to care for one's own dead without the help of a funeral director and was eager to write a book on the subject. Her book was the first we published."

Since then, Lisa has left publishing to become executive director of a national nonprofit organization to protect the rights of consumers in their dealings with the funerary industry. Steve has developed other businesses for small presses, including a fulfillment, or order-filling company, that he's since sold and a business software program called Publisher's Assistant.

"Publisher's Assistant is used by hundreds of publishers, mostly relatively small presses," Steve says. "However, that has now become a partnership with my programmer's company, so my involvement is reduced. As a result, my publishing house is now a full-time, one-person company, and I am devoting almost all of my working hours to publishing books."

Fun Fact
Good writing transcends age, gender, and time. The eternally popular tale of mankind's botched attempts at creation, *Frankenstein,* was written by Mary Wollstonecraft Shelley when she was just 21 years old.

Horrors!

June H. in Rochester Hills, Michigan, specializes in horror stories but hopes to branch out into other genres as her company grows. She has been nominated for the coveted Bram

Stoker Award, presented by The Horror Writers Association. "I currently have four books in the stores and on Amazon.com and Barnes & Noble.com," June says. "At the moment, it is my intention to do a yearly book of short horror stories, with which I hope to find undiscovered talent. [June's anthologies showcase the works of previously unknown writers.] I am also working on a ghostly novel.

> ## Smart Tip
>
> An unsolicited manu-script—one sent to a prospec-tive publisher by an unknown author who is not represented by an agent—is a said to be received over the transom.

Tip...

"The idea of forming my own company came to me in the middle of the night, after a frustrating day of rejections and also a frustrating day of finding the same old themes in bookstores," recalls the work-at-home mom of a high school senior. "I wanted to tap into the talent that the large publishing companies weren't willing to take a chance on because the writer was unpublished."

Machine Guns and Memoirs

Gary S. in Panama City Beach, Florida, is a state environmental protection agent by day and self-publisher by night. Gary's niche is the biographies of World War II veterans—not the celebrated captains and generals, but average soldiers with their own exciting stories to tell from the front lines. "I started to self-publish in 1999, after I wrote my father's World War II account, and soon realized there was a need for this type of product for veterans," Gary says. "Self-publishing worked best because the men for whom I was writing wanted their stories out as soon as possible, and this was the quickest way to accomplish this goal."

Baby Hearts and Books

You have already met Anna J., who started her publishing company shortly after her baby was diagnosed with a life-threatening heart defect. This traumatic event catapulted the home-schooler and mother of two in Temple, Texas, to self-publish-ing success. Anna now has three books in print. "Two books deal specifically with congenital heart defects, although one is inspirational in nature. The other is a children's book for the stay-at-home sibling of a child who must be hospitalized," says Anna.

Anna is now working on another inspirational title, branching out to publish the works of other authors who write on similar health-related topics. She is transform-ing her one-woman sole proprietorship into a nonprofit organization with a staff to help with the workload.

SPAWNing a Successful Start-Up
An Interview with SPAWN President Patricia Fry

Patricia Fry has been writing for publication for about 33 years. She has contributed hundreds of articles to about 260 different magazines such as, *Writer's Digest, Writers' Journal, Cat Fancy, PMA Independent, Entrepreneur, Mature Outlook, The World and I, Your Health* and many others. She is also the author of 25 books, including eight related to writing and publishing. Her latest is the 300-page *The Right Way to Write, Publish and Sell Your Book*, (Matilija Press, 2006). She established Matilija Press in 1983 and has produced several of her books through this company. She also has books with traditional royalty publishers.

Currently the working president of SPAWN, Patricia was in on the ground floor of SPAWN 11 years ago working alongside founder Mary Embree as she established this networking organization.

Today, the articles she writes pertain mainly to writing and publishing. She also works with other authors and freelance writers on their projects and speaks at several writers conferences throughout the U.S. each year.

1. What are the hot trends in small publishing?

For inexperienced, hopeful authors, the fee-based POD publishing service is big. Typically, when someone finishes his or her first book manuscript, they will immediately start searching for a publisher. A Google search takes them promptly to iUniverse, AuthorHouse, PublishAmerica or other such companies. The author sends his manuscript as requested, it is accepted on the spot and, in his exuberance, he signs any contract that is put in front of him.

For the slightly savvier author, the trend I see most often is an attempt to get representation by a literary agent and/or land a contract with a major publisher. This author typically quits too soon and either self-publishes or gives up altogether. (Self-publishing means to establish your own publishing company.)

For established small publishers, the trend seems to be toward much greater involvement, more industry savvy through research, more creativity in the way they promote their books—more enthusiasm, more hands-on, more success.

2. Are there any categories that stand out sales-wise? Is non-fiction still tops?

I see more memoirs produced by small publishers and one-title authors than practically any other category. These are military memoirs as well as stories of abuse, illness, death of a loved one, overcoming mental illness, spiritual encounters, ancestor history, and even a journal of a Little League parent.

Memoirs had their day, but I understand that they are not popular with publishers now unless the author is a celebrated person.

Overall, in the industry, religious/spiritual/inspirational topics are always high on the list of best selling books. Young adult and juvenile books are on the rise. But, yes, it looks as though nonfiction does sell in greater numbers than does fiction.

3. What are your thoughts on e-books? Is it a viable market for small/self-publishers?

There are publishers who absolutely live and breathe e-books. I met a man in Atlanta a few weeks ago at a writers' conference who is all about e-books. He said current statistics illustrate that e-books are alive and well and the industry is growing by leaps and bounds. We're not seeing that here at SPAWN, however.

Is it a viable market for small publishers? I have some of my books in both print and e-book form and this is what I suggest to SPAWN members: It costs virtually nothing to produce an e-book, so why not produce a print book and also make it available to overseas customers and others who like to read their books on a handheld device?

4. Would you recommend print-on-demand? Why or why not?

By print-on-demand, I assume that you mean the many fee-based, POD self-publishing services that are around today. I rarely recommend them to authors, but I don't bad-mouth them, either. We here at SPAWN strongly recommend that any author who is contemplating a relationship with a fee-based POD publishing service take two important steps first. Study the publishing industry so that you know your publishing options and the consequences of your decisions. And write a book proposal so that you are acutely aware of the validity of your book, your target audience, and how you will reach this audience. In other words, don't rush blindly into publishing. Do your homework.

Once armed with enough knowledge to make an intelligent decision on your book's behalf, no matter which publishing option you choose, make sure that everything you discuss with the sales rep or publisher is in writing and have an intellectual properties attorney look it over.

5. Where should a prospective new small/self publisher start in regard to market research?

In regard to searching for a publisher, I suggest my book, *The Right Way to Write, Publish and Sell Your Book* as well as market directories such as *Literary Marketplace* and *Writer's Market*. Also, look at books similar to the one you are writing in local mega-bookstores and see who published them. Contact those publishers.

In regard to book promotion, start by writing a book proposal. Your book proposal will reveal your target audience. Where are they? Where do they shop? What web sites do they visit? What magazines do they read? What conferences do they attend? Answering these questions is your first step toward creating your book promotion plan.

6. What's your best advice for someone considering their own publishing business?

In most cases, I would rather see an author self-publish (establish his/her own publishing company) instead of go with a fee-based POD publishing service. I believe that a self-published author is generally more committed to his book—has a more intimate relationship with it—than one who turns the responsibilities over to a publishing service. In most cases, a self-published author generates more sales and more profit than does one who goes with a fee-based POD publishing service.

My hallmark presentation at writers and publishers conferences revolves around the book proposal. And I strongly recommend that any author of any type book write a detailed book proposal. This is especially important when you decide to self-publish. Publishing is a business and a book proposal is your business plan.

7. Are there any organizations (besides yours) that you think are valuable for a small publisher?

I would recommend Publishers Marketing Association (PMA) and Small Publishers Association of North America (SPAN).

8. Tell us a bit about your organization.

Mary Embree founded SPAWN (Small Publishers, Artists, and Writers Network) 11 years ago in Ventura County, California, as a face-to-face networking organization for anyone interested in publishing. She envisioned having meetings where authors could connect with illustrators, where graphic artists could connect with freelance writers who needed brochures designed, etc., and where writers could meet publishers, for example. Within a few months, there were three chapters meeting once a month each in three different counties. Authors were sharing information and resources with one another, working relationships were formed and everyone was learning from the various expert speakers at every meeting.

About six years ago, we ceased the face-to-face meetings and turned to the internet where we continue to provide information, resources, and networking opportunities. We have a free monthly newsletter. Sign up for *SPAWNews* at www.spawn.org. Members receive the newsletter, plus a *Market Update* that is absolutely brimming with opportunities and information for anyone interested in or involved in the publishing field. We have an online discussion group and a forum. Plus we offer members the opportunity to include their books and services in the SPAWN Catalog of Members' Books and Services and display and sell their books at various book festivals throughout the year.

Check out Patricia's web site at www.matilijapress.com and her blog site at www.matilijapress.com/publishingblog. She welcomes dialogue with other writers and publishers, so drop her a line at PJfry620@yahoo.com.

Seeing into the Future

One final issue to consider is the industry prognosis: Will self-publishing be around well into the future, or will it go the way of the eight-track tape and pet rock in a matter of months?

Self-publishing has slowly and progressively become "legitimate" over the course of the last two or three decades, but has really come into its own in the past four to five years. And with new outlets for self-publishers, from dotcom bookstores to print-on-demand and e-publishing service providers, the path is being paved for the self-publisher to compete on a far more even footing with the big guys than ever before.

Technology has also made it possible for small independent publishers to succeed. With home desktop computers and publishing programs, self-publishers can do much of the work that once had to be farmed out to somebody else at considerable expense. This, coupled with the demise of many of the major publishers, has forced wholesalers and distributors to take self-publishers seriously. It has also forced major publishers to take small presses seriously.

Since many major publishers no longer have the go-ahead to nurture new talent and take creative chances in their own corporate worlds, they leave it to independent publishers to do so and then negotiate lucrative deals for successful new titles. This is a win-win situation that isn't likely to change in the near future. In short, the self-publishing trend is poised to take off in a very positive way.

Self-Publishing 101

OK, you've read through Chapter 1 and decided that self-publishing is the business for you. Terrific! But before you can produce that bestseller, you have to know what you're doing. So don your virtual school jacket and step into the hallowed halls of Self-Publishing 101.

Ah, Vanity

We've already explored the differences between traditional publishing houses and the self-publisher. You know that the self-publisher not only pens that great novel or nonfiction book, but also sees it through every step of production and printing, and then nurtures its sales and promotion. As a self-publisher, you can keep your books in print for as long as you can make sales—even if those sales are as few as five or ten per month. In contrast, traditional publishing houses may not keep your book alive for more than a year or two, despite the fact that a considerable untapped market may still exist.

Self-publishing isn't new. It's been practiced for hundreds of years. Writers we now consider literary luminaries—including Edgar Allan Poe, Virginia Woolf, and James Joyce—have gone the do-it-yourself route with great success.

But until fairly recently—within probably the last 20 years—self-publishing was basically the jurisdiction of the eccentric few. The literary world turned up its collective nose at writers who were self-published. It generally meant that your work was so awful that no one else in his or her right mind would print it, and that you had turned to a vanity publisher—always a bad move.

Vanity or subsidy publishers are publishers only in the loosest sense of the word. They're actually printers who promise to take on a publisher's tasks but rarely, if ever, follow through. Where the traditional publishing house pays an author an advance and royalties for his work, a vanity publisher has the author pay for the privilege of seeing his work in print. Vanity publishers have a sad reputation for failing to print more than a few hundred copies of a book and failing to distribute them to bookstores. As for promotions, the key words are "Forget it." In addition, the prices charged by vanity or subsidy publishers are exorbitant.

As a budding self-publisher, don't let anyone confuse your own legitimate publishing business with a vanity house. And don't get confused yourself. Vanity publishing is a venture to steer clear of.

The Three Graces

One really favorable aspect of self-publishing is that it forms a perfect bond with two other hot businesses for the new millennium—seminar promotions and mail order, which lend themselves ideally to one another and to the business of self-publishing. Together, these businesses make the ultimate trio.

> **Tip...**
>
> **Smart Tip**
>
> New titles that a publisher has just released are called its *front list*. Old standbys, the books that are no longer new but are steady sellers, are called the *back list*.

All Fired Up

One of the best ways to promote your books and encourage sales is by giving seminars, workshops, and lectures. People who listen to your presentations get fired up. They are excited about the subject and want to take immediate action. And what better action than to buy your books, conveniently displayed at the back of the room? Seminar professionals have long understood this concept, which is known as making *BOR* or *back-of-the-room sales*.

You might think that giving talks is not your style, but think again. As an author/publisher, you'll be promoting your products at everything from mini workshops at your local library and bookstore, to media appearances on local TV. Seminars are a logical extension, and they can be fun!

Books by Mail

Another top-notch way to sell your books is through *direct mail*, which is another term for mail order. Traditionally, publishers have sold their products to their readers indirectly—through special book distributors who sell the products to bookstores (that sell them to consumers). This method isn't always the best one for the new self-publisher, and indeed it should not be the only one.

Distributors typically demand 40 to 60 percent discounts off the cover price of a book, which effectively skims the cream off the publisher's profits before he or she has even considered other costs, like shipping and promotions. In addition, book distributors frequently don't work as hard to sell for small presses as they do for the giants like Random House.

As a self-publisher, you don't have to go solely with the distributor route. You'll have targeted a special market niche that's already interested in your particular topics even before you print your first book. It makes sense to sell directly to those readers via mail order. You don't have to cough up distributor-heavy discounts, and your readers even pay the shipping costs.

We'll come back to seminars and mail order in Chapter 10. For now, keep these options in mind, since they can work wonders for the self-publisher.

Anatomy of a Bestseller

Now that we've investigated who will publish your book and how you'll sell it, let's talk about its anatomy. Take a stroll through any bookstore and you'll see that there are dozens, if not hundreds, of variations on a theme. True, they all have a front and back cover with text and occasionally some graphics in between. But they come in all sizes, shapes, and subject matters.

Fib or Fact

Perhaps the biggest difference in the types of books that are commonly sold is whether they're fiction or nonfiction. People are often confused about which is which, but it's simple, really: Fiction is make-believe, a story the author invents for the purpose of entertaining his readers. Nonfiction, on the other hand, is fact—it can be entertaining to readers, but it relays true information rather than an invented tale.

A romance novel is fiction—an invented story about a make-believe hero and heroine. A biography can be romantic, for instance the love story of Princess Grace and Prince Rainier of Monaco, but since it's about real people, it's nonfiction.

Mysteries like those written by Agatha Christie are fiction. The "who" in whodunit, as well as the "what" of what was done, is pure invention. However, a book dealing with a real-life mystery, like who killed the woman known as the Black Dahlia in 1940s Los Angeles, is nonfiction, so it's classified as "true crime."

Stat Fact

Do men really read more nonfiction than their female counterparts do? According to a recent report from the National Endowment for the Arts (NEA), yes. Just over 62 percent of men who read choose non-fiction. Women choose literary works a little more than half the time, at a rate of about 55 percent. Consider diversifying your title list to meet demands of both genders.

The Nonfiction Edge

Which should you write? Industry experts tend to agree that nonfiction is a far wiser choice for the self-publisher than fiction. If you've been scribbling away at a heart-pounding mystery, a heart-wrenching romance, or some other invented tale, this may seem like exactly what you did not want to hear. But take heart—there are new options for you that have only recently become available.

Before we get to them, let's explore why nonfiction is generally a better bet for the self-publisher.

Stat Fact

According to a recent report from R. R. Bowker, book production in 2005 was the second highest ever recorded, second only to 2004.

First of all, Americans read far more nonfiction than fiction. In a Gallup survey, 46 percent of respondents said they have nonfiction books on their night stands, while only 35 percent have their noses stuck in novels or other works of fiction.

Nonfiction categories are experiencing strong gains in both production and sales. According to a recent report from R.R. Bowker, North America's leading resource for bibliographic data, the sports/recreation category enjoyed an increase in new titles of 22 percent. Health and medical titles also grew, with an 18 percent increase in title production.

Secondly, you don't have to be a "name" to sell nonfiction. When readers head to the bookstore on the prowl for a good story, they look first for a name they already recognize, like Stephen King, Jackie Collins, or John Grisham. So if you have penned a tale of horror, lust among the monied classes, or a legal whodunit, you've got stiff competition. However, when readers go to the bookstore to find a book on cooking hors d'oeuvres or creating healthy relationships, they look for content rather than celebrity authors. Sure it helps if you're Martha Stewart or Dr. John Gray, but it's not everything. If your book gives readers information they can use, chances are they'll probably buy it.

Constants with Clout

Nonfiction comes in all subjects, everything from connecting with your computer to communicating with your dog to conducting electricity—and lots more. Some genres,

Hold the Autobiography

The more time you spend in the publishing business, the more you'll hear people proclaim that their life story would make a great book. And while most people's lives—due to the very nature of life itself—contain lots of drama, trials, and tribulations, they're not necessarily the stuff of great prose.

If you harbor this thought yourself, think carefully before committing fingers to keyboard. Have you lived through some great natural disaster or historical trauma? Do you have a truly dramatic story, like having survived frostbite, gangrene, and/or cannibalism on a snowy mountain peak; sailing around the world single-handedly; or being dead for four hours and coming back to tell about it? Have you overcome a terrible physical or mental handicap? Do you have a really interesting and extraordinary job or hobby, like bounty hunter, movie star, Mafia hit-person, CIA spy, or ghostbuster?

These are not all requirements for autobiographical success: People have written winning tomes based simply on growing up a child of the Depression in the 1930s or a Beaver Cleaver-clone kid in the 1950s. But as with fiction, unless you're a stellar writer with an excellent hook on which to base your tale, you're facing an uphill road to self-publishing success.

however, have more clout with readers than others. Take a look at these constants of the bookstore shelves:

- *Cookbooks.* Cookery books, as the British call them, were an "acceptable" self-publishing avenue long before any other genre. Today they are even considered collectibles in some circles. Think back to all those spiral-bound volumes you have seen through the years that were put together as fund-raisers by countless junior leagues, church groups, and chambers of commerce. They sell! But you do not have to be a nonprofit organization to write a cookbook. If you've got a flair for food, you might consider this genre, especially if you can target a special niche, like heart-healthy, diabetic, vegetarian, vegan, picky-kid/spouse, or harried working parent.

- *Self-help.* This is a perennial favorite on the nonfiction shelves. Americans are always looking to improve their own self-esteem or their children's self-confidence, to strengthen good relationships or cut off bad ones—in short to build psychological well-being. If you are a psychologist, psychiatrist, minister, social worker, or other mental health professional with a theory to propound, self-help can be a good nonfiction base for you.

- *How-to.* Another enduring favorite, the how-to guide runs the gamut of topics. You can write—and probably sell—a book on anything from woodworking to quilting, car repair to computer repair, flea market decorating to scuba diving. If you're either a schooled or self-styled expert in just about any hands-on activity, chances are you can turn it into a book.

- *Inspirational/motivational.* Also perennially popular, inspirational and motivational books can be mega-sellers. Just look at all those *Chicken Soup for the Soul* (Health Communications) books—of which there are now an astounding 100-plus volumes and counting! Peruse the scores of minibooks displayed on and around bookstore checkout counters (where they make terrific impulse buys), and you'll see that most of them are inspirational: *A Sister Is a Kindred Soul, Love Notes of the Great Poets, Grandbabies Are for Spoiling.* The list goes on and on. If you can come up with inspirational or motivational material that strikes a chord in readers, you might do well with this genre.

- *Regional.* This is a relatively unsung genre in which the self-publisher can often excel. If you live in a big city or a heavily touristed area, consider writing a restaurant or attraction guide. Or how about a volume featuring local history, local lore, or even area ghost stories? You might target the book toward families with young children, seniors, or the physically challenged. Use your imagination!

The Format

Nonfiction doesn't necessarily mean a 400-page volume of closely spaced text. It can encompass books—or perhaps more accurately, documents—of all lengths and sizes. You can format and sell your text as any one of the following:

- *Full-length books*. We'll explore book sizes and page counts in depth in Chapter 7. For now, let's say that a book by traditional definition is a collection of bound material that contains 49 or more pages, not including its front and back covers.

- *Pamphlets and reports*. These are smaller than books (unless they're produced by an office of the federal government) and focus on a single narrow topic. Bookstores

> **Smart Tip** — Tip…
>
> What book genres sell best? Jan Nathan of Publishers Marketing Association recommends business/career, personal finance, health, psychology/self-help, parenting, specialized crafts, cookbooks, religious/inspirational, animal, and gardening titles.

won't buy reports, but some intrepid self-publishers do very well selling them via mail order or on the internet as e-publications. Self-publishing guru Dan Poynter, for instance, sells 51 specialized reports on different aspects of the business at his web site, plus offers quite a bit of free information (see Appendix for contact information). You might publish reports on aspects of foreign or domestic travel, the how-tos of clearing up your credit or obtaining college scholarships, producing various handcrafts, designing a web site, or grooming different breeds of dogs—or anything else that's short, informative, and will interest a specific audience.

- *Minibooks*. These are generally of the inspirational/motivational variety we talked about earlier and are impulse buy and/or gift-oriented: *10 Cool Things About Cats*, *Daughters Are Perfect People*, or *The Fairies' Flower Language*, etc.

Back to the Fiction

> **Fun Fact**
>
> In the 19th century, *penny dreadfuls* were inexpensive, sensational novels of crime and adventure, so called because you could buy them for mere pennies. They didn't have a reputation as literature, but they sold like mad!

Now let's take another look at fiction. As we have explained, fiction has traditionally been a harder sell for the self-publisher. This doesn't mean it can't be successful. What it does mean is that you'll need to double up on your marketing smarts.

You need to consider how to make a novel commercially viable, advises Marilyn Ross of SPAN. How? Make it regional so it will sell regionally. Give your protagonist an interesting job, like spelunking, that other cave-explorers will want to read about. Really project what the important topics of the day will be when your book comes out so you can serve as an authority on those subjects. "You need to be calculating," Ross says. "You need a hook and you need publicity."

Jan Nathan of the Publishers Marketing Association agrees. "I think it's much easier with nonfiction, but specialized fiction [e.g. gay/lesbian, mystery, western, and sci-fi] can stand a chance of success as an independent. But general mainstream fiction still needs lots of dollars invested, in most cases, to tell the world about the book and to make a star of its author."

With the recent advent of e-publishing—which we will explore later in this chapter—the fiction-writer's handicap has begun to fade. As with just about every other kind of business, the internet seems to be leveling the playing field for writers. E-publishing is making fiction a more viable proposition by opening up new avenues of distribution. However, keep in mind that for most self-publishers it's still not anywhere near as profitable as nonfiction.

Fictional Formats

OK, so what kinds of fiction should you publish? There are many formats to choose from, but some are more popular among readers than others.

- *Novel.* This is the one everybody recognizes as a "book," a full-length tale by the likes of Danielle Steele, Dean Koontz, or J.K. Rowling. Novels come in genres like mystery, thriller, romance, horror, sci-fi, or "general fiction," which loosely includes any story that doesn't fit neatly into any of the traditional categories. And being the most recognizable, as well as the most popular type of fiction, novels are also the easiest to sell.

- *Short story.* Once upon a time, short stories were the lifeblood of many a successful author. Then this fiction format fell on hard times: A scant few were published in magazines, and even fewer found their way into books. Recently, however, the short story has bounded back to life due perhaps to the trendiness of 1950s art and artifacts, and traditional publishing houses are pumping out the collected short stories of various writers with zeal. Keep in mind, however, that the general public isn't nearly as interested in short fiction as in novels—if this is what you want to publish, you'll have to market assertively.

- *Novella.* A novella is shorter than a novel but longer than a short story. It's often grouped with two or three other tales of the same length by the same author, into a full-length book. Again, unless you're Stephen King or Nora Roberts, this format is going to be a tougher sell than a novel, but with e-publishing it is more of an option than ever before.

- *Serial.* Long, long ago in a century far away (the 19th to be exact), serials were very popular. They were actually novels divided into several installments and printed in successive issues of magazines or newspapers. Eagerly devoured by legions of devoted readers, serials were a sort of pre-electronic version of the TV miniseries. Today, after a very long hiatus, the serial has been resurrected, thanks in no small part to e-publishing.

- *Poetry.* Let's face it: Most folks consider poetry to be "arty" and basically unreadable, except as high school or college penance. Even with e-publishing, this is not going to be a major seller. If you're a poet at heart, do it for enjoyment but don't plan on it as a source of sufficient income.

- *Children's picture book.* People often have the misconception that writing a children's book is easy. It's not! A successful picture book is a carefully designed mélange of artwork and words that creates a verbal as well as a visual world. It has to speak to kids, as well as to parents on several levels, who will have to read it over and over and over again. But this doesn't mean you should give up before you start. Children's books can be timeless bestsellers, and there is always room for one more. If you're not an illustrator yourself, find one whose vision matches your own. Plan each scene on each page with care and with its own message, just as Anna J., the self-publisher in Temple, Texas, did with her children's book.

Outsourcing Options

If you're reading this book, you're probably a writer already—or you've at least got a pretty fair idea of the topic(s) you plan to write about. However, if you love the idea of publishing but are not sure you can pen an entire book on your own that people will actually want to read, fear not. There are several other sources from which to choose that will still give you the creative power of the press, while letting someone else do the brunt of the writing:

- *Out-of-copyright books.* Haunt garage sales, flea markets, and used book stores, and you can turn up terrific old books that are now in the public domain. When exactly a work is out of copyright can be complicated. Go to the Library of Congress web site at www.loc.gov/copyright for more information and always check with your attorney. With a little imagination and a catchy introduction, you can turn all sorts of dated material into a charming or clever outing. How about a 1890s "Boys Own Paper" book on camping skills or a sweet foray into Victorian manners with an antique wedding planner?

- *Anthologies or collections.* Take a noodle from the bowl of the prolific *Chicken Soup for the Soul* (Health Communications) publishers and put together an anthology of tales by various authors. Each story should have a common theme, like Victorian ghost tales, yarns for sailors, or gems for gardeners. Alternatively, you could take a more factual approach and put together a collection of articles on a particular topic—anything from dyslexia to the business of jewelry design to the truth about UFOs. You might commission

> **Fun Fact**
> Charles Dickens' immortal tale of lost boys and larceny among the lower classes, *Oliver Twist*, was originally published as a serial.

new material, or reprint stories or articles that have already appeared elsewhere. If you take the latter approach, make sure the rights to the story are actually available before you include it (see the section on subsidiary rights in Chapter 12).

- *Other writers' books*. Once you hang out your publishing shingle, you'll discover that authors will flock to you. You may already know several writers who would love to have you publish their books. If you don't, join a few writers' groups, which you can find in your hometown or in the global village of the internet. You'll probably find an author in one of these groups whose work is worth nurturing and then publishing.

The Potential of e-Publishing

We've made enticing allusions to e-publishing throughout this chapter. So now, without further ado, let's delve into e-publishing and find out what it involves.

e Is for Internet

The "e" stands for "electronic," but what it means to you is "internet." When you publish a book the traditional way, you have it printed on paper and bound between cardboard covers. Then you take your *dead tree*, paper-and-ink books and distribute them to bookstores, libraries, specialty stores, and direct mail customers.

When you e-publish a book, you place your text on an internet web site where it can be purchased directly by readers. This neatly eliminates two of the self-publisher's biggest costs: printing and distribution. Most e-publishers offer consumers several options for transforming their work from electronic bytes to readable book. Consumers can:

- Download material onto their computer's hard drive and then read the text on the computer's monitor, or print a hard copy using their own printer
- Purchase the material in CD form so they can read it using their computer or print a copy

- Purchase the material as a printed dead tree or p-book that will be mailed to them (an option not offered by most e-publishers)

- Download the material onto an *e-book reader* (a hardware device about the size of a paperback book, which allows material to be read on-screen)

Stat Fact

According to *Publishers Weekly*, e-book sales average between $12–15 million per year. The medium isn't exactly setting the world on fire, but is slowly gaining ground.

The e-Advantage

As a self-publisher, you can put up your own site, or you can upload your book on one of the dozens of e-book sites that are springing up all over the internet. There are numerous advantages to the latter:

1. You let somebody else do all the work of converting your text to a *PDF file*, a language computers use to translate your text into a downloadable format and then back again to plain English.

2. Some e-book sites provide "cover" art for your book, which saves you the expense of finding and then paying an illustrator.

3. The site acts as a virtual bookstore where readers will hopefully choose your title from among all the others offered, thus providing you with "shelf space" without having to go through traditional avenues of distribution.

4. E-book sites offer generous royalty schedules—generally from 30 to 70 percent of the list price of each title. Keep in mind, however, that e-books often sell for less than conventional p-books. The norm is anywhere from $5 to $8.95, although prices can soar to $19.95.

5. Some sites have editorial guidelines and don't accept every author and every title, while others are happy to let anybody upload anything.

6. Most e-book sites are more than happy to accept fiction!

Too Good

If all this sounds too good to be true, it's not. E-publishing is phenomenally exciting. But the jury is still out. The dawn of the e-book has come and gone without the earth-shattering sales many industry spectators were anticipating. According to *Publishers Weekly*, at least 20 clashing e-book formats have popped up in recent years, making it difficult to reach a mass audience. E-book sales trail behind traditional book sales by the billions, and much of this has to do with the e-book industry's failure to adopt standards that would make downloading and reading an e-book as easy as downloading songs on iTunes. However, industry experts remain hopeful, believe it's here to stay, and are working at securing a slice of the pie. According to the *Communications Industry Forecast* (CIF), publishers have slowly been testing the digital and online markets, and spending on e-books, online versions of printed copies, and audio podcasts—rose 68 percent in 2005, to $74 million.

Like any other form of publishing, e-publishing demands scads of promotional time, effort, and talent to achieve true success. If you're not willing to make that commitment, your title will probably languish on the virtual shelf of the e-book site just as it would languish on the racks of a brick-and-mortar bookstore.

Fun Fact

Stephen King's writing career almost ended up in the wastepaper basket. After suffering the rejection of two earlier novels, King tossed a work-in-progress into the trash. His wife, Tabitha, dug it out and convinced him to forge ahead. In 1974, Doubleday bought that manuscript—called *Carrie*—providing the King of horror with enough money to quit his day job as a schoolteacher and write full time.

Plotting Your Bestseller
Market Research

Authors often believe that they should write a book first, then find an audience later. This may be a viable proposition for the writer who's a dabbler or hobbyist, but it's not necessarily profitable. As a self-publisher, you're writing and producing a book with a specific goal in mind: to make money. You may have other goals in mind as well, like

Anna J., in Temple, Texas, whose primary goal is to help the families of critically ill children. But if you can't make that venture pay for itself or earn a profit, you can't be successful.

So your first mission in becoming a self-publisher is to conduct market research. This will help you determine whether there is in fact an audience, or market, for your book. Your research should tell you how large that market is and even narrow down what specific elements your target market wants to read about in your book.

The First Task

The first task you will have is to decide what exactly your book will be about. You may already have made this decision, down to the tiniest detail, or you may still have a wide-open field in front of you. Either approach is fine, so long as you keep in mind the following guidelines:

- *Be a cheerleader*. Enthusiasm sells books. You can't write a winning book on a subject you think is dead boring. Cast your mind back to the agony of all those fatally dull high school and college term papers. It's no fun to write about something you're completely uninterested in, and it will show in your text. But if you write about something you feel truly passionate about, you stand a better chance of excelling at it.

- *Be in the know*. You must have a thorough knowledge of your subject. Knowledge gives your words confidence and credibility—the first steps to best-sellerdom. If you do not know everything about your subject, get out there and research, research, and research some more and build some credentials for yourself.

- *Fixate on your focus*. Make sure your book has a well-defined subject. A cookbook called *Good Food* won't attract anybody in particular—it isn't focused on any specific interest, need or goal. But a cookbook called *Festive Parties for Frazzled Folks*, or *Brain-Booster Cookery*, or even *Cooking Lean* will attract a legion of readers with their promises of stress-free party giving, boosted brain power, or slim and trim tummies.

- *Quench a thirst*. Remember that readers buy books based on their wants and needs, thirsts that you as a self-publisher can slake. These can run the gamut: a desire to retire rich at age 40 or a need to find a better-paying job; a desire to find a husband or a need to save a marriage; a desire to grow bigger flowers or a need to feed a family on home-grown vegetables. Besides hard-core nonfiction topics, readers of all ages, genders, and walks of life have an unquenchable thirst for entertainment and inspiration in the form of fiction, biographies, autobiographies, and humor.

Your Target Market

Now that you've decided what you'll write about, you've probably already figured out—at least in part—who you're writing it for. This is your target market. And it's very important. You would not write a book on *Home Driveway Auto Repair* with the goal of selling it to urban New Yorkers who do not have driveways, or to people who think Makita is a furniture style and not a Sears hand tool.

If your target market is too small, your book is unlikely to be lucrative. If you write a genealogical history of your immediate family, for instance, you'll have eliminated your entire market once your parents, your siblings, and Aunt Ethel and Uncle Bill buy copies. (And they probably won't actually buy those books anyway. They'll insist that as family they should get complimentary copies.) But if you write a history of the Celtic families of California (with yours just one among them), you may find you have thousands of readers to sell to.

Smart Tip

Tip...

If you are serious about finding the most accurate, up-to-date sales and market information, consider purchasing a membership to Nielsen Bookscan. Yep, this is the same group responsible for the Nielsen television rating system. Now, they've extended their reach to books, music, and even software. You can harness the power of Nielsen research and search for sales information by title, author, category . . . you name it. Though pricey, the information is worth its weight in 60-pound natural paper! Check out www.bookscan.com to find out more.

Nudging into Your Niche

As you target your market, start thinking *market niche*. This is your special corner of the market, the area of expertise and interest that makes your book, and what you have to say in it, stand out from any competition you may have. There are lots of books on the shelves, for instance, on crafts. But if yours is specifically for busy working people who don't have the time to fashion Christmas tree decorations or Independence Day doodads (until you show them how), then that's your niche: crafts for the constantly hectic.

If you write a self-help guide on the power of positive thinking, you'll have to compete with the scads of similar volumes already out there. So you will want to consider a market niche that makes yours special. Is it positive thinking for the hopelessly pessimistic? Is it positive thinking for families to practice together? Or is it positive thinking for teachers?

Spend time online and in bookstores finding out more about what's already out there on the shelves and find a totally new spin on the subject. See what sells well and what doesn't, and consider the customer comments of your competitors. Many times,

Clarity Sells

Once you decide on a subject for your book, you'll want to narrow its focus. The clearer you are about your topic and who you're writing it for, the easier it will be both to write and sell. If you're an avid gardener, for instance, you could choose any one of several intriguing directions to focus on:

○ A guide for the after-work gardener

○ A children's book for the young beginning gardener

○ A manual on gardening in your specific region of the country

○ An anthology of inspirational stories by gardeners of all ages and walks of life

○ A gardener's cookbook

○ A book on gardening as therapy for the elderly

○ And lots more! Use your imagination!

those comments provide clues on what worked in a similar title and what didn't, giving you a roadmap of where to take your unique approach.

Gary S., the self-publisher in Panama City Beach, Florida, has a found his market niche in books that deal with the experiences of World War II veterans. His books are oral histories, personal stories told directly by participants in the action—which sets his works apart from the tomes written by historians who hadn't "been there and done that" themselves. Anna J.'s market niche is that her books are written for families that have a child with a heart defect—a special group for whom no other books exist.

Researching Your Reader Base

Once you target your market and develop your special niche, you'll want to research it to make sure it's large enough to support your publishing efforts. There are all sorts of ways to go about this, from gathering statistics to taking informal surveys.

Send Me a Letter

One sure-fire way to ascertain the size and interest level of your target market is via direct-mail surveys. You won't blanket the entire state of Mississippi or the San Francisco Bay area (or wherever you live) with questionnaires; this would be extremely

Stat Fact

What moves readers to open their wallets at the bookstore? Forty-nine percent of people polled by Spier NY, an advertising firm, bought books based on a friend's recommendation. Familiarity with the author was a close second at 45 percent, followed by being moved by the jacket copy (32 percent), reviews (22 percent), and advertisement (21 percent). Other factors playing a role in purchasing decisions are placement on a bestseller list, reading group influence, and the design of the cover art. Seems some people do judge a book by its cover.

expensive, as well as unproductive. Instead, you'll narrow your focus to the very potential readers you want to attract.

If you're writing an alternative therapy book for people suffering from arthritis, for instance, you would send surveys to members of local, regional, and national arthritis support groups. If you are penning a book on closing techniques for real-estate agents, you'll send your surveys out to the members of various real-estate boards.

If you belong to an association, organization, or listserv (an electronic mailing list), and it just happens to be affiliated with your target market, you have it made. You may already have a directory packed with names and phone numbers at hand. If not, you may be able to beg, borrow, or buy a directory from the organization's main office. If your market niche is something more general, like a volume of inspirational thoughts for each month of the year, you might still start off with the members of your club or group. Your common membership will act as your proverbial foot in the door. If you don't belong to any groups, how about a church roster or neighborhood association? Use your imagination!

What should you ask? Check out the "Market Research Survey" on page 37. Your queries will relate to your own target market and written product, but you can use this as a starting point for what and how to ask.

Hello Central

Another way to reach potential customers is through telephone surveys, which are basically the same as direct-mail or listserv surveys—with one important difference. People don't always react kindly to unsolicited calls these days when telemarketers are striving mightily to drive us all around the bend with their poorly-timed appeals. Unless you've got thick skin, it can be difficult to make cold calls to people you don't know and pick their brains.

Smart Tip

Tip...

Anna J., the self-publisher in Temple, Texas, used *listservs* (e-mail message-sharing groups) to help determine her market. Since she belonged to several listservs for parents of kids with heart defects, she was able to judge the number of families who needed her books.

An Added Bonus

There's a secret bonus to taking market research surveys. It's that your respondents help you write your book! When you ask what specific elements prospective readers would like to see addressed, you know what to include in your book.

Of course, you have to be selective about the results. If one person out of a hundred claims to want to read about growing deadly nightshade in a garden text, you can safely leave that topic aside. But if 95 people out of the same 100 ask for information on growing tomatoes in a shade garden, you can assume this is a subject most readers will genuinely be interested in.

You can also use this survey information in your back-of-the-book blurb—the sales material you print on your back cover. How? Write up something like, "*Shade Tree Gardening* answers the questions America's home gardeners want to know!" Or, "*Shade Tree Gardening* is the book America's home gardeners helped design!"

However, if you use a membership list from an organization you belong to, you may have a foot in the door. Your call won't seem quite as unsolicited if you can say that you (or your sibling, spouse, or child) belong to the Upper Peninsula Chapter of the Antique Car Restoration Society or the Michigan Educators Society, etc.

Statistics on Tap

Besides going directly to your prospective readers for your market research, you'll also want cool, calculated statistics. For that book on alternative therapies, you will want to know facts like the number of arthritis sufferers there are in the United States. For a regional title on coastal home design, you may need to know how many people build second homes on the Florida Gulf Coast.

The answers to questions like these will help you determine just how many prospective readers you can expect and if that number is large enough to be lucrative. Where do you get all this statistical stuff? Try the following sources.

Smart Tip

Tip...

People are unlikely to return a mail survey unless you offer them an incentive. So get creative! Give them a coupon for 10 percent off your book when it comes out. This gives you a head start on advanced sales and also helps spread the word about your book.

Market Research Survey

This sample survey is designed for market research for a book on affordable housing for seniors.

1. If you're a senior citizen, what is your age? _____

2. Are you living on a fixed income? _____

3. Have you experienced difficulties finding affordable housing? _____

4. If yes, what avenues have you explored and what were the results? _____
   _____

5. Where are you living now (i.e. apartment, house, condominium, etc.)? ____

6. What do you pay for rent per month?
   a) $200 to $700   b) $701 to $1,400   c) $1,401 and up

7. Is your rent subsidized by the government or another agency? _____

8. Do your children or other relatives help to pay your rent? _____

9. Would you be interested in a book that would guide you to find affordable housing? _____

10. How much would you be willing to pay for such a book? _____

11. What specific information or problems would you like to see addressed in relation to this topic? _____
    _____
    _____

12. Have you read a book or pamphlet of this type in the past? _____

13. If so, did you find it helpful? Why or why not? _____
    _____

14. Please comment on the title *Affordable Housing on a Fixed Income* (love, like, dislike, or detest, and why): _____
    _____
    _____

15. Please comment on the title *Home Alone: Affordable Housing for Seniors* (love, like, dislike, or detest, and why): _____
    _____
    _____

Library Look-Up

Ask your local reference librarian, a person well worth making friends with. Pay her a visit and explain what you need to know and why. Librarians live for books, so the fact that you're writing one gives you extra brownie points. Tell your librarian that you need to know how many florists, bed-and-breakfast inns, or adults with Alzheimer's there are in the United States. She will provide you with stacks of demographic statistics; more facts and figures than you might imagine could possibly exist.

Get on the Net

You'll find the answers to all sorts of fascinating questions on the internet. For starters, check in with the U.S. Department of Commerce (www.doc.gov) and the U.S. Census Bureau (www.census.gov). You can check out the stats from all those millennium census surveys! Click on any number of general and specialized search engines, from Yahoo! to Google to InfoJump, and get the scoop from millions of articles, publications, and web sites that relate to your area of interest.

Try the Target

Sometimes the best place to go for information on a target market is the target itself. If your market is crafters, for instance, you'd contact the National Craft Association and the Association of Crafts and Creative Industries for counts of their members. To find out the number of dog breeders, you'd talk to the folks at state and regional breeding societies. You get the idea.

Check Out the Competition

While you're doing your market research, don't forget to check out what sort of competition your book will face. Ask any literary agent, and they'll tell you that's one of the first things they consider. Specifically, you want to look at these key questions:

- How many books are already out there on your subject?
- What are their strengths and weaknesses compared with the one you plan?

Beware!

Those up-to-the-minute rankings on Amazon.com are great, but keep in mind that they don't tell the whole story of a competitive book's sales. They provide snapshots of how a particular book is performing on a particular day. Complete the sales picture with comprehensive sales information from Nielsen Bookscan.

- What sets your book apart from the crowd?

This part of your market research is fun—it means that, darn it, you'll have to abandon doing the laundry, mowing the lawn, or preparing your income tax return, and spend time in the bookstore. Peruse the shelves. Look at any book that could conceivably match yours and see how it stacks up in respect to the key questions above.

Keep in mind that the bookstore is where you want to be. The library is not the best place to do this kind of research because most of its volumes will be several—or several dozen—years old. You want to know what readers will see today or tomorrow that will compete with your volume, not what was popular 5, 10, or even 20 years ago. You want to know what other publishers' market research has shown to be worthy of stacking on those bookstore shelves today. And that is what bookstore crawling will tell you.

Tip...

Smart Tip

The fact that there are no books the least like yours on the shelves can be a plus—or a minus. If you find a dozen titles on financial investments, it doesn't necessarily mean the market is saturated; it means people are eager readers on the topic. If you can't find even one volume about cockroach farming, this can be a valuable clue that there's no market for the subject.

Your Publishing House
Office and Business Structure

Every publisher, from the mighty Warner Books to the smallest small press, has a "house," or office. As a self-publisher, you'll need one, too. You'll also need a sound business structure that will take you from novice book producer to seasoned publisher. In this chapter, we'll investigate the issues involved in getting established, including your legal business structure, company image, and domain name, as well as dealing with zoning regulations and Uncle Sam. It's not all drudgery, and it is crucial for getting your business off to a good start. So let's get to it!

Creating an Image

Even though self-publishing has come out of the closet and is now a respected segment of the industry, it can still carry a stigma of amateurism. So the image your company will have is important. You'll want to craft one that will tell readers, reviewers, distributors, bookstores, and everybody else you'll deal with on a business basis that you're a professional.

The Name Game

The first element of your image is your company name. It's going to reflect not only your first book but also all the others to come; so plan it carefully. You might choose a name based on the types of books you'll publish, like "Gardeners Press" for a publisher of gardening guides, or "Cookbook Nook Publishing" for a cookbook publisher. The upside of this technique is that readers know exactly what to expect from you—and that's a plus. The downside is that if you decide later on to add to your repertoire by publishing quilting books in addition to cookbooks, your name will be misleading.

You might try naming your company after a local or regional feature, perhaps "Three Trees Press," "Seaside Publishing," or "Moonlight & Magnolias Press." Instead, you might decide on something quirky like "Glitterbug Press" or "Three Jakes Publishing," which is perfectly fine—just make sure that your name properly reflects your products. If you will publish serious works like surgical manuals for physicians, a name like "All Thumbs Press" won't give you much credibility.

Beware!

If you name your company after yourself, as in Joe Doaks Publishing or Doaks Press, book reviewers and other industry movers-and-shakers will likely brand you an amateur self-publisher and refuse to take your book seriously.

Name Fiction

Once you've decided on a company name, you'll need to register it with your local authorities. In doing so, you make sure that no one else in your area is already using that name. You also ensure that no one else in your area can legally take on your business name at a later date, and you give your company its first legal status. This is important: Banks will not give you a business account without a *fictitious business name statement*, also called a DBA, which stands for "doing business as." And without a business account, many vendors will not deal with you.

Obtaining a DBA is easy, although the process varies a bit in different regions of the country. In the state of Florida, for instance, you call the office of the Secretary of State, and after enough time on hold to file all your nails, watch two "I Love Lucy" reruns, and read a chapter of *Harry Potter*, you're given the opportunity to check up to three potential business names. When you hit on one that hasn't already

> **Tip...**
>
> **Smart Tip**
> Don't panic if your domain name has already been taken; there's usually a way around it. If your company is called "Bell Book Press," for instance, and there's already a www.bellbook.com, try something like www.bb press.com or www.bellbook xpress.com. Get creative!

Business Name Brainstorming

List three ideas for a business name based on the type of books you plan to publish (paranormal, romance, children's fantasy, auto repair, etc.).

1. _____

2. _____

3. _____

List three ideas for a name combining a favorite theme with your planned products (i.e., New Age, eco-awareness, empowering women, etc.).

1. _____

2. _____

3. _____

After you've decided which name you like best, have you:

❏ Tried it aloud to make sure it's easily understood and pronounced? (Has it passed muster with your family? Have you had a friend call to see how it sounds over the phone?)

❏ Checked your local Yellow Pages to make sure the same or similar name is not already listed?

❏ Checked with your local business name authority to make sure it's available?

Your Domain

While you're registering your company name, you should also consider registering your business web site name, or *domain name*, which is the www.whatever.com thing people type in to access your virtual office. There can be only one company per domain name, so you'll have to think up several versions of the name you want in case one has already been taken.

Here's what you need to do: Go into your web browser and type in www.networksolutions.com. Once you're at the Network Solutions web site, which is very user-friendly, follow the easy directions and check to see if the domain name you've chosen has been taken. If it has, keep choosing alternatives until you find a permutation that's available; then register it online. The cost—if you already have a web host for your site—is $35 for a one-year registration.

been appropriated, the Secretary's office sends you a registration form. You mail back the completed form, the registration fee, and a form from your local newspaper verifying that you have advertised your DBA for one week. In return, you receive your business name certificate.

In other areas of the country, you might simply pop down to your city or county clerk's office, thumb through the roster of business names, and then complete the registration procedure at the clerk's window.

Of Logos and Letterhead

There's more to image than a name. Your visual image—the colors, graphics, typefaces, and paper stocks you choose for everything from stationery to brochures—also plays a starring role in how people perceive your company.

If you'll publish books for the home handyperson, for instance, design a logo that says home repair with saws, wrenches or hammers embellishing your company name. If you'll publish travel books, splash your materials with travel stickers, suitcases, or a stylized cruise liner. And if you publish sci-fi tales, how about a logo featuring a UFO or an extraterrestrial?

> **Tip...**
>
> **Smart Tip**
>
> If you choose to have your stationery professionally printed instead of going with your own desktop publishing, check prices with a variety of vendors: local printers, quick-copy centers like Kinko's, and also office supply supercenters like Office Depot.

Since you'll carry out most of your negotiations with customers, vendors, and suppliers via snail mail (U.S. Postal Service) when you're not using e-mail, you should take care that your stationery is high quality. You can design and print everything from letterhead and envelopes to business cards using your own computer system, so it does not have to be expensive. Use papers with oomph—those with weight, class, and distinction:

- Letterhead paper weight should be about 24 pounds—not the copier-grade see-through stuff that's 20 pounds. You might try a style that's specially-textured for added interest.
- Business cards that you print off your computer come in sheets with each card perforated so you can tear them out easily. Go for stock with fine perforations so they look professionally printed; avoid the sheets with raggedy "punched" edges.
- Envelopes should match your letterhead and your business cards.

Laying Your Foundation

Your publishing house will need more of a foundation than a business name and a domain name. You'll need to decide on a legal structure, check into sales tax, get insurance coverage, and line up an attorney and an accountant—all the nitty gritty stuff that will give your company a solid base on which to grow.

The Soul of Your Proprietorship

To appease those hard-working IRS employees, your business must have a structure. You can operate it as a sole proprietorship, a partnership, or a corporation, with variations thereon. Many self-publishing newbies go with the simplest and easiest version, which is the sole proprietorship. If you'll be starting out on your own, you may choose the same option. It's the least complicated and the least expensive.

You can always switch to another format later on, if and when you take on partners and employees. Anna J., the self-publisher in Temple, Texas, for example, has chosen to reformat her company as a non-profit corporation, after four years as a sole proprietor. This is time-consuming and expensive, and it's not a do-it-yourself option—you need the assistance of an attorney. But Anna decided to go for it because the money she saves on taxes will enable her to help many more families with sick children.

Tip...

Smart Tip

When you contact your local municipality, don't forget to ask about a business license. Getting one generally involves filling out a simple form and paying a nominal annual fee. It's easy!

A Taxing Affair

If you plan to sell books by mail order (which includes internet sales) or in person at seminars and workshops, you will need to register to collect sales tax by applying for a state sales license or permit. Sales taxes vary by state and are imposed at the retail level. This can all get a bit complex. You only charge sales tax to mail order customers who live in your state—when you ship out of state you don't charge tax.

The best way to handle the situation is to check with your accountant when you get to that point. He or she can advise you on where to get your license and who to charge for what.

Expert Advice

Attorneys are like plumbers: You don't want to think about them until you need one, but as a business owner, you should have a good attorney on call—one that knows the intellectual property business. You will want her to check over any contracts you

Mission Style

While you're setting up the elements of your publishing house, you'll want to design a *mission statement*. This is a short and sweet summary of your company's products, philosophy, market niche, and goals. The mission statement is the business version of the positive-thinking "sticky" notes you put on your bathroom mirror. It gives your company a plan—and a style—which are easily referred to and easily remembered.

A mission statement for a self-publisher of parenting books might look something like this:

Parent City Press is devoted to helping parents raise a new generation of caring kids. Our mission is to foster a feeling of community among parents and children around the world with a series of books by and for parents of smart, happy young people. Our goal is steady and incremental growth and annually increased profits that will fund us in teaching the global village to raise its children wisely.

write with wholesalers, distributors, book clubs, printers, and other authors or publishers. You'll also need your lawyer to advise you on the fine points of general small-business law. You won't need to call her every week, or even every month, but there's no point in waiting until you've got a problem to establish a relationship.

Along with that on-call attorney, you'll want to look into hiring an accountant to fill out your tax returns and advise you of any special ways you can save money with your business structure.

And don't forget your insurance agent! He can be an invaluable source of information and expertise. If you'll be homebased, you'll need to find out if your homeowners' package covers your business assets, inventory, and equipment, or if you need additional coverage. If you're based outside the home, you need coverage for these same items, as well as your physical location.

On Location

One of the great perks of being a self-publisher by trade is that you can work at home. You don't need a high-traffic or high-visibility location, so you don't need to set up shop in a trendy part of town. Because all your business is virtual, you won't need an executive office with client seating or a Lucite-and-chrome conference room. The only space requirement is an area large enough for your desk, your chair, your filing cabinets, and your bookcase.

The home office is convenient: It cuts commuting time and expense down to zero. It's also economical—you don't need to spend money on leased space, extra utilities, or lunches in the building cafeteria.

Working at home is not compulsory for the self-publisher, but it's a definite plus, and one that you should not ignore. Unless you've got a boisterous family or a roommate who's an aspiring rock-and-roll drummer, wait until your company has outgrown your home work space to shop around for something else.

The Home Office

The self-publishers we interviewed for this book have home offices. If you go the same route, you can locate your office work space anywhere in the house that's convenient; but ideally, you should have a dedicated office, a room that's reserved just for the business. You can locate this room in a den, a FROG (finished room over garage), the garage itself, or a spare bedroom. Keep in mind that whatever space you choose will be your work station and command center.

If a dedicated office is not an option for you, you can also station yourself in a corner of the kitchen, or at the dining room table. If you've got a noisy family, however, a cubbyhole in your bedroom is liable to be much more conducive to quiet, clear thinking than a nook in the family room with the TV blaring at all hours.

The Big Write-Off

A big advantage to the home office is the ability to wear two hats—to be at home with your family and be at work at the same time. Another advantage is the ability to count your home business as a tax write-off. The IRS will graciously allow you to deduct money from your income taxes if you're using a portion of your home as your income-producing work space. You can deduct a percentage of expenses equivalent to the percentage of space your home office occupies. If, for example, you're using one room in an eight-room house, you can deduct one-eighth of your rent or mortgage, plus you can deduct one-eighth of your utility bills.

There is an "if" involved here. You can only use this deduction if you're using a space in your home that serves solely as your office. If you have turned your spare bedroom into your office, and you don't use it for anything but conducting your business, then you qualify. If, however, your office is tucked into a corner of the kitchen, and you're still feeding people in there, you don't qualify for the home office deduction (unless you can convince the IRS that the microwave oven is actually some sort of quick-dry printing device).

Organized and Efficient

Even though you will be working at home, it's important to remember that you are still a professional. Your work quarters, like yourself, should be organized and efficient. If at all possible, designate a separate room with four walls and a door. Aim for pleasant, quiet, well-lit surroundings. You're going to be spending a lot of time in this space, so you want it to be comfortable.

Find a desk or a table large enough to hold your computer, keyboard, phone, pencil holder, stapler, etc., and that will be big enough to have room to spread out your working papers.

Make sure you have enough space to neatly file bids from printers, distributors, and other vendors. You'll also need a place to file manuscript pages in various stages of revision, artwork, and order forms from customers. You'll probably need a separate room or storage area to stash your company brochures, catalogs, and other direct-mail materials, as well as industry magazines you'll subscribe to and copies of your own books!

> ### Tip...
> **Smart Tip**
> If you plan to work from home, you'll want to check into zoning regulations. Find out from your city government whether any permits are necessary. If you need a zoning variance, apply for that, too.

The Home Office

Use this handy worksheet to locate and design your home office.

Start by listing three possible locations in your home for your office, which should include a work area for you and enough space for your desk, computer, and telephone.

1. _____

2. _____

3. _____

Make a physical survey of each location.

❏ Are phone and electrical outlets placed close enough to your equipment so that they can be accessed easily? Or will you be faced with unsightly, unsafe cords snaking across the carpet?

❏ Measure your space. Will your current desk or table (or the one you have your eye on) fit?

❏ Do you have adequate lighting? If not, can you create or import it?

❏ What is the noise factor?

❏ Is there room to spread out your work?

❏ Optional: How close is it to the kitchen? (This can be either a plus or minus, depending on your current waistline.)

Take a survey of possible home storage spaces for books.

❏ Is there adequate lighting, ventilation, and space for you to easily access books?

❏ What is the humidity factor?

❏ Will you need to construct special shelving or add other storage space? If so, make notes here: _____

_____

_____

_____

_____

_____

Whether you use the fanciest hanging file folders in mahogany drawers, or simple manila ones in cardboard boxes, you must be able to access this information quickly and easily. It's no fun digging through the back of the clothes closet or running out to the garage every time somebody calls with a question.

The Storage Space

You'll need storage space for your books after you get them from the printer. We'll explore this issue further in Chapter 8. For now, consider having to store a print run that's anywhere from 150 to 5,000 books. Do you have a garage or spare room where you can store them in clean, dry, low-humidity splendor?

If not, you'll have to look into renting a space, as Anna J. in Texas does. "I used to have all my books in my house, but since I printed 5,000 copies of each of my last two books, I have had to rent a climate-controlled storage facility," Anna says.

Tip...

Smart Tip

You'll need enough space for your company "shipping department," an area you'll use to package your products for shipping. It doesn't matter if it's the kitchen table or a special workstation in your office, so long as there's adequate room to spread out your materials and wrap that package professionally.

The Commercial Office

This worksheet will help you plan your commercial office.

Start by listing three possible locations for your office based on proximity to your home, rental price, and storage space for your books:

1. _____

2. _____

3. _____

Make a physical survey of the interior office space of potential locations.

❑ Is there enough room for desks, computers, and telephones for you and for employees who may need their own units?

❑ Can phone and electrical outlets be accessed easily at potential workstations?

❑ Is there adequate lighting and proper ventilation?

❑ Is there adequate storage space?

❑ Optional: Where will you place a coffee maker? A refrigerator?

For Steve C. in Hinesburg, Vermont, storage is not a problem. "I live in the country on a big piece of land, and my favorite hobby is building and remodeling," Steve says. "So I've built whatever storage facilities I need. If I lived in a city apartment, that obviously wouldn't be an option. More and more publishers are signing up with the kinds of fulfillment services that store large quantities—companies like Publishers' Shipping and Storage, Rayve, and Pathway. When they get an order from Ingram [a book wholesaler] for 90 cases of books, they just call the storage company and have the books shipped from there. Of course, there are still lots of self-publishers with one or two titles who find their garages adequate for storage—as long as they don't mind parking in the driveway."

The Commercial Office

If you decide to go for an office outside your home, you can choose just about any spot, so long as it's clean, dry (books don't like dampness), quiet, and accessible to the UPS man for those book deliveries.

You could go with a downtown loft, a space in a light industrial park, or an older house in a quaint historic district. Since you won't need visibility, you could even start out by subleasing space from another aspiring businessperson who could use help with the rent.

Outfitting Your Space

Whether your office is in an historic building, a modest office plaza, a downtown office, or a barn by the river, you'll need the same basic setup as in a home office. You'll need plenty of room for your files, plus your desk, chair, a few pieces of visitors' furniture, and desks and chairs for any employees you may hire.

Whether in a home or commercial office, your computer should occupy a place of honor, away from dirt, drafts, and blinding sunlight. The same applies to your printer and fax machine. And don't forget to outfit your office space with every worker's favorite piece of equipment—the coffee maker!

Take into consideration, too, book storage and shipping issues. If you go with a light industrial site, it will likely include a warehouse or work space in the back that can serve as an ideal storage and packaging space. But if you'll take on a quirkier alternative, like a room in somebody else's office, you might need to go with an off-site, climate-controlled storage unit to hold all your books.

5

Your Start-Up
Finances

As you know, one of the really grand things about self-publishing is that your costs can be relatively low. You won't need a commercial space, workroom, or equipment for scads of employees, and you won't need thousands of dollars of inventory to put on store shelves. But self-publishing isn't cost-free, either. Your expenses will fall into three basic categories:

1. *Company expenses.* These are the expenses like a computer, software, telephone, and membership fees to various organizations that you'll incur whether you produce one book or a hundred.
2. *Book production expenses.* These costs will be different for each title you publish; they include things like printing, illustration, and copy editing fees (see Chapter 6).
3. *Sales and promotion expenses.* The costs associated with sales and promotion will be covered in Chapters 9 and 10. Distributors' fees and shipping costs will also fall under this category (see Chapter 8).

In this chapter, we'll explore the costs involved in starting your self-publishing company. We'll return to the costs associated with book production, and selling and promoting your books in later chapters.

Computer Caveats

Perhaps the most important item on your start-up list is a computer system—a hard drive, monitor, mouse, modem, and printer, plus whatever peripherals you choose to tack on. A good system will allow you to shine as a self-publisher by taking on all these tasks on your own:

- Writing and editing your manuscript.
- Writing and editing promotional materials like press releases and reviews. (Yes, you will sometimes create your own for reviewers to print!)
- Creating your own brochures, display ads, and other direct-mail pieces.
- Generating stationery, invoices, and order forms.
- Tracking royalties (your own from e-publishing sites and/or those you pay to other authors).
- Performing accounting functions and generating financial reports.
- Maintaining customer databases.
- Accessing research materials and other resources online.
- Selling via an online or "virtual" brochure or catalog.
- Communicating with repeat and potential customers, suppliers, vendors, and distributors via e-mail.

Your new computer should be Pentium-class with the latest version of the Windows operating system, since this is what the majority of software packages are geared toward. To run your software properly, you will need at least 64MB RAM, plus at least an 8GB to 10GB hard drive, a CD-ROM drive and/or Zip drive, and a 56Kbps modem. You can expect to pay from $1,500 to $3,500 for a good name-brand computer system (not including a printer), with prices increasing as you add on goodies.

Soft on Software

As beneficial as your computer is, it can't help you unless you give it software to make it sing. A stunning array of software lines the shelves of most office supply stores, ready to help you perform every business task—design and print your own checks, develop professional-quality marketing materials, make mailing lists and labels, even act as your own attorney and accountant.

Most new computers come pre-loaded with all the software you'll need for basic office procedures. You'll also need to look into the following programs:

> **Smart Tip** _Tip..._
>
> Monitors are often sold separately. You will want an SVGA high resolution color display and a screen large enough to make long-term viewing comfortable, say 17 inches and up. Remember that a few extra dollars spent upfront will save hours of squinting over the long haul. You can expect to dish out $200 to $300 for a solid, mid-range model.

- *Word processing*. A good basic program such as Microsoft Word or Corel WordPerfect can be had for around $100. With this software, you can write your book, as well as correspondence, contracts, press releases, articles, and whatever else strikes your fancy.

- *Accounting*. These software programs are a sort of checkbook on a CD, and they make record-keeping a breeze. You assign categories such as office supplies and business travel to the checks you write, and at tax time you print out a report showing how much you spent for what. Your accountant not only thanks you but also gives you a discount for not having to wade through all your receipts. You can expect to pay $30 to $180 for a program like Intuit Quicken for Home and Business, Intuit QuickBooks or Peachtree Accounting to track your business finances.

- *Desktop publishing*. This type of program will help you transform the manuscript you generate with word processing software into a format that book printers will accept. You can also use this software for creating sales and promotional materials. The two true publishing programs available are pricey and often considered challenging to use. So be prepared to work at it, and eventually you will learn to love them. Choose Adobe InDesign or Quark Xpress, which both dent your wallet for around $700.

- *Mailing list management*. For those mailing lists you're developing of past and potential participants, you'll also want to purchase a list management program like My Mail List and AddressBook from Avanquest for around $30. You can organize mail lists, create and import databases, and design a variety of mail pieces.

- *Software designed for publishers*. Instead of going amateur with a mailing list program and a general-purpose accounting program, you might opt to start off with the real thing: software designed especially for publishers. Publishers' Assistant by Upper Access Inc. gives you everything you need to track invoices, royalties, and inventory; handle billing and order entry; and manage your mailing lists. Pencil in about $495 for the "Sonnet" version, or be ready to shell out big bucks to the tune of $2245 for the "Epic" edition. You can download a free trial of any version of the program, but you are limited to 24 uses (see the Appendix for contact information). Other popular publisher software programs include Publishing Solutions from Quality Solutions, Inc. and Publishing Manager from Trilogy.

Dollar Stretcher

When you purchase your new computer, you can often buy it pre-loaded with word processing and accounting programs that will suit your needs. If you negotiate wisely, you might save valuable software dollars.

Go ISP!

As a self-publisher, you must have a safe and reliable ISP, or internet service provider, such as America Online, AT&T, People PC, Net Zero, or countless others. With the power of the World Wide Web at your command, you can go anywhere on the globe instantly, all from the comfort of your own desktop. You can research, promote, and sell books, as well as communicate with customers and vendors. And it's cheap! Most internet service providers, or ISPs, charge about $20 to $25 per month and give you unlimited web and e-mail access.

Web Weaving

Several of the self-publishers we talked with for this book have their own web sites. If you plan to sell by mail order (which includes internet sales), a company site can be a boon. And even if you don't go this route, a web site can help promote your books.

The cost of putting up and maintaining a business site can vary considerably. If you're lucky enough to have a computer brain in the family, or if you take the time to become your own computer expert, you can pencil in a zero under web site design and construction costs. There's a definite learning curve, but once you

Smart Tip

Web site design and hosting fees may be higher in large urban areas. Shop around. It doesn't matter if you're in Atlanta, Chicago, or Los Angeles. You can hire a webmaster in Pipsqueak, South Dakota, and work with the designer as easily as if he or she were next door.

have it, you can make all the changes you like whenever you like, without having to rely on an outside source.

Many entrepreneurs opt for outsourcing this task instead. What can you expect to pay if you outsource web site construction? You can pencil in about $300 to $500 for hands-on help from a web site designer. As a third option, you may be lucky enough to have a qualified friend or relative who'll put up your site in exchange for lawn mowing, baby-sitting, or a steady supply of home-baked cookies. Don't forget that you'll also need a web host (see Chapter 11 for more information). For now, plan on spending $10 to $75 per month for basic web hosting.

Doing It Digitally

If you plan on producing your own web site or your own advertising materials (or both), you might want to spring for a digital camera. With one of these gadgets, you simply snap photos of, say, the slim-and-trim participants in your aerobics book, or the crafts projects in your candle-making title. Then you connect the camera to your computer, move your mouse around a bit—and presto! You've got the picture right in your desktop publishing program. Expect to pay from $200 to $500 for a good-quality digital camera.

You may also want to consider a scanner, a nifty gadget that imports or "pastes" graphics from just about any printed medium—books, photographs, brochures, original art, or postcards, for example—into your desktop publishing program. You can pick up a basic scanner for about $100 to $200; look for one with resolution of 4800 x 9600 dpi (dots per square inch) or better.

Photo Finish

Once the photo is in your computer, you can manipulate it in all sorts of interesting ways, acting as your own photofinishing expert. You can crop it; expand it; zoom in or out on various features; blur the edges for that shot-through-gauze look; make it look like a watercolor, pastel, or oil painting—ad infinitum. This stuff is not only great for business purposes, it's a heck of a lot of fun! Some digital cameras, like Kodak, come complete with this software. Or you can purchase any number of programs, from Corel's Paint Shop Pro Photo, priced at about $100, to Adobe's Photoshop, which costs about $600.

Printer Mania

A good printer is a must. Not for your manuscript, which your printer or e-publishing site will want sent by e-mail or on a Zip drive, but for all the other materials you'll produce. You'll have promotional materials, order forms, mailing labels, contracts, statements, and sundry other materials that will need to look polished and professional. The materials you produce will be a direct reflection of your company.

Faint dot-matrix printing looks amateurish. You'll want sharp, bold graphics and print to give your business an aura of confidence and success. You'll also want a

---

Take a Number

You'll also want to figure in the cost of buying ISBNs (International Standard Book Numbers) as part of your company set-up expenses. The ISBN is a number that is used to identify a book by edition, binding, and publisher. There's a price tag attached to the ISBN. It costs $269.95—but before you start gasping, realize that this is for a group of 10 numbers that you can use whenever you're ready to put out a new title or new edition of a previous one. Yes, you must buy 10 numbers at a time, unless you want to purchase them in bulk: 100, 1,000, or even 10,000 at a gulp. You will pay extra for expedited processing.

Where do you get your ISBN numbers? You can purchase them only through one source, R.R. Bowker in New Providence, New Jersey, which acts as the ISBN databank, as well as the purveyor. Go to www.isbn.org to order your numbers online or download a snail mail order form.

To make your publishing life *sans souci*, or carefree, you may want to spring for a SAN or Standard Address Number. This is a number used by publishers, libraries, bookstores, and other industry buyers, vendors, and suppliers to give them instant computerized billing and shipping information. With a SAN on your letterhead and invoices, any library or bookstore that purchases from you can immediately plug your address into their system and pay you ASAP.

SANs cost $150 per address. If you have separate payment and shipping addresses, you'll need two SANs. Go to www.isbn.org and then click on the SAN button to order your number(s).

printer that's fast. There's nothing quite like the frustration of waiting for material to trickle out of a slow-going printer: One page per minute can seem like one page per hour.

Fortunately, the really hot-stuff printers are much less expensive now than ever before. You can purchase an inkjet, many of which can produce all the wonderful colors of commercial artwork. Color-capable models print more slowly than black-and-white models do, but if you'll be printing lots of marketing materials, like brochures and newsletters, then color should be a consideration. You can expect to pay from $150 to $300 for a color inkjet printer, and from $200 to $1,000 or more for a basic laser printer.

Fax Facts

Now that just about everybody communicates by e-mail, a fax machine is not a hard-and-fast necessity, but it's a nice touch. Customers who can't—or won't—order products on the internet can fax their book orders to you. And you can fax *RFQs* *(request for quote)* to printers, who usually have pre-printed forms on which you check the services you want.

You can purchase a basic plain-paper fax for as little as $50 to $150, or a fancy multifunctional machine incorporating fax/copier/scanner/printer from $250 to $800.

Phone Fanatic

Beware!

Don't "enhance" your voice mail message with background music or a cutesy script. It's just not professional. Keep it simple. Give your business name—spoken clearly and carefully—and ask callers to leave a short message and a phone number. Thank them for calling and assure them that someone from your office will return their call as soon as possible.

We assume that you already have a telephone, in which case you already know all about phone bills. As a self-publisher, you'll learn even more. You'll want at least two separate, dedicated lines for your business: one for handling phone calls, and another for your fax machine and internet connection. If you've ever tried to call a friend who has his phone line tied up surfing the internet, you know how important this is. And as a businessperson, you can't let phone calls go unanswered—it's unprofessional and results in lost orders. If customers can't reach you, they give up and don't order books. The phone company's line installation fee should run you in the range of $40 to $60.

Check with your local phone company to determine exactly what these costs are in your area.

If you're working from a home office (or even from a commercial one), you'll want a two-line phone so you can put one line on hold while you are answering the other. A speaker is also a nice feature, especially for all those on-hold forever calls to your banker, attorney, insurance company, or whoever. Your hands are free to work on financial data or your latest advertising materials, your shoulder remains unhunched, and there's no earring jabbing you in the side of the head while you listen to Muzak and wait your turn.

You can expect to pay about $70 to $150 for a two-line speaker phone with auto redial, memory dial, flashing lights, mute button, and other assorted goodies. Add another $20 to $100 for an answering machine, or $6 to $12 per month for voice mail service.

Misery

If you've read Stephen King's *Misery*—or seen the movie—you know how really traumatic it can be to lose that book you have been working on so diligently. (If you aren't up on your King, take our word for it. You do not want to chance losing a manuscript. It's every writer's worst nightmare.)

Why are we suddenly discussing the subject? To convince you to invest in an uninterruptible power supply or UPS (not to be confused with UPS, the package service), for your computer system. This is especially important if you live in an area where lightning or power surges are frequent phenomena. (Or if you have a pet or small child who thinks disconnecting the power is kind of fun.)

If you're a computer newbie, you may not realize that even a flicker of power loss can shut down your computer, causing it to forget all the data you have carefully entered during your current work session, or—the ultimate horror—fry your computer's brains entirely. With a UPS in your arsenal, you won't lose power to your system when the house power fails or flickers. Instead, the unit flashes red and sounds a warning, giving you ample time to safely shut down your computer.

If you'll be spending a large amount of time on the internet, which accesses the World Wide Web through the telephone, you want to be

Smart Tip

Even though your computer probably has an onboard calculator program, you'll want to have the real thing close at hand. You can do quicker calculations without complex mouse maneuvers, and if you have a calculator with a paper tape, you can check your work, too! Expect to pay under $15 for a battery-operated model and $25 to $75 for the printing type.

sure that your UPS includes phone line protection. You can expect to pay between $70 and $200 or up for one of these indispensable units.

A surge protector safeguards your electronic equipment from power spikes during storms or outages. Your battery backup will double as a surge protector for your computer's hard drive (or CPU) and monitor, but you'll want protection for other valuable office equipment, like your printer, fax machine, and copier. They do not need a battery backup because no data will be lost if the power goes out, so a surge protector will do the job for a lot less money (expect to pay in the range of $15 to $60). If you've got a fax machine, be sure the surge protector also defends its phone line.

Electronic Money

An electronic credit card terminal can be a major boon to your business. Remember that you'll likely be selling your books on the internet, by direct mail, or to specialty stores, as well as through a book distributor. So you'll need a method of accepting payments, and credit cards are the method of choice. They make payment easier and faster for customers and for you because you can take credit card information over the phone, on the web, or by fax, and send out the order immediately.

More and more merchant card service firms are springing up that cater specifically to the SOHO, or small office/home office, and to the internet entrepreneur. Shop around (especially on the web), and you'll find a variety to choose from.

What can you expect to pay for an electronic terminal? Fees depend on several factors, including the company you go with and your personal credit history. Take a look at the chart on page 62 for an idea, but also keep in mind that this is an industry that's growing rapidly with better deals all the time. You can lease or purchase the terminal itself from the merchant bank, or you can go the bargain hunter route and buy a used (but still serviceable) machine from a company that's gone out of business or has upgraded its unit.

Smart Tip

Tip...

The copier is an optional item, but as you grow you may find it a necessary luxury for running off forms, brochures, fliers, and other goodies. It's far easier to run off a few copies in your own office than having to run down to the copy center every time the need arises. Copiers range from $200 to $2000 and up. If you feel the need to collate to your heart's content, consider leasing a higher-end model.

Domain Décor

Office furniture for your publishing domain is another optional item. It's important that

Electronic Card Terminal Fees

Item	Fees (Swiped*)	Fees (Mail, Phone, or Internet Order)
Discount rate *(Multiply each transaction by this rate, i.e., $200 ticket fee x 1.59% = $3.18 that the bank charges you to process the transaction.)*	1.18% to 1.89%	2.09% to 2.50%
Transaction fee *(another fee the bank adds on for each transaction processed)*	20 cents	25 to 30 cents
Monthly statement fee	$5 to $10	$5 to $15
Monthly minimum *(If your monthly sales are less than the minimum amount, you pay this amount.)*	$10 to $20	$10 to $20
Application fee	$0 to $75	$0 to $75
Programming fee	usually free with equipment lease or purchase	usually free with equipment lease or purchase
Electronic card terminal	$300 to $600 purchase or $19 to $72 per month lease option	$300 to $600 purchase or $19 to $62 per month lease option

*Merchant card services charge higher discount rates for orders taken by mail, internet, or phone than for those handled in person, or swiped, through the credit card terminal. Why? Because if a customer signs for your product or service while he's standing there, you and the merchant service run less risk of a charge-back.

In addition to the fees shown here, you may be charged an *address verification* fee per transaction, a *daily batchout* fee to send charges from the electronic terminal to the merchant service in batches or chunks, and an annual membership fee. Be sure to ask and negotiate before you sign up!

your work environment is comfortable and ergonomic, but if you are homebased it's perfectly acceptable to start off with an old door set on cinder blocks for a desk and an egg crate for your files. When you're ready to go the big step toward real office furniture for that oh-so-professional look, you've got a stunning array of possibilities to choose from.

Not Going Postal

If you plan on selling via direct mail, a postage meter may keep you from "going postal." Depending on how snazzy a model you choose, you can fold, staple, insert, seal, label, weigh, sort, stack, wrap, and stamp your mail. Phew! And, it used to be that you'd have to lug your postage meter down to the post office and stand in line to get it reset, but you don't have to any more! Now you simply reset it via phone or computer.

The fancier and faster the machine, the more expensive it will be to rent, lease, or purchase. As a ballpark figure, you can expect to rent a combination postage meter/electronic scale for about $18 to $100 per month.

The big office supply warehouse stores typically offer midrange desks from $200 to $300, computer work centers for around $200, printer stands from $50 to $75, two-drawer letter-size file cabinets (which can double as your printer stand) from $25 to $100, and bookcases for $25-$70.

Chairs are a very personal matter. Some people like the dainty secretary's chair for its economy of space; others want the tonier, high-back executive model. There are chairs with everything from kangaroo pockets to pneumatic height adjustments. Prices range from $60 to $250 and up.

Pen and Paper

Don't forget that you'll also need paper—lots of it—to print various drafts of your book as well as press releases, and correspondence, envelopes, business cards, pens, pencils, and all those miscellaneous office supplies like paper clips, cellophane tape, and staples. Plan on allocating about $45 for a box of good-quality printer/copier paper. This will give you ten reams of 500 sheets each. (It might sound like a lot of paper, but it goes quickly!)

And if you'll do any sort of mail order (which includes internet sales), you'll want shipping materials in which to send off your products. You'll spend in the range of $100 to $150 for a starter collection of shipping supplies, including sturdy bubble-lined envelopes, sealing tape, and a gun-style tape dispenser.

Spawn of Publishers

While you're investigating professional associations, check out SPAWN, which is the acronym for Small Publishers, Artists and Writers Network. This group has a slightly different mission, as its name implies. SPAWN seeks to give authors, illustrators, graphic designers, and photographers, as well as editors and self-publishers, a place to share information and ideas.

SPAWN's $45 annual membership fee includes a newsletter, a member directory, chapter meetings, discounts on seminars and workshops, discount supplemental health benefits service, an online bookstore for small publishers, discounts on web services, and your very own web page. Plus—as an added bonus—SPAWN members get a discount on their Publishers Marketing Association membership.

Get Professional

We've now given you a shopping list of every office gizmo you'll need to get up and running as a self-publisher—including two take-along checklists to have in hand when you hit the office and computer superstores. You will find "The Self-Publisher's Office Equipment Checklist" (page 66), and "The Office Supplies Mini-Shopping List" (page 65).

But there's still more to come! You should also budget for membership in professional organizations and subscriptions to industry publications. Taking these steps gives you up-to-the-nanosecond information on news, reviews, and issues in the publishing world. You'll also have access to industry gurus who can answer pressing questions, as well as a support team of other publishers who are actively "being there and doing that."

"It's good to belong to as many organizations and networking opportunities as you can spare time for," advises Steve C. in Vermont. "They provide opportunities to keep abreast of the constant changes in the book businesses and to share insights and ideas that will help you sell books."

"I belong to Publishers Marketing Association (PMA), Small Publishers Association of North America (SPAN), National Association of Independent Publishers (NAIP), the Vermont Book Publishers Association (VBPA), and Independent Publishers of New England (IPNE)," Steve says. "I'm also an associate

Dollar Stretcher

Membership in professional associations often qualifies you for discounts on a variety of services, from insurance to shipping.

The Office Supplies Mini-Shopping List

Items

- ❏ Computer/copier/fax paper $_____
- ❏ Blank business cards   _____
- ❏ Blank letterhead stationery   _____
- ❏ Matching envelopes   _____
- ❏ Shipping materials (for mail orders):
  - Bubble-lined envelopes   _____
  - Sealing tape   _____
  - Tape dispenser   _____
- ❏ File folders   _____
- ❏ Return address stamp or stickers   _____
- ❏ Extra printer cartridge   _____
- ❏ Extra fax cartridge   _____
- ❏ 3.5 inch floppy disks   _____
- ❏ Zip disks   _____
- ❏ Mouse pad   _____
- ❏ Miscellaneous office supplies (pencils, paper clips, etc.)   _____

Total Office Supplies Expenditures $_____

member of American Booksellers Association (ABA) and an active member/participant in the pub-forum listserv [a forum for independent book publishers offered through eGroups, a free service that lets you create or join e-mail lists (www.egroups.com/group/pub-forum)].

"Among the magazines I take (other than those associated with the organizations I belong to) are *ForeWord* and *Publishers Weekly*. Another group I belong to that is not specific to a book business is Vermont Businesses for Social Responsibility. If that didn't exist I'd probably join the Chamber of Commerce and Better Business Bureau, but being a member of a BSR group establishes to the public that you are a highly ethical business," says Steve.

Spanning the Industry

The Small Publishers Association of North America (SPAN) is a terrific place to start your professional hobnobbing. With more than 1,100 members, this group offers all sorts of membership perks including:

The Self-Publisher's Office Equipment Checklist

Use this handy list as a shopping guide for equipping your office. It has been designed with the one-person home office in mind. If you've got partners, employees, or you just inherited a million dollars with the stipulation that you spend at least half on office equipment, you may want to make modifications.

After you've decided what you want to buy, fill in the purchase price next to each item, add up the total, and use this figure in "Your Company Start-Up Costs" worksheet on page 71!

❏ Windows based Pentium-class PC with
   SVGA monitor, modem, and CD-ROM $ _____

❏ Laser or inkjet printer   _____

❏ Fax machine   _____

❏ Software:
   Word processing   _____

   Desktop publishing   _____

   Specialty software, like Publishers' Assistant   _____
   Accounting   _____

   Mailing list management   _____

❏ Phone(s), two to three lines   _____

❏ Answering machine (or voice mail)   _____

❏ Uninterruptible power supply   _____

❏ Zip drive (if not included in computer)   _____

❏ Surge protector   _____

❏ Calculator   _____

❏ Electronic credit card terminal (cost to lease or buy)   _____

❏ Postage meter (cost to lease)   _____

Not on the critical list

❏ Digital camera   _____

❏ Scanner   _____

❏ Copier   _____

❏ Desk   _____

❏ Desk chair   _____

❏ Filing cabinet   _____

❏ Bookcase   _____

Total Office Equipment/Furniture Expenditures $ _____

- A monthly newsletter packed with public relations and sales strategies
- Annual conferences (with CDs available for those who can't be there in person)
- Discounts on industry publications
- Participation in book expos, fairs, and other exhibitions
- Royalty-free sales of your books on SPAN's online bookstore (i.e., you do not have to pay them royalties for being listed on their site)
- Discounts on book freight and shipping
- Co-op advertising program
- Waiver of book wholesaler fee

What does it cost to join SPAN? Annual membership tallies in at $105 per publishing house, which isn't a bad investment!

PMA Pals

Another handy organization to be affiliated with is the Publishers Marketing Association, or PMA. With over 4000 members, PMA advances the efforts of book, audio, video, and CD publishers worldwide. Like SPAN, it also offers many perks for its members, including:

- Various discounts on publishing/advertising/marketing services
- Dispute resolution program
- Exhibit opportunities at book trade shows
- Discounted freight and mailing services
- Health insurance
- Liability insurance
- Merchant credit card acceptance program
- Discounted rate for Nielsen Bookscan
- Monthly newsletter

The cost for all these member services depends on the number of employees in your company. For a publisher with one to nine employees (which will more than likely describe you at this point), the annual membership fee for PMA is $95.

Read All About It

There's no dearth of reading material in the publishing industry—in fact, there's so much that you could easily spend all your time perusing other people's texts instead of producing your own. But as a savvy self-publisher, you will want to stay up to speed in the field. We recommend you start with subscriptions to the following three publications. (You can check out many more that are listed in the Appendix at the back of this book.)

1. *Foreword.* Who couldn't like a publication with world headquarters over a chocolate shop? Besides understanding one of the truly important food groups, ForeWord does a wonderful job of providing news and reviews specifically about small and independent presses. A must-read, so budget $40 for 12 annual issues.

2. *Writer's Digest.* This venerable publication is as the name implies written more for writers than publishers, but it is always full of helpful tips and hints. An annual subscription of 13 issues costs about $20.

3. *Publishers Weekly.* The name says it all—news, reviews, and lots more for the publishing trade. It's pricey at $240 per year, but read by everybody who's anybody in the field.

Are You Insured?

Don't forget insurance. Since your office will most likely be in your home, you'll need to find out if your homeowner's package covers your business assets, inventory, and equipment, or if you need additional coverage. As a ballpark figure, allow from $100 to $500 annually over your existing homeowner's policy. Then you'll want to add special publisher's liability coverage to cover you for horrors including errors and omissions or defective advice. Budget $1,200 to $2,500 per year; costs vary depending on your gross annual revenues.

Tally It Up

OK, now it's time to don your bookkeeping cap and tally up the company set up expenses we've investigated in this chapter. Besides the ones we've already checked into, you will want to add other expenses like business licenses, business insurance, legal advice, and all the other costs intrinsic to any company's birth. To give you an idea of how much you can expect to budget, check out the "Equipment Expenses" and "Self-Publisher Company Start-Up Expenses" charts for two hypothetical self-publishers, Glowworm Press and Bell & Candle Publishing (see pages 69–70).

As you peruse these publishers' setup costs, you will see that Bell & Candle is spending significantly more than her colleague, even though both companies will be homebased with the owner as the only employee. The biggest cost differences can be attributed to computer and web site related items. Bell & Candle, for instance, will go with an all-new, top-of-the-line computer system and software, while Glowworm will use the owner's existing system and software. And Glowworm's computer-savvy owner will also design and put up the company's web site, while Bell & Candle's owner will outsource these functions.

Equipment Expenses

Furniture, Equipment & Supplies	Glowworm Press	Bell & Candle Publishing
Computer system (including printer)	0	$2,500
Fax machine	$150	$250
Software	0	$995
Phone system	$70	$90
Uninterruptible power supply	0	$125
Surge protector	0	$34
Calculator	$25	$75
Postage meter	$24	$117
Copier	0	$500
Electronic credit card terminal	$300	$450
Desk	0	$300
Desk chair	0	$100
Printer stand	0	$70
File cabinet	0	$50
Bookcase	0	$70
Printer/copier paper	$25	$50
Blank business cards	$6	$12
Letterhead paper	$30	$30
Matching envelopes	$35	$35
No. 10 blank envelopes	$3	$6
Shipping materials (for mail orders)	$117	$150
Address stamp or stickers	$10	$10
Extra printer cartridges	$70	$70
Extra fax cartridge	$80	$80
Mouse pad	0	$10
Rewritable CDs	$7	$12
Zip disks	$25	$50
Miscellaneous office supplies	$50	$100
Total Expenditures	**$1,027**	**$6,341**

Self-Publisher Company Start-Up Expenses

Costs	Glowworm Press	Bell & Candle Publishing
Professional associations	$190	$235
Equipment and office supplies (see chart on page 69)	$1,027	$6,341
Licenses	$100	$100
Phone (installation/line charges)	$90	$90
Subscriptions	$50	$219
Legal services	$375	$375
Miscellaneous postage	$50	$50
Internet service provider (six months)	$120	$120
Web site design and marketing	0	$500
Web hosting (six months)	$180	$300
Insurance (six months)	$850	$1,150
ISBN (set of 10)	$205	$205
SAN	0	$100
Subtotal	**$3,237**	**$9,785**
Miscellaneous expenses (add roughly 10 percent of total.)	$324	$979
Total Start-Up Costs	**$3,561**	**$10,764**

You can use the worksheet, "Your Company Start-Up Costs," on page 71 to list the expenses you will have for setting up your own company. If you make a few copies of this sheet, you can work up several options, compare them all, and decide which will be the best one for you.

Your Company Start-Up Costs

Costs

Professional associations $ _____

Office equipment (insert total from "The Self-Publisher's
  Office Equipment Checklist" on page 66)   _____

Licenses   _____

Phone (installation/line charges)   _____

Subscriptions   _____

Legal services   _____

Internet service provider   _____

Web site design and marketing   _____

Web hosting   _____

Office supplies (insert total from "The Office Supplies
  Mini-Shopping List" on page 65)   _____

Miscellaneous postage   _____

Insurance   _____

SAN   _____

ISBN   _____

Subtotal $ _____

Miscellaneous expenses (add roughly 10 percent of total)   _____

Your Total Start-Up Costs $ _____

▲

Romancing the Bank

Now that you've done all the arithmetic, you can determine just how much capital you'll need to start your company. If you find that your bank account falls short of the necessary funds, you can show all these beautifully executed figures to prospective lenders. This will help you convince them that your business is a good risk, and that you'll be able to repay a loan without difficulty.

You might want to consider financing through your bank or credit union. In this case, your projected start-up costs, as well as projected income figures (see Chapter 11) will be extremely important. The bank will want to see all of this information neatly laid out and carefully calculated. You'll also want to show them all the statistics you can gather about the bright future of the self-publishing industry.

Friends and Family

Most entrepreneurs use a very exclusive source to finance their start-up expenses—family and friends. You may choose to go this route yourself, especially because bankers are generally not very gung-ho about so-called nontraditional businesses like self-publishing.

If you go with someone from your own inner circle, you'll have less paperwork to fill out, and you can let your financier share in the excitement as your company takes off. But remember that you'll still need to figure the repayment of borrowed funds into your costs, and that you should treat your repayment agreement as seriously as you would any bank loan.

Going Plastic

Another route many entrepreneurs take to obtain financing is through an entity as close as your back pocket—the credit card. Before you choose this option, take a look at your available credit balance and at the annual percentage rate. Card companies frequently offer low, low rates as an incentive to sign up or to use their service; they usually raise these interest rates after a certain period of time. Go with the one that offers the best rate for the longest period.

More Bookkeeping
Production Costs

In the last chapter, we explored the costs involved in setting up your business office, including everything from computer equipment to memberships in professional organizations. But there's much more to the excitement—and the expense—of self-publishing. There are

▲

also the actual costs involved in producing a book, from proofreading to printing to illustrations, and that's what we'll investigate in this chapter.

Pre-Production Basics

Prospective self-publishers always want to know: How much does it cost to print a book? This is a very good question, but one that might be better asked is: How much does it cost to *produce* a book? A lot of elements go into a book's production long before it's ready for the printer, things like cover and interior art, copy editing, and proofreading.

These are important elements that you do not want to skimp on. If your book looks amateurish—if the artwork is clumsy, the layout is awkward, and the text is riddled with typos and grammatical glitches, nobody is going to buy it. Distributors, booksellers, and librarians will perceive your book as the worst form of self-publishing, and prospective readers won't buy it. If you're a professional who can competently perform some of these services yourself, terrific! If not, it's worth it to pay someone else to do them for you.

Look at the chart called "Book Production Costs" on page 85 as you read through this chapter. You can use the costs incurred by our hypothetical publishers, Glowworm Press and Bell & Candle Publishing, as a guide for what your costs may be. Glowworm Press is going with a 6-by-9 softcover (or *trade paperback*) that will be 192 pages, with a four-color cover and no interior artwork. Bell & Candle is going for a snazzier presentation, with a 6-by-9 hardcover (or *case bound book*) that will be 288 pages, with a four-color dust jacket, and no interior artwork. We've also provided a work sheet for determining your own book production costs on page 91.

A Book by Its Cover

The old adage that you can't tell a book by its cover doesn't hold true in the publishing world—at least not as far as readers are concerned. The average consumer spends an astonishing eight seconds perusing a book's cover before moving on to the next selection on the shelf. That means your book has eight seconds to make a positive impact—eight seconds to communicate its value as a source of information or entertainment. That is not much time. And it's the reason that many savvy publishers turn to professional book designers to produce their covers.

"A designer who specializes in book covers knows about the appropriate positioning of text and graphics, the power of the spine and back, the "rules" for bar codes, how to prepare artwork for specific book manufacturing methods, how to speak the book printer's language, and understands the critical scheduling and positioning of your book cover design in the marketing process," explains Kathi Dunn of Dunn & Associates Design in Hayward, Wisconsin. "If you choose to hire a graphic designer who is not experienced in book cover design, be sure you have time to invest in supervision and are willing to take responsibility for the results."

How much does it cost to have a cover professionally designed? Prices vary with the type of cover, colors, images, graphics, and effects. A one-color softcover book will be far less expen-

> ## Smart Tip
>
> When discussing graphics, *four-color* actually refers to all the colors in the rainbow. It's called four-color because every hue and shade is derived from a specific mix of four basic colors: red, blue, yellow, and black.

sive than a fancy four-color dust jacket with multiple images or graphics embossed with foil lettering. As a ballpark, pencil in a minimum of $1,000 to $2,500 for a "full-service" design. There are many design companies offering cover design for as low as $300, but do your homework. They may not offer original designs or might make liberal use of stock photography that you are likely to see pop up on other covers. Be sure you know what you are getting for your money.

Designer Search

Since the cover design of your book is so critical to its success, how do you find a designer that will do your project justice? Choose one with whom you can forge a healthy relationship, counsels Pam Terry, owner and senior designer at Opus 1 Design in Beverly Hills, California. "Feel that she's enthusiastic about your work. See if you like her style. Make sure she's open for comments, suggestions, and critiques.

"Don't expect free work beforehand to see if she understands your idea," Pam adds. "Pay to see roughs only—maybe $200 for some very rough sketches to see if she's on the right track. If you have an idea about how you want your book to look, and there's another book that looks similar, bring it along or let the designer know the title. She can look it up on Amazon.com."

Drawing the Line

If you plan to produce a children's book, or other title that includes drawings and other artwork, you will have yet another reason to think about hiring a professional. If you're an artist or have one in your family, you're home free. If not, you'll need to hire an illustrator.

"I hire a graphic artist to do my covers and have hired other artists for interior illustrations," says Steve C. in Vermont. "If you're not good at packaging, you should hire a professional. The biggest mistake many new publishers make is producing a book that looks like amateurs threw it together. It doesn't matter how good a book it is—if it doesn't look professional and attractive, bookstores and distributors won't carry it, and it won't get reviews. You'll die with a garage full of copies."

Prices for professional illustrators are all over the map and depend on whether you'll need a few black-and-white line drawings or dozens of pages of four-color, full-page splendor. The only real way to pencil this expense into your book budget is to get quotes based on your particular needs. Shop for an illustrator by going to the Society of Children's Book Writers and Illustrators or the Graphic Artists Guild. (See contact information in the Appendix).

> ### Tip...
> ### Smart Tip
> "Don't take any changes by the copy editor personally," counsels Laura Poole of Archer Editorial Services in Durham, North Carolina. "We don't mean to hurt your feelings or slight your writing skills. We want you to sound good on paper!"

Copy Quality

The *copy editor*, also called a *content editor*, is another professional you should turn to. This behind-the-scenes expert will read your text or copy to make sure that your material isn't garbled, inconsistent, or otherwise confused.

Copy editors look for all sorts of manuscript problems, like the fact that you change tense from present to past and back again throughout your text, or the fact that your character's mom is named Thelma in Chapter 2 and Nonie in Chapter 6. (Hey, it happens. You change the name in mid-manuscript for whatever reason and forget to go back and correct earlier pages.) They can catch errors like the fact that you said cold cereal is unhealthy in Chapter 3, but that granola is good for you in Chapter 4.

> ### Tip...
> ### Smart Tip
> Text in a finished book should be single-spaced. But when you submit your manuscript to a copy editor or proofreader to be worked on, send it double-spaced. This gives them room between the lines to make corrections and also marks you as a professional.

Copy editors also look for style glitches. Say you put tip boxes in every chapter except Chapter 8, or that you start each story with a quote but stop doing so halfway through the book. In other words, they nit-pick—but in the best way. When you're writing a manuscript, it's hard to see the forest for the trees, but a good copy editor can do just that.

"I was a professional editor before I started this business, but even so, when I'm editing a book I become too close to it to see all the mistakes, the awkward phrases, the gaps in information, etc.," says Steve C. in Hinesburg, Vermont. "I usually do the heavy editing, then send it out to two or three freelancers. Some of the freelancers are professionals, others are English majors who love books and offer their services for cheap. The more literate people who go through a book to make corrections and suggestions, the better book it will be."

Anna J. in Texas agrees. "I hired an editor and proofreader for my third book, which had a lot of text," she says. "I'm glad I did. She has a degree in English, and she was wonderful. Hiring her was good for a number of reasons. She was a stickler for perfection and looked things up when she wasn't sure if something was "stylistic" or just plain wrong. She worked with me throughout the process and asked me what kind of editing/proofreading I wanted and adhered to what I said. But most importantly, she was unfamiliar with the jargon and experiences of the authors, and her fresh perspective brought to the forefront any passages that to a layman were a bit unclear."

How much should you pencil in for a copy editor? Ink in $2 to $3 per manuscript page—which is double-spaced with one-inch margins and standard 10-point to 12-point font (see Chapter 7), advises Laura Poole of Archer Editorial Services in Durham, North Carolina. You may also see prices quoted by the hour; a ballpark range is $25 to $50 per hour.

How do you know whom to choose? "Find someone who has experience editing the type of book you've written," says Laura Poole. "Use someone with whom you are comfortable. Be willing to submit a sample (from two pages to a whole chapter) for an editor to do, and be willing to pay for their time."

Proof Positive

Some copy editors, like the one Anna used, also act as *proofreaders*. Others do not, in which case you'll want to hire one. These detail-oriented types scan your text with an eagle eye, seeking out typos, misspellings, punctuation pitfalls, and other typesetting traumas. The big difference between a copy editor and a proofreader is that the former looks at the big picture—style and content omissions, contradictions, and other goofs, while the latter concentrates on spelling and punctuation. It's extremely difficult to detect these sorts of mini-glitches in your own work—you're so close to it that you can be completely blind to a blatant typo even when it has stared you in the face through ten revisions. Rates for a good proofreader range from $1 to $2.50 per page.

By the Numbers

Every book, like every good secret agent, has to have a number to go along with its name. For books, this number is the *ISBN* or *International Standard Book Number*. Every book has its own individual 13-digit ISBN printed on the back cover or dust jacket as well as somewhere in the front matter or first few pages.

The ISBN is like a fingerprint—it identifies you as the publisher and also identifies each of your products as a specific version of a specific title. The classic hardcover first edition of *Raising Radishes for Fun & Profit* will have a different ISBN than the revised second edition. The paperback edition will carry its own ISBN. The Japanese-language version will have a different ISBN than the English one. And the audiobook of *Raising Radishes* will have its own separate ISBN, different than both the book and videocassette versions.

We placed basic ISBN costs under your company setup expenses since you will need to purchase these numbers in groups of at least ten at a time, regardless of when you intend to use the numbers. They must be purchased through R.R. Bowker in New Providence, New Jersey (www.isbn.org).

Lucky Number 13

On January 1, 2007, the book industry converted its 10-digit ISBN system to 13 digits. Why? In short, there is a number shortage. So many books are being published, the amount of 10-digit numbers was running low. The new 13-digit system will allow the ISBN system to grow its numbering capacity and allow for more numbers that can be assigned. In addition, the new system will make the book numbering system complement the global EAN.UCC ID system that most other consumer goods use for identification purposes.

There will be two new prefixes—978 and 979. The 978 prefix will be added to the front of current ISBNs and one new digit will be added at the end. Voila! The 979 prefix will only be used once all of the 978s are gone and cannot be used to convert back to a 10-digit ISBN.

If you have already purchased a boatload of ISBN-10 numbers, you can convert them to ISBN-13 by visiting www.isbn.org and clicking on the "ISBN-13 Support" link. There, you will find a handy-dandy converter tool that's a snap to use.

Another facet of the change is that all publishers will cease using the UPC barcode on the back of books and will instead use the EAN barcode. Since some consumers will continue to reference old ISBN-10 numbers when ordering books, be prepared to transact with that number, but discourage its use and spread the word about the new system.

For more information, you can download a PDF of *ISBN-13 For Dummies* on the ISBN web site.

Name, Rank, and Serial Number

If you plan to publish serials—which include magazines, newspapers, annuals, frequently revised directories, and other ongoing publications—you'll need an *ISSN* or *International Standard Serial Number*. ISSNs are basically just like ISBNs except that:

- Their eight digits don't mean anything in particular (see "Anatomy of an ISBN Number" for comparison).
- They describe the whole of a series, like *The Butterfly Breeder's Home Companion* magazine, issues No. 1 through No. 25, instead of one specific issue. They also describe "continuing resources" that most publications make available online. There are specific restrictions on what internet-based content does and does not require an ISSN, so check the web site for more information. For example, different language versions and media outlets get different ISSNs.)

There's no charge for an ISSN. For more information, check out the ISSN International Centre website at www.issn.org.

Bar Codes in Bookland

In addition to your ISBN (or ISSN), you'll need a bar code for each book title that you publish. This is simply the book's ISBN and its price, rendered in store-scanner format and called the *Bookland EAN number with price code*. Unless you absolutely, positively plan to sell only to passers-by at flea markets or at your annual church bazaar, you must have a Bookland bar code. Bookstores and their wholesalers insist on them so they can ring up books at their registers equipped with scanners.

You buy one master film of the Bookland bar code for your book, and then you have it printed on the back cover of each copy. The cost is reasonable, and you can get them from a variety of sources. Check out the Appendix at the back of this book for contact information.

Advanced Information

Once you've received your ISBNs, you'll need to fill out an ABI, which is an *Advanced Book Information* form. This step is critically important because the ABI form gets your book into the bible of the publishing industry, R.R. Bowker's *Books in Print*. Booksellers and librarians, as well as everybody else in the trade, use Books in Print as the source for information about titles in print and their publishers. If your book is not listed here, it might as well be lost in the ether.

You can fill out an ABI form on the internet for free, so there's no reason not to do so. Go to the R.R. Bowker web site for publisher services, www.bowkerlink.com, and click on the "Books In Print" link at the left of the screen. Make sure you apply about six months before your

Smart Tip

If you go with a graphic artist who specializes in book covers, she'll handle the Bookland bar code assignment for you so you won't have to worry about it.

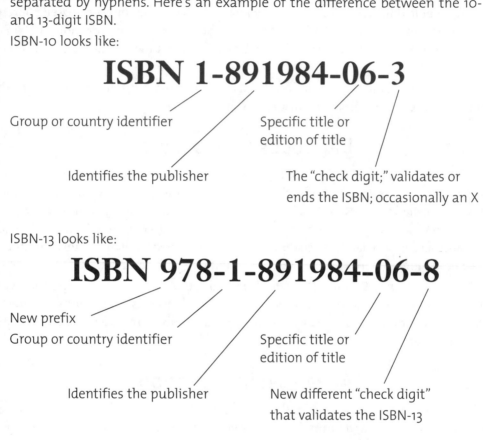

Anatomy of an ISBN Number

As of January 1, 2007, the entire book publishing world converted to using a 13-digit ISBN. Each ISBN is divided into five sets of numbers of various lengths, separated by hyphens. Here's an example of the difference between the 10- and 13-digit ISBN.

ISBN-10 looks like:

ISBN 1-891984-06-3

Group or country identifier

Specific title or edition of title

Identifies the publisher

The "check digit;" validates or ends the ISBN; occasionally an X

ISBN-13 looks like:

ISBN 978-1-891984-06-8

New prefix
Group or country identifier

Specific title or edition of title

Identifies the publisher

New different "check digit" that validates the ISBN-13

book rolls off the printing press. You must have an ISBN before you can fill out your ABI, so don't procrastinate on that either.

Getting Carded

Yet another alphabet item to tackle is applying for your book's *LCCN* or *Library of Congress Catalog Card Number*. This is like an ISBN for the library trade. It's assigned by the Library of Congress and allows librarians all over the country to order books by the numbers from the Library's catalog. Since the majority of public and private libraries subscribe to this catalog and order freely from it, your book will lose out if it's not listed.

Newly Revised

Plan ahead when you write that nonfiction book. If it contains material that should be updated every few years, you can make the necessary changes and reprint it as a revised edition. The beauty here is that it will be a brand-new book (with a brand-new ISBN), and you can start your pre-publication marketing campaign all over again. You'll have new reviews from book industry publications, niche industry publications, and other opinion molders.

Don't get confused about the difference between *reprints* and *revised editions*. A reprint is another printing of a book with no changes made to it (except perhaps to fix a few previously unspotted typos). A revision is a book in which a significant amount of material has been changed—because new information has been added, new research has been done, contact information (like addresses and phone numbers) has changed, or any combination thereof.

The Library of Congress is a bit picky about what types of publications it chooses to assign LCCNs to. Among the materials that get the thumbs down are: books under 50 pages in length, except for picture books; religious school materials; workbooks; mass market paperbacks (which are the kind of novels found on supermarket and drugstore racks); and e-books.

You can find a complete list of unacceptable materials on the Library of Congress LCCN web site at http://pcn.loc.gov/pcn005.html. (Don't be misled by the fact that, in true government-speak, the LCCN is called the PCN here. It means *Pre-assigned Card Number* because the number is assigned before the book is printed.) You can also apply for your number on this site. It's free—all the Library asks is that you send a complimentary copy after publication. This means your book will be on the shelf at the nation's library in Washington, DC!

This is another task that you'll need to complete well before your book goes to the printer. If you wait until after printing, you can't list your LCCN on the copyright page where it belongs.

The CIP on Your Shoulder

One more item to concern yourself with before your book goes to print is the *CIP* or *Cataloging in Publication record*, which is also issued by the Library of Congress free of charge. This is the block of text you find on the copyright page of LCCN-registered books that gives all the technical stuff librarians love, including Library of

▲

Congress subject headings, Dewey decimal numbers, and Library of Congress classification numbers.

The CIP is important for any book that has an LCCN—but there's a catch. Even though the Library of Congress hands out LCCNs to books from even the newest of publishers, it won't give out CIP records until you already have three previous titles under your belt. And the Library of Congress will want proof in the form of front matter (the pages that precede the main body of a book) for several forthcoming books from your company, by more than two authors. For more information, check out the CIP web site at http://cip.loc.gov/.

But there's hope. You can also develop your own *P-CIP*, which is a CIP made up by a publisher or its agent. For a fee, Quality Books, a distributor based in Oregon, Illinois, which specializes in library sales, will provide a P-CIP record for you for around $150. It also provides an excellent explanation of CIP information on its web site. (You'll find Quality Books listed in the Appendix of this book.) If you want to go it alone, ask your local librarian for help.

Print Talk

Now that we've explored your book's pre-production costs, it's time for the issue that first-time publishers are most interested in: printing costs. Here again, there's no set cost for all books. Each book is a separate entity and can be radically different from the next. A 32-page children's book, with full-color graphics on each page, will cost a heck of a lot more than a 32-page, text-only pamphlet on opal hunting in Arkansas. And a 192-page softcover book of house plans will carry a different printer's price tag than a 288-page hardcover romance novel that has a glossy, gold-embossed dust jacket.

In addition, printers' bids can vary wildly from one company to the next, or even from one job to the next. Printers are notorious for raising their rates on a whim, so it's extremely important to get a variety of bids each time you have a book printed.

There are over 40 book printers in the United States. Get estimates from as many as possible—it's perfectly acceptable to send an *RFQ* or *request for quote* to them all. You can send a letter; however, many print shops have "quick quote" forms you can fill out and submit online. This is a great convenience, except that you immediately realize there are an overwhelming number of choices, all of which are set out in terminology only printers (and seasoned publishers) understand.

As we go through this chapter, we'll delve into the most common printing choices that you'll need to make. You'll soon be speaking printer lingo like a pro. For now, though, take a look at the sample "Quick Quote" form on page 83, and then see the response that you would get from the printer in the form on pages 86–87, "Price Quote from Printer."

Keep in mind that you can't know everything about book printing your first (or even second or third) time out. Book printing companies, on the other hand, do this for a living. They know it all, and they're usually quite willing to help. Find a printer you trust and can communicate with; then explain your project and don't hesitate to ask questions.

Vital Statistics

Before you can get any sort of printing estimate, you must know the vital statistics of your proposed book including:

- *Trim size*, or outside dimensions
- Number of pages
- Cover (hard or soft)
- Type of binding
- Number of ink colors for text
- Number of ink colors for graphics
- How material will be supplied (on disk or camera-ready)
- Paper stock
- Cover stock
- Type of cover finish
- Type of packaging (shrink-wrapped, in cartons, etc.)

Wow! Where to start? We'll delve into all the details in Chapter 7. For now, let's look at our hypothetical publishers' costs in the "Book Production Costs" chart on page 85.

Glowworm Press, seeking a niche in gardening books, plans to start off with a print run of 3,000, 192-page, perfect-bound (softcover book binding in which the cover is glued onto the page ends), trade paperbacks with four-color covers. Its first title will be *The Night Garden*. Bell & Candle Publishing will ignite its sales with a print run of 5,000

Quick Quote

Thomson - Shore, Inc.

phone (734) 426-3939 ● fax 800-706-4545

Remit Quotation To:

Company_____

Address _____

City_____ State ____ Zip _____

Contact Name _____

Phone _____ Fax _____

E-mail _____

Book Specifications:

Title_____

Author_____

Page Count_____ Quantity_____

Trim Size_____

Expected date job would arrive at T-S _____
                                        Month/Year

TEXT COPY
- ○ Output-Ready PDF   ○ APP/PostScript/PDF
- ○ Bluelines   ○ Halftones #_____
- ○ Digital Bluelines   ○ Camera Ready Copy

TEXT STOCK

Recycled* ○ Yes   ○ No *Available for certain trim sizes

Natural	○ 50 lb	○ 55 lb	○ 60 lb
White	○ 50 lb	n/a	○ 60 lb

○ Other_____

TEXT INK
- ○ Black Ink Only   ○ Black & 1 PMS
- ○ Bleeds   ○ No Bleeds

BINDING
- ○ Perfect Paperback   ○ Smyth Sewn Case
- ○ Sewn Paperback   ○ Notch Case
- ○ Other_____   ○ Cloth Type _____

SHRINKWRAPPING
- ○ Individually   ○ In Groups

— COVER —	— JACKET —
FURNISHED COPY	*FURNISHED COPY*
○ Camera Ready	○ Camera Ready
○ Trouble Free Disk	○ Trouble Free Disk
○ Composite Film	○ Composite Film
○ *T-S* to Separate	○ *T-S* to Separate
STOCK	*STOCK*
○ 10pt C1S	○ 80lb Enamel
○ 12pt C1S	○ 100lb Enamel
○ 65 lb White	○ Other_____
○ Other_____	
PRINTING	*PRINTING*
○ Black ink	○ Black ink
+____ PMS colors	+____ PMS colors
○ 4-color process	○ 4-color process
COATING	*COATING*
○ Gloss Lam Coating	○ Gloss Lam Coating
○ Matte Lam Coating	○ Matte Lam Coating
PROOFS	*PROOFS*
○ Blue	○ Blue
○ Waterproof	○ Waterproof

Provided courtesy of Thomson-Shore Inc.

Beware!
A local, general-job printer is fine for printing up church newsletters, wedding announcements, and neighborhood garage-sale fliers. However, they don't know much more about book printing than you do, and their prices are astronomical. Go with an established, experienced firm that specializes in printing books.

of its inspirational-genre book titled *Soaring on Invisible Wings*. Bell & Candle will go with 288-page hardcovers with four-color dust jackets for this inspirational volume.

As with the company setup costs, Bell & Candle will spend significantly more than her colleague will. The greatest cost difference is in the printing—Bell & Candle's print run is 2,000 copies higher and almost 100 pages more per copy than Glowworm's. And while Glowworm is going the inexpensive trade paperback route, Bell & Candle will spring for hardcovers with dust jackets, both of which are pricey options. You'll note that the inspirational publisher is also spending considerably more than her garden-buff colleague for cover art and for copy editing—the latter because she's got more pages to edit.

Front Line Wisdom

"The biggest mistake many new publishers make is to have a book printed by a local general-purpose printer," advises Steve C. in Vermont. "You need a short-run book printer, because the cost will be half or less, and the quality will be better. Always go for several bids—the one that had the best price last time may not this time. There are some printers every small press learns about, such as Bang, Data Reproductions, McNaughton and Gunn, and Hignell. That's not a comprehensive list, but they are among the small number of printers that would be on anybody's bid list. Another smaller one that I like is Master Printers of New England. There are others that are well-known because they advertise heavily in small-press publications, but which, if you network with other small presses, you'll learn to avoid. The above are regular short-run book printers, good to use if your first printing will be in the 1,000 to 10,000 range or more."

Covering the Spectrum

"Visit your printer," urges Anna J. in Texas. "I haven't done that yet, but I've had three different printers; two worked out beautifully, and one did not. I had to hire a lawyer and in the process have learned that I should have

Tip...

Smart Tip
If you have color illustrations, the printer will send *match prints*, which are like color copies, for you to proof and send back. These are preferable to e-mailed PDFs because color is not typically "true" when viewed on a screen. Sometimes, the old school is the best school.

Book Production Costs		
Costs	**Glowworm Press**	**Bell & Candle Publishing**
Bar codes	$20	$20
Copyright	$30	$30
Cover art	$1,500	$2,500
Copy editing	$384	$625
Proofreading	$192	$250
Indexing	$384	0
Printing	$5,032	$15,801
	for 3,000 copies	for 5,000 copies
Total Production Costs	**$7,542**	**$19,226**
Per-Book Cost	**$2.51**	**$3.85**

taken the time to travel to the printer to visit with them *before* sending them my manuscript.

"I would also suggest getting a lot of bids and a lot of samples," Anna says. "I was amazed at the differences in bids I got for my projects. The quality of printing and binding also covers the spectrum. I also kept track of how long it took printers to get their bids to me after I sent them an RFQ. If it took them a long time to get a bid to me, that told me something about that company.

"Join a publishing listserv (online) and ask other publishers for recommendations. That's how I got my second printer (and I would have used them for my third book, but it wasn't cost and time effective because they're an overseas printer).

"Another must for a new publisher is to develop a good working relationship with your printer before you send the manuscript," the mother of two suggests. "I thought I put everything in writing, but my lawyer says that we need to do more than what printers traditionally do. The contracts we sign benefit the people drawing up the contracts—the printers. My lawyer suggested that next time I work with a printer, I have some clauses added which benefit me—just in case mistakes are made during the printing process. It might cost a couple of hundred dollars to hire a lawyer, and you may not even need those clauses; but when you have a problem, you lose a lot more than a couple hundred dollars, not to mention a lot of sleep.

"Along those lines: Keep a phone/communication log. Every time you talk to your printer, write down the date, time, and what was said. This way if you have problems

Price Quote from a Printer

Thomson-Shore, Inc.
7300 West Joy Road Dexter, MI 48130-9701
734.426.3939 Fax 800.706.4545
www.tshore.com

Read carefully and call immediately with any changes or questions!

9999
Glowworm Press
1 Firefly Lane
Luminescent, FL 10000

DATE: 04/06/07
QUOTE NUMBER: 178476
ACCOUNT NUMBER: 9999

Peter Moss
Ph:
Fax: (000)000-0000

TITLE:	THE NIGHT GARDEN
AUTHOR:	MOSS
QUANTITY:	1000, 3000, 5000
TRIM SIZE:	6 x 9
PAGES:	192
COPY:	Text - Customer furnished trouble free postscript or application files. Cover - Customer furnished TS supported, trouble free application files with 4 color image in place. Price will be confirmed upon review of disk. Proofs - 1 Full text proofs (Digital) and 1 Set(s) Digital Color proof of cover included.
PRESS:	Text - Black ink throughout, without bleeds. Covers - 4 color process plus Matte Lamination on outside. Note this coating is subject to scuffing and marking at the slightest pressure.
STOCK:	Text - 60# Natures Natural - (50%PCR), 360 ppi. Covers - 10pt. C1S.
BINDING:	Perfect binding in 32's.
PACKING:	Bulk Pack - Single Wall Carton
SHIPPING:	FOB Dexter, MI.
TERMS:	To avoid delays, arrange credit prior to sending job.

PRICING:	1000	3000	5000
PREP/PLATE	628.00	628.00	628.00
COVER	800.00	927.00	1,053.00
PAPER	473.00	1,340.00	2,202.00
PRESS	297.00	507.00	717.00
BINDING	485.00	926.00	1,364.00
	==========	==========	==========
	$ 2,683.00	$ 4,328.00	$ 5,964.00

OVER/UNDERS $ 0.82 each.

For new titles, T-S to archive digital files for an additional one-time fee of $40 per title.

Please Contact:

These prices will be honored for thirty (30) days from the date of this quotation. Signing and returning this quotation or the submission of your Purchase Order within those 30 days will secure the pricing for ninety (90) days from the date of this quotation. Any job received after ninety (90) days will be subject to new pricing. A confirmation, including new prices for any changes, additions, or alterations to the above specifications, will be sent to your after your order is received.

Accepted by:_____ Date:_____

TERMS AND CONDITIONS

The following "Production Procedures" constitute a binding agreement between you and Thomson-Shore. By signing the price quotation, submitting a purchase order and/or letter of specifications for work to be performed by Thomson-Shore, you agree to be bound by all terms in this document. In addition, by submitting a job to Thomson-Shore as described on its "Confirmation of Specifications and Price" (CSP) form, you agree to be bound by all our "Production Procedures".

1. When your job is received, we will acknowledge its arrival within one day of receipt. The notification will be emailed/faxed and provides you with the job number, and the name of your customer service representative at Thomson-Shore. When your job is scheduled, your CSP will be emailed/faxed; the CSP provides your projected ship and proof date.

2. If your job has any changes from the specifications on our quotation, the CSP will indicate your revised prices based on the final specifications. If this price change is less than $200.00, we will email/fax the CSP to you. If it is more than $200, we will contact you with details. When the CSP is emailed/faxed, production has started. If you have any questions or concerns at this point, it is important that you call us immediately.

3. If your Thomson-Shore customer service representative has questions regarding your expectations, he/she will call you before proceeding. This will be done before we send you the CSP.

4. If you have not requested a proof, we will print and bind your book without submitting anything for you to check. If you require digital proofs (a proof of the text pages submitted for approval prior to printing) there is a cost for this and it will add a minimum of one week to our production time. If you originally requested a digital proof of the text, it will be included in our quoted price and will show up on our quotation in the category of "prep/plates". The digital proof is meant to show you the margins, order of pages and the location of any strip-ins you might have. It is not meant to be proofread for typos. Our schedule assumes you will approve the digital proof, as well as other proofs, within 24 hours. We send out all proofs for approval via Federal Express, standard overnight, unless otherwise instructed. The cost of this mailing is not included in our quotation.

5. If you prefer, you could request digital proofs of just the first 32 pages instead of the entire book. This would be less expensive than a complete digital proof and it would let you see how we interpreted your margin instructions. T-S also has the capability of providing proofs via email or FTP

6. To work efficiently and commit to reliable schedules, we need your entire job and final specifications at one time. We will not begin production of your order until the complete job is in our plant.

7. Your schedule could be affected if you require changes during the production process i.e., quantity change, an additional proof, new copy submission. If changes are made and your schedule is a concern, please let us know immediately.

8. When your job is complete and ready for shipment, we will ship it motor freight. Accessorial charges, i.e., inside delivery, residential delivery, lift gate, are additional and will be invoiced accordingly. Shipping time is not included in our production schedule and will usually add from one to five working days to get from Dexter to locations in the continental U.S. Please refer to our online Shipping Terms and Procedures Guideline located on our web site for more detail.

9. When a Thomson-Shore estimator quoted your project it was most likely quoted F.O.B. Origin, freight prepaid and charged back. In simple terms, F.O.B. (Free On Board) refers to the responsibility for freight cost and transit risk. F.O.B. origin means that under the terms of sale the buyer bears all freight and associated charges, owns the goods in transit, and is responsible for any claims that may arise as a result of transit.

10. If we have an email address for you, T-S will email a delivery confirmation the evening of your shipment. If you have other requirements, please let us know.

11. We will ship the quantity you order with a maximum possible overage or shortage of 10%. These will be charged or credited at the over/under price.

12. Thomson-Shore works with several area vendors that can help you with the distribution of your books. The following applies to drop shipments (transportation via UPS, FedEx, USPS). Any job that requires shipment to more than two destinations and requires more than two cartons (if shipped via any method other than motor freight) will incur additional charges as follows: $6 for each additional destination greater than two plus $6 for each carton more than two for shipments other than motor freight (such as UPS, FedEx, USPS, etc). Shipments of advance copies for approval are not included. Please contact your Customer Service Representative for more information regarding distribution vendors or handling charges.

13. Your CSP will include a one-time fee of $40 for the archival of your digital files. The fee includes storing your electronic files in the archive library and providing online reporting; it must be paid at job invoice. If you prefer not to store electronic files at Thomson-Shore, please let your CSR know. Negative storage will continue to be invoiced a yearly storage fee (Jan-Dec) of $30 per title (first two years of storage are gratis).

14. Your agreement with Thomson-Shore is made at Dexter, Washtenaw County, Michigan. The prices in the quotation on the other side of this page shall remain in effect for thirty (30)days; we may, in our discretion extend this period beyond thirty (30) days. You should obtain credit approval prior to sending the job to us; this will eliminate a possible delay. Thomson-Shore reserves the right to reject any order within ten (10) days after receiving complete text copy, digital files, or furnished film; Thomson-Shore may reject the order based on content, or any other issues which, in Thomson-Shore's sole discretion, Thomson-Shore believes justify rejection of the order. These reasons may include, but are not limited to, rejection of content, which Thomson-Shore finds objectionable, illegal, or offensive.

Provided courtesy of Thomson-Shore Inc.

later, you can refer back to your log and say who you talked to and what was agreed upon. You have to have this kind of documentation in case you have problems later," offers Anna.

Proof Is in the Pudding

June H., the horror-story maven, concurs. "Do get at least three bids from printers and look at some of the work they produce," she says. "The packaging of a book can make the difference between whether a prospective customer picks up your book to look at the content. You can't sell a book if no one picks it up off the shelf.

"Once you've made a decision on a printer—and I recommend one as nearby as possible because you'll be working closely with them—make sure to get a contract in writing that covers everything from artwork (including covers), to the size of the book and typesetting.

"You can save yourself a few dollars if you typeset your own work and present it to the printer in camera-ready format," the Michigan resident explains. "This means all they do is reproduce what you give them. This can be accomplished on any computer by setting your margins to the size you want, say 5 by 7, or whatever you choose.

Smart Tip

Tip...

A *hickey* is not what you get from smooching on the front porch after dark, at least not in the printing world. Here it means a speck or a blotch on a page.

Get with the Program

An important book-printing issue is the format in which you'll deliver your manuscript to the printer. The more work the printer has to do, the more he'll charge you for. If you send your work on CD as a Microsoft Word file, the printer will have to typeset it, import it into Adobe InDesign and then into PDF or portable document format files for you. This is expensive—about an extra $2 to $3 per page.

If you do the work yourself and send the book to the printer on a CD-ROM or Zip disk as an InDesign file, already formatted in PDF, the printer has to do far less work. It saves him a step and saves you money, as much as 15 percent, says Maria Smith of Thomson-Shore, Inc., a book printing company in Dexter, Michigan.

As an added bonus, when you format your book in InDesign and then PDF, what you see is what you get. There's no guessing about how it will end up looking. You'll be able to see it and make any changes long before you send it off to the printer.

"As a last note, if you do your own typesetting, you are responsible for proofing the galley, or final copy, before the book is bound; so do proof carefully. What you give them is what they print. On important issues such as ISBNs, take along a copy of the correct number when you go to the printer to proof. I once had an incident where the printer had put the wrong ISBN on my book, and since I did not catch it, I had to pay extra for stickers with the correct number and do each book by hand. Your ISBN is your book's identifier; if it's incorrect, bookstores will have a difficult if not impossible time trying to find it for the consumer," says June.

After you submit your book to the printer on Microsoft Word (even better if you can submit it on Adobe InDesign as a PDF file), he goes to work performing the magic that turns it into a real book. What the printer does exactly is mysterious and involves all sorts of cameras, printers, binderies, and other pieces of heavy machinery. Basically, he sends your text to a digital image center, which transforms your pages into signature-size flats of paper. What was formerly known as *bluelines*, so named because they look exactly like those blurry blue-ink plans architects and engineers are so fond of, are now printed digitally in (usually) black and white. In this case, the proofs look exactly like your book, down to the trim size. These digital prints are your final opportunity to make any changes to the book before it goes into production.

The printer will send these digital prints to you for proofing. Be sure you examine them with X-ray eyes. Make sure no pages are missing, that they're all in the right order, and that they're all properly numbered. Look for missing lines of text, and text or images that are not where they're supposed to be.

If you find errors the printer has made and point them out immediately, they can be corrected free of charge. But if you shrug, pronounce the digital prints as OK without really checking carefully, let the book go to print, and then find errors—it's too late. And if you decide at this point that, hey, maybe you'd like to add two pages or move that sidebar from page 7 to page 12, it will cost you money. So don't get creative at this stage—do it before you submit your manuscript.

Once you send back the digital prints, the book goes to print. When the printing is all done, it's shipped to you. Take a moment out from all the heady excitement to examine not just one book or two, but several boxes of books. It doesn't happen often, but printers do goof. Your books can arrive with the covers glued on upside down or an entire signature missing. It's better to catch these errors in your garage than after books have been shipped to your customers.

Printing Price Tag

We're not done yet. The price tag for each job will change, depending on how many copies you want—the more you order, the cheaper the per-book cost. So you have to decide how many books you can afford for your initial run, as well as how many you estimate you can sell.

Take another look at the "Price Quote from a Printer" on pages 86–87, and you'll see that the bottom line jumps each time the quantity gets larger. At the same time, however, the per-book cost gets smaller. If Glowworm press has 1,000 books printed, the per-book cost will be $2.68; for 3,000 copies, it will cost $1.44 per book; and for 5,000 copies, the price plummets to $1.19 each. If Glowworm prints even more, say, 6,000, 8,000, or 10,000 copies, the price will go even lower.

But don't get too carried away. Industry experts generally recommend that you go with an initial print run of at least 3,000 books, but no more than 5,000. It takes about 3,000 to get

Smart Tip

In the printer's RFQ (request for quote), you'll be asked if you want your books shrink-wrapped. Your answer should be, "Yes." Shrink-wrapping protects your books from damage in transit. Have them wrapped in bundles of two to four—the staff at the local bookstore will be less inclined to unwrap individually shrink-wrapped books, which means customers won't be able to browse through your book to see if they want to purchase it.

the first good price break, but going with radically more than 5,000 is unwise until you get a feel for how fast and how well your book sells.

Overs, Unders, and Other Quirks

Print runs never come out to an exact count. If you order 5,000 books, you may end up with 4,923 or 5,106—or some other number entirely. The difference is called *overs* and *unders*, and printers are routinely allowed a 10 percent margin either way. If your run comes out over, you'll be charged a flat fee for every extra copy. Look for it on your invoice. Your quote from the printer should tell you how much you would have to pay for overs and unders. The sample quote on pages 86–87 shows that Glowworm will be charged 82 cents each for extra copies.

While you might not particularly want overs, asking for overruns is a smart idea. These are extra copies of your cover that you can request, which cost as little as $20 per 100 for the four-color, perfect-bound variety. You can use these overruns as publicity and advertising tools (see Chapter 10), or to send as tokens of appreciation to people who helped bring your book into the world, like a mentor, editor, designer, or artist—and do not forget Mom and Dad!

The POD Effect

"An option used by a lot of small presses is *print on demand* or *POD*," says small-press pro Steve C. "Books are printed one at a time, and they look just exactly like conventionally printed books. The per-unit cost is higher, of course, but you run no risk of dying with 5,000 books in your garage; you can just print them as they sell.

"The most popular [POD] printer by far is Lightning Source," Steve explains. "There are probably others that are as good and cheaper. But the advantage of Lightning Source [see Appendix for contact information] is that it's a division of Ingram [a major book-wholesaler]. If you are printing a book that may sell only 300 copies, you may have a hard time getting it listed with Ingram, so it would be hard for people to special-order at bookstores. But if it's printed by Lightning Source, it will be automatically listed by Ingram, and bookstores will be able to easily obtain copies."

Bright Idea

Instead of filling out a different "quick quote" for each printer with different variables, format your own RFQ (request for quote) as Anna J., the self-publisher from Temple, Texas, does. Send it to all the printers on your list so you get a standard bid for comparison, instead of having to make sense of the jumble of possible choices.

Your Book Production Costs

Use this form to develop your own book production costs. Make several copies and get estimates from several different sources, then choose the best—and least expensive—option.

Bar code	$ _____
Copyright	_____
Cover art	_____
Illustrations	_____
Copy editing	_____
Proofreading	_____
Indexing	_____
Printing	_____
Your Total Production Costs	$ _____
Divide by number of copies	_____
Your Per-Book Cost	$ _____

Why POD?

A recent study in *Publishers Weekly,* produced by Vista International, ranks the top reasons for going with POD. They are:

- ○ Generating profitable business
- ○ Satisfying customer demand that would otherwise go unsatisfied
- ○ Creating sales from backlist titles that would otherwise be lost
- ○ Reducing investment in inventory
- ○ Reducing risk in printing decisions

Print-on-demand providers are proliferating as quickly as e-publishing sites, and POD has been around for a little over ten years. They act much like e-publishers—as a virtual bookstore for your title—but with an all-important difference. In addition to "shelf space on their sites," they also print actual perfect-bound paper copies of your book. Because books are printed with state-of-the-art laser copiers that use regular paper, instead of on web presses that must be fed huge signature-size sheets, POD sites can provide as few—or as many—copies as you like on request. And they look just like traditional p-books.

Like e-publishers, each POD provider has its own pricing and royalty structure. Generally you can expect to pay nothing or up to $1,200 in setup fees, depending on how much you want to spend on add-on services like copy editing, layout, and cover design, and your own web page. Specific costs vary radically, depending on the POD provider and the service program you choose, so you may or may not be saving on the add-on costs as opposed to outsourcing these tasks on your own. The bottom line, however, is the cost for the books themselves. With rising production and printing costs for traditional publishers, the POD option is looking more attractive each day.

The upside of POD is that you don't pay for books until you have orders to fill. The downside is that they're a lot more expensive than traditionally printed books. Trade paperbacks printed POD cost from $6 to $10 each, which is a far cry from the $2 and under costs you get when you go with a conventional run of thousands at a time. Some POD sites, like Xlibris (www.xlibris.com), don't charge printing costs, but their royalties are far less—10 percent to 25 percent of a set list price—as opposed to sites like Trafford (www.trafford.com) that charge for printing but offer up to 60 percent royalties.

So why would you want to go with this method? It's cheaper in the short haul. You might print 100 to 500 copies, send half (or more) of them out for review to opinion molders, and then sit back and wait for orders before committing to a larger print run. This way you get an idea of how many books you'll want to order from the traditional printing press before you invest in a large run.

In that case, why wouldn't you go with POD and forego conventional printing? The traditional large-print run, remember, is far less expensive on a per-book basis. Unless you're doing a very limited book production, you're much better off with a conventional order of 3,000 copies or more. Another reason is that POD providers supply the ISBNs for your titles, which is not necessarily a good thing. Although you get the copyright for your book, the *ISBN identifies the POD site as the publisher—not you!* You'll find a list of some POD providers in the Appendix at the back of this book. You can locate others by doing a search on the internet.

More Bang for Your Book

You can get even more bang for your book by producing it in a few alternative formats. You can transform those printed words into an audiobook package, a video production, or even create your own merchandising goodies.

Easy Listening

Audiobooks are particularly popular with people who attend seminars and workshops, and they make terrific *BOR* or *back-of-the-room* sales products. You sell the CDs immediately after your seminar, while your audience is still hyped up and eager to hear more on your subject. You can make even more profit by offering a downloadable version (like those available on iTunes or Audible.com, for example) that requires less production cost.

Since almost everybody is a commuter these days, audiobooks are in demand as antidotes to highway hypnosis. Audiobooks are also a wonderful way to provide your title to people who have poor vision or who are blind. In addition, they make fun gifts for children when accompanied by simple picture books so kids can "read aloud" to themselves. Even for adults, audio books are read-aloud versions of the print version—it's not necessary to fancy them up with actors playing different roles or with expensive sound effects. In fact, the simpler the better, since adding too many special effects tends to muddy the clarity.

Audiobooks are fairly simple to produce—you've already got the ready-made script to follow. Many audiobooks, however, are *abridged* (or condensed) to keep both costs and retail price down. You can go with either version, but do your market research to determine which your niche market is more likely to purchase. Digital audio files, like those available on iTunes, for example, have allowed more publishers the leeway to record books in their entirety, since there is no CD duplication cost involved. Today, you can find most complete books available in this format, with the abridged versions available on CD.

Keep in mind that you will pay for a full-fledged audio production as well as for having the sound files mastered and *duped* (duplicated). Recording the program yourself with a home voice recorder at your kitchen table is not a good idea (the end result will sound dreadfully tinny and amateurish). However, there are many brands of quality voice recording software currently on the market that do a remarkably professional job—if you have the most updated equipment to use with it, including a higher-end computer with CD duplication capability and a studio-quality microphone. Your best bet is to check with your local music or audio solutions store to find the most economic and professional recording equipment.

Spring for a professional in-studio job if you are unsure of your technical skills. You will find audiovisual production services listed in your local Yellow Pages as well as on the internet, or contact a local radio DJ who will have access to professional equipment and will be delighted to take on the job at a discount rate. As with printing and most other services, the more CDs you buy, the cheaper your costs.

Speaking of improving your bottom line, give serious consideration to offering only a downloadable version of your audio book. Listening on the go with your iPod or other MP3 device is quickly gaining popularity. According to a January 2007 article in the *New York Times*, Audible.com's membership has grown 54 percent over the last year, to 345,200, while the site also sells titles through iTunes and Amazon. The savings for publishers of going exclusively downloadable (in duplication, packaging, and distribution) is passed directly to the consumer in the form of a cheaper, more accessible medium. Take a look at the "Audiobook Production Costs" chart on the next page to get an idea of price range for both CD and downloadable options.

> **Smart Tip** *Tip...*
>
> If you're the brave soul who wants to record his own audiobook in a home studio, there are some great computer programs that will help you add professional polish. Try Sony Sound Forge Audio Studio for around $70, or on the higher end, use Adobe Audition for around $350—it's said to be tops for Podcast production.

> **Stat Fact**
>
> According to the Audio Publishers Association, downloads have risen to 9 percent of audio book sales in 2005—a 50 percent increase over the previous year.

Lights, Action, Camera!

Unlike audiobooks, video productions won't fit every book format. Since your audience is not likely to be fascinated by a tape of you sitting in a chair reading your own words,

Audiobook Production Costs

Book on CD or Electronic File

Studio time	$250–300 per finished hour
Sound engineer	$125–200 per finished hour
Producer	$200–1,000 per finished hour, based on experience
Narration talent	$275–400 per finished hour
Editing	$200–300 per finished hour
Post-production	$100–200 per finished hour
Duplication (CD only)	$1–3 per CD, depending on total number of units

DIY Recording

Laptop with CD burning capability	$1,100–2,500
Audio recording/editing software	$70–400
Recording equipment	$100–1,000, depending on make and model
Duplication (CD only)	$1–2 per CD
Design software for creating cover art	$100–700
Jewel cases	$.50–1.00

○ Duplication cost per CD will decrease as total units increase

○ Don't forget that you'll want artwork for your J-cards or album covers. Some studios will handle the printing for you; at others it's up to you.

you'll have to carefully consider what—if anything—you can do to make this a viable product.

Fiction is probably out. Unless you already own a full-fledged production company and have (or can get) the budget for actors, sets, location shooting, a director, a cameraperson, film, etc., the costs are entirely too prohibitive.

But lots of nonfiction lends itself to fairly inexpensive video. The cheapest of all is the type produced by seminar professionals who hire a videographer to film them during an actual session. The tape is then edited, packaged, and sold as a BOR product.

Cookbooks, exercise manuals, and how-to books can also lend themselves to video productions. People like to see a live person demonstrating how to frost a cake, crunch those abs, build a deck, or make gift wrap with rubber stamps. Because you don't need actors, special sets, or any of the rest for these types of productions, you can keep your costs down. Make sure you keep it interesting, though. Keep things moving, use humor when you can, and talk to your audience as if they're actually in the room with you.

As with audiobooks, you must hire a video production professional. Even if your brother-in-law has a nifty camcorder and does all your family's reunions, he most likely doesn't know enough about sound, lighting, and duping to produce a saleable product.

Merchandise Madness

You can develop all sorts of merchandise to tie in with your book—everything from calendars and note cards, to T-shirts and toys. Again, you will have to take your book's genre and subject matter into account, but you can also get creative.

Anna J. sells heart-shaped pins to readers of her books for and about families that have a child with a heart-defect. You might design a simple cloth doll from a character in your children's book. You might sell coffee mugs imprinted with an adage from your motivational or inspirational book, a calendar based on your gardener's diary that shows readers when to perform various garden tasks, or a chef's apron emblazoned with the name of your cookbook.

You can buy all sorts of goodies, from coffee mugs to mouse pads to tote bags, fairly inexpensively and have them imprinted with whatever you like. You can also have products like dolls and other toys made up by specialty manufacturers. Look for suppliers and giftware manufacturers in your local Yellow Pages or on the internet.

Going e!

E-publishing is yet another venue for your book. Although still in its infancy, e-publishing is hot and getting hotter by the nanosecond, with everybody from giant publishers to small independent publishers to stars like Stephen King getting into the act. E-books are exciting for publishers because the cost of printing and binding is eliminated. Readers download titles directly onto their computers and print them out on their own machines. They're exciting for readers because they allow instant gratification: You can browse books and then download and read them immediately. And e-titles are usually cheaper than their paper counterparts. Publishers pass on to their readers the money they save by not using a printing house.

There are three ways to produce your own e-book:

1. Set up your own web site and sell online.
2. Sell through an e-publisher like Booklocker.com (www.booklocker.com).
3. Sell through an e-book reader site.

The main thing they all have in common is that you must make your book available in PDF or *HTML* (hypertext markup language) format so it can be downloaded.

Do Right, Copyright

Neophyte writers frequently worry that someone will steal their work if they don't copyright it. This is rarely a problem. In the United States of America, your work is automatically and immediately copyrighted as soon as you've created it. And just about any creative work is copyright-protected, including the following:

- ❍ Literary works, which can encompass computer programs
- ❍ Songs and other musical works
- ❍ Plays and other dramatic works
- ❍ Movies and audiovisual works
- ❍ Pictorial and graphic works, as well as sculptures
- ❍ Sound recordings

However, since you'll be publishing your book, you will want to file a formal registration with the U.S. Copyright Office. All you have to do is fill out a form obtainable on the office's web site at www.copyright.gov. Send the form, a copy of your book once it's printed, and a check for $45 to the Copyright Office. Your copyright is effective on the date the Copyright Office receives all of the materials, and you should receive a certificate of copyright within about four months. Copyright law is complicated, but as a rule of thumb you can figure that your protection exists until 70 years after your death. For specifics, consult your attorney.

In addition, your niche market must be computer-savvy—if they're not, they'll never find your book much less be able to read it. Let's take a look at the advantages and disadvantages of each of these approaches.

The Do-It-Yourself Site

Since you'll probably have a web site anyway, you may want to offer your title in downloadable format. You will already have your book in PDF—that's how you delivered it to your printing house—so it's not much more of a step to upload it to your web site.

The big advantage here is that since the book is yours and the site is yours, you don't have to share the profits with anybody. The disadvantage is that you'll have to take readers by the e-hand and lead them to your site. Unless you do stellar marketing, they won't find you as easily as they might if you go with a big e-publisher.

Beware!

Read all contracts carefully. Most e-publishers are more than happy to give you all rights to your book so that when a trade publisher comes along with that five-figure offer, you're free to snap it up. But some sites are not so kind, and some manufacturers of e-book readers have reputations as downright rights-annihilators.

e-Book Publishers

You may choose to go with an established e-publishing site (see the Appendix for a listing of several e-publishing providers). The advantage here is that they're like big e-bookstores and thus have the capability of attracting lots of browsers. People who may be surfing the site, not looking for your book in particular, may happen upon it and decide to buy it. Another advantage is that some e-publishers will translate your text into PDF for you. This is a plus if you decide to put up new titles that haven't already been made PDF-ready.

The disadvantage is that you will have to pay royalties for the privilege of being on the site's e-list. Royalty rates vary from 20 to 70 percent, depending on the site. And remember that royalties are based on the book's price, which will be lower than the version found in brick-and-mortar stores. Some sites are free, but with others you'll pay a setup fee of up to $500.

The important thing to remember about e-pub sites is that even though your title is "on the shelf," you must still do just as much promotion as you would for your print version.

e-Book Reader

The technology of "Star Trek: The Next Generation" is already here—at least as far as those nifty little computers-as-books are concerned. You can now buy e-book readers, gadgets the size of mass-market paperbacks on which you can download dozens of titles at a time. You can read a book on-screen, on the go—at the airport, in the supermarket checkout line, or wherever you happen to be. While some e-book readers are set up to accept PDF format, others demand HTML (the language web designers use to set up and edit sites) or *OEB*, which is *open e-book* (a language used to produce some e-book content).

Consumers can buy texts specifically formatted for e-book readers online at virtual bookstores. Or they can go directly to the e-book reader manufacturers' sites to purchase texts.

The makers of e-book readers are not anywhere near as receptive to purchasing texts from small presses as their e-publisher compatriots are. While most e-publisher sites are openly eager for your business, the makers of e-book readers like to deal only with the major players in the industry. You can certainly approach them, but don't look for an easy sale.

Writing and Designing Your Book

At this point, you've done your market research—you know what type of book you want to publish and in what genre. You've done the math—you know what efforts and expenses are involved in setting up your office and producing your first title.

▲

Now it's time to actually put pen to paper, or fingers to keyboard. In this chapter we'll explore the facets of book creation and design, from organization to paper stock and cover design.

Exhilaration and Panic

Writing a book is one of the most exhilarating and also one of the most daunting things you can do. If you're a born writer—one of those people who's been scribbling stories and publishing "newspapers" since the age of eight, then you already know all about the joys—and terrors—of authorship. If you've never tackled any written project other than the ones forced upon you by school or your job, you may face the prospect of actually producing a book with the same sort of anxiety you'd feel building your own space station!

Writing 101

The key to any successful writing project, fiction or nonfiction, is organization. The more planning you do before you actually begin writing, the easier and faster it will go. Try these tips for sorting your germ of an idea into a completed, savvy manuscript:

- *Give your book a working title.* It's much easier to think of your project in terms of a finished, polished book when it has an identity.

- *Draw up a chapter-by-chapter outline.* Give each chapter a title and a paragraph that describes what information you'll cover.

- *Now go one step further and make a detailed outline of each chapter.* You don't have to write a magnum opus but list, item by item, the points you intend to cover.

- *If you'll use quotes and statistics, start gathering material.* Make up files for your research and interviews, and stash your materials in folders labeled for each chapter. Carefully note where you got the information from and when.

- *Make a deliberate effort to start writing.* Pour yourself a nice, fresh cup of coffee, sit down at your desk, take a deep breath, and start writing. Keep in mind that starting a brand-new book is usually the hardest part. You haven't found your voice yet, and you and your book have not really gotten to know each other. It will get easier as you go along.

- *Keep in mind that every writer has good days and bad days.* The trick that separates real writers who finish books from dilettantes who do not is that real writers keep slogging ahead, even on days when the task seems hopeless. Set a weekly goal for yourself and stick to it: three pages a day, two hours a night, or six hours every Saturday—whatever you can fit into your schedule.

Beware!
If you quote people in your book, you must get their permission first. If you use statistics, you must cite the source where you found them.

Ghosts and Other Writers

What if, despite your very best efforts, you can't write your way out of a paper bag? Or you don't have the time to devote to writing an entire book? You've got options. You can hire a ghostwriter or a co-author. You provide the ideas, information, and research, and leave the writing to them.

A ghostwriter is a writer who works behind the scenes to put your material into professional prose worthy of publishing. Your name goes on the book, and you are touted as the author. Celebrities often "write" their autobiographies using the talents of ghostwriters. There's no reason you can't do it too—except the added expense.

A co-author is like a ghostwriter, except that he or she shares writing credit with you on the book's cover and title page. Where the title page of a ghostwritten book might read "*Do It Yourself Divorces by King Henry VIII*," the title page of a co-authored book would read, "*Do It Yourself Divorces by King Henry VIII*, with Irving Levine."

The cost for a ghostwriter or co-author is entirely dependent on who you hire, how much of the manuscript you may already have written, how much sprucing up and organizing it needs, how much additional research you want done, and what financial arrangements you make. Most ghostwriters or co-authors expect to be paid royalties, or they expect to be paid on a *work-for-hire basis* (which means you pay a flat fee and no royalties). But as a self-publisher, you can make any arrangement that suits you and your writer.

You can find a ghostwriter or co-author at the American Society of Journalists and Authors, within the pages of *Literary Marketplace* (R.R. Bowker), or by nosing around in various publishing and writing web sites (see contact information in the Appendix at the back of this book).

Layout and Design Decisions

If you write a book that's published by someone else, you turn in your typewritten manuscript, and that's it. The book's design remains a mystery until your complimentary copies arrive in the mail. But as a publisher, you need to be every bit as concerned with the book's design, layout, and appearance as you are with its message.

The design will affect your book's production costs and ultimately your profit margin. As you already know, all sorts of factors—from the number of pages and the type of cover, to the amount and style of artwork—play a role in printing expenses. The higher your costs, the smaller your bottom line. Your book's design also plays an important role in whether potential readers perceive it as a title they want to purchase. People judge a book not only by its cover but by whether it is:

- Too long (too much of a reading task to tackle)
- Too skimpy (not enough material for the price)
- Too expensive
- Too cheap (priced significantly lower than other books—may be perceived as not being very good)
- Too amateurish

Your printer can help you with some of these elements. Your graphic designer or cover artist can help with others. But the final decisions—and final appearance—are up to you. So, ready? Here we go!

All books have basically the same layout, which makes it easy to plan yours. You always have lots of room for creativity within your text, of course, but if you deviate from the basic setup, your book will look unprofessional, not to mention strange.

Some sections are standard format: All books have them in roughly the same place and except for how you design the actual page and what you actually say, there's not a lot of decision-making to do. Other sections are optional—you can leave them out, or you can put them in if you like for information or design purposes, or if your page count demands them. Why would your page count "demand" an optional section or two? Because of signatures.

The Signature

Book pages are not printed one at a time the way you run a typewritten page through a copier. Instead, they're printed on *signatures*, huge sheets of paper on which 16 or 32 book pages are laid out and run through the press at once. After printing, the signatures are neatly sliced into 16 or 32 individual pages and then sewn together.

When you lay out your book, you strive for an even signature, one that's a multiple of 16. That's why our hypothetical publishing companies chose to go with a 192-page book (12 signatures, 16 pages per signature) and a 288-page book (18 signatures, 16 pages per signature). The further away you veer from an even signature, the more expensive your print job will be because the printer has to chop pages from that huge sheet of 16 or 32. And printers don't like to do that.

You can always add material to the front or back of your book to fill out a signature, like

Fun Fact

Winston Churchill, who wrote 14 books between the end of World War II and his death at age 90, began every day at 8:30 A.M. with a work-in-progress, a glass of whiskey, and his signature cigar—in bed.

quotations, author or publicity blurbs, and extra order information. You can always leave a couple of blank pages at the front or back if absolutely necessary. And you can go for a partial signature of eight pages—which is not the ideal, but isn't too drastic either.

You won't know exactly what your page count is until you finish writing the book in your word processing program, import it into in a publishing program like Adobe InDesign, and then lay it out. But that's OK. You can add or delete material as you go along.

Use the "Book Layout Checklist" on page 105 to see what goes where and to check off the sections of your book as you complete them. Remember that the standard elements you would include in a fiction book differ from those you would include in a nonfiction book.

Page Primer

Now that we've discussed some of the basics of book design and layout, let's investigate what the inside pages of your book will look like.

Front Matter

The pages at the beginning of your book are called the front matter and consist of everything up to the copy that makes up the body of your text. The best way to decide how you want your front matter to look and feel is to peruse books whose style you admire, and see how they're laid out. Then, keeping in mind signatures, page counts, and standard book layouts, set your own similar style for addressing the elements that go in the front matter of your book:

- *Book blurbs*. This is optional publicity material and can consist of one page or several pages. Use this section for any pre-publication endorsements from opinion molders—quotes like, "*The Night Garden* should be required reading for anyone who enjoys gardening, entertaining, or just a soul-soothing brush with Mother Nature at the end of the day. —*Horticulture Magazine*." You need at least one page and preferably two or more of these blurbs. If you have only a few, save them for the back cover.

- *Half title page*. The half title page is the first standard page of your book. It contains your title and subtitle, and that's all.

> **Bright Idea**
> You can often get a busy opinion molder to "pen" your foreword if you offer to write it for her. Then all she has to do is approve it and put her name to it.

- *Title page.* This is your title and subtitle again, with the author's name, as well as the publisher's name, logo, and city/state.

- *Copyright page.* Here's where you put your copyright date, the person who owns the copyright (you as the author, the author whose work you're publishing, or perhaps your family trust if that's how you've set up your legal organization). You should also add the words "All Rights Reserved" and a statement that your material cannot be reproduced without your permission. You may want to add a disclaimer to the effect that you have not intentionally made any errors or insulted anybody. If you've included excerpts from someone else's work that need to be attributed (like song lyrics or poetry), you say so here. This is also where you put your ISBN, LCCN, and CIP record.

- *Dedication.* Here's your chance to thank your spouse for selflessly washing dishes and minding the kids while you've been writing, or to show your appreciation to a mentor for opening your eyes to the joys of gardening or whatever. A dedication is short, sweet, and to the point—just a few lines on the page.

- *Acknowledgments.* This is where you recognize everybody who helped make your book a reality—the industry experts who shared information, the reference librarian who looked up countless statistics, and the editor who caught all those nasty copy goofs. Acknowledgments should also be brief—no more than a page, tops.

- *Quotations.* You may want to set out a topical quotation from a great thinker (or Bart Simpson, depending on the tone of your book) or an excerpt from a poem or song. This can have a very nice effect, so long as it relates to the book as a whole. Don't add something just to fill space, especially if it doesn't really enhance your book.

- *Table of contents.* List each chapter in your book by title, with the page on which it begins. This usually applies only to nonfiction. With the exception of the wonderful Harry Potter (Scholastic Inc.) books and some other juvenile works, it's no longer fashionable to give titles to fiction chapters.

- *Foreword.* This is a sort of pre-introductory blurb about why your book has merit, and why you as its author are a pro on the subject. It's not a must, but if you can coerce a mover and shaker in your target market to write a foreword for your book, you can use it as a terrific PR piece on your front cover. An example would be writing a book about architecture and putting "Foreword by Frank Lloyd Wright" on the cover. Forewords are not long (three to four pages).

- *Introduction.* This is a brief section in which you explain why you penned the book and what it will help the reader achieve. Again, it does not have to be long; five pages or so is fine.

Book Layout Checklist

Book Section	Fiction Book	Nonfiction Book	Element Completed
Front matter			
Book blurbs	*Optional*	*Optional*	
Half title page	***Standard***	***Standard***	
Title page	***Standard***	***Standard***	
Copyright page	***Standard***	***Standard***	
Dedication	*Optional*	*Optional*	
Acknowledgments	*Optional*	*Optional*	
Quotation(s)	*Optional*	*Optional*	
Table of contents		***Standard***	
Foreword		*Optional*	
Preface		***Standard***	
Body			
Your text	***Standard***	***Standard***	
Back matter			
Afterword		*Optional*	
Appendix/ references section		*Optional*	
Glossary		*Optional*	
Index		***Standard***	
Author bio	*Optional*	*Optional*	
Order form/ contact information	*Optional*	*Optional*	

Beware!

Publishing programs like Adobe InDesign and Quark Xpress are notoriously not user-friendly. Don't force yourself into a deadline situation where you have only a short span of time to lay out your book. Instead, give yourself time to get acquainted with one of these programs and up to speed on using it. And realize that no one learns this stuff overnight.

The Body

This section contains the meat and potatoes of your book. It should include your chapters, charts, illustrations, and whatever else goes into giving your readers the information and inspiration you've promised.

What you decide to include in the body of your book will largely depend on what your subject matter is and what treatment you have chosen (fiction or nonfiction, poetry or self-help, etc.). Some authors may need more chapters than others to effectively communicate their message. Some authors may want illustrations to accompany their text; others will not. Look at similar books in your topic area or genre to see how other authors have approached putting together the body of their book.

While you're laying out your book, decide if you'll add tip boxes and/or sidebars to the body text. Tip boxes are one-sentence to one-paragraph factoids that you can scatter throughout the text to add extra comments, comic relief, or highlight important points. Sidebars are one-quarter page to one-half page mini-articles that complement the text.

In addition to imparting information, tip boxes and sidebars also serve to break up the text and create visually interesting pages. Pull quotes are another element that can serve this purpose. A pull quote is a particularly interesting phrase or sentence from your text that you "pull" and reprint elsewhere on the page in a much larger font, usually in bold face or italics, to draw reader's interest to that page.

Back Matter

The sections that come after the body of your book are called the back matter. As with the front matter, the best way to decide how you want this material to look is to get ideas from books that have a style you admire already. The back matter of your book may include the following elements:

- *Afterword*. Also called an *epilogue*, this is the finishing note of your book, the wind-up in which you leave your reader with some final thoughts and messages. Like the foreword and introduction, the afterword should be fairly short. A half dozen pages is more than adequate.

- *Appendix*. Here's where you give readers resource information so they can go on to tackle their own projects. You might list handy reference materials, organizations and associations, helpful vendors, web sites, or pertinent government bureaus. If you have more than one appendix, you call them *appendices*.

- *Glossary*. This is a mini dictionary in which you list the buzzwords specific to the topic you have explored throughout your text.

- *Index*. If you're writing nonfiction, an index is practically a must. Readers will refer to the book often over the course of weeks, months, or even years, and it's nice to give them an easy way to access specific information. If you're extremely detail-oriented, you can put together your own index. If not, it's best to hire a professional. Ask other professionals in your field for referrals or approach publishing organizations/associations that you belong to for suggestions.

> **Smart Tip**
>
> Tip...
>
> When you list sources in your appendix, make sure you are as accurate as possible with your contact information. If you get sloppy and neglect to check the information twice before you go to press, your readers will call you—repeatedly—asking why they can't locate your source. Make sure nobody has changed phone numbers or URLs (web site addresses), etc., before you declare the appendix ready for print.

- *Author bio*. People always want to know something about the author, so give them the groupie-info they crave. Keep it short, though; a few paragraphs is fine. For a hardcover book, the author's bio may be placed on the inside of the dust jacket at the back of the book.

- *Order form/publisher contact information*. Always put an order form at the back of the book so readers can send for an extra copy—this works more often than you might imagine. People who like your book will want to order copies for friends or relatives, or someone who sees your book in an office or shop may want to order one for themselves. You might combine your order form with your company contact information, especially if you have other products to sell.

Fit and Trim

The *trim size*, or outside dimensions of your book, will naturally play a major role in your page count. This is one of the first things your printer will want to know. The bigger the book, the more text will fit on a page, and the fewer pages you'll need. There are exceptions, of course, such as children's picture books that have minimal text despite a larger trim size.

The most common trim sizes are:

- 5.5 inches by 8.5 inches (most popular)
- 6 inches by 9 inches (also very popular)

- 7 inches by 10 inches
- 8.5 inches by 11 inches

The first two trim sizes are *trade paperback* sizes, which means simply that they're standard for books sold to the trade—in other words to bookstores, libraries, and other publishing industry types.

One other trim size you'll see bandied about is *mass market paperback*, which refers to all those novels measuring 4.5 inches by 6.75 inches that you see in the supermarket checkout lanes and airport newsstands. Unless you believe your book will sell primarily to these types of markets, it's best to stick to the larger trim sizes.

Paper Stock

Now you'll need to decide what stock, or type of paper, you want for your text pages. Like choosing which color of white you want from the house paint swatches at the home improvement center, this can be tough. There are lots of choices.

First you need to decide on the weight of the paper. Your choices range from 40- to 70-pound papers, with a higher number indicating a heavier paper. As a general rule, you should go with 60-pound paper. Anything less is on the flimsy side, and anything more will probably be more expensive than what you need. Colors run from cream to white.

More Color

Next, you'll need to decide on the ink color for your text. This is generally pretty simple: black. But if you are planning something different, or you've got a kid's book, you might want to use another color or two. Don't get too carried away with ink colors. The more you choose, the more expensive the print job will be. And ink colors other than black—unless used cleverly—can make your book look unprofessional.

If you have color or black-and-white photos that you'll want reproduced in black-and-white, the printer will have to re-shoot them as *halftones*. This means, in a nutshell, that they get re-photographed through a fine screen to make them sharp and clear on the printed page. If you don't use halftones, you end up with the muddy mess you can achieve yourself by running a photo through a copier. If you want color photos in your pages, you'll need to ask for *color separations*, which simply means that the printer separates each photo into four separate negatives, one for each of the four print process colors.

While we're on the subject of artwork, if you've got photos or graphics that are centerfolds (covering a two-page spread), you'll need to tell the printer you've got bleeds. This means you have to account for the portion of your material that's tucked within the binding.

Fantastic Fonts

There are hundreds of *fonts*, or typestyles, to choose from, from the mod and trendy to the staid and stalwart. You can have a lot of fun playing with different fonts for chapter heads or title pages, but when you're producing running text, stick with something simple. Don't force your readers to strain their eyes trying to decipher a weird typeface—they won't. Different fonts take up surprisingly different amounts of space on a page, so this can be a factor in your final product, too.

Point Taken

Typed characters are measured in *points*—72 points to one inch. The smaller the point, the smaller the type, and the more print you can fit on a page. Most books are printed in 10 pt (or point) to 12 pt fonts (unless it's a children's book or large-print edition for the visually impaired). If you go smaller or larger, your print gets more difficult to read.

Shaving Points

Book design is as much art as technique. There's a lot to learn, but it's also a lot of fun. While the material we're exploring here may sound daunting, it's really not. Remember that with your publishing program, you'll be able to view your final product more or less as it will come from the printer in book form. You can always re-size margins, change fonts, and move graphics—whatever it takes to give your book a professional sparkle.

If you end up with 205 pages, for instance, which is an awkward 13 pages more than an even 12 signatures (16 pages per signature), you might tinker with your fonts, your margins, or your points to shave off those extra pages. You could eliminate your running heads or bump your folios (page numbers) onto the same line as your running heads, instead of placing them at the bottom of the page.

▲

Take the Lead

Leading (pronounced "ledding") refers to the amount of space between lines of text. Word processing and publishing programs usually figure the leading for you. This is a nice feature since a page with cramped leading or with oversized leading looks amateurish and is hard to read. Leading is measured from baseline to baseline (from the bottom of the first line to the bottom of the second line). Standard leading consists of your font's point size plus 2. For instance, if you have 10 pt type, you'll go with 12 pt leading, which is written as 10/12.

Going Marginal

You've got four margins to consider: top, bottom, left, and right. How you proportion them makes a big difference to the final size of your book. The more margin, or white space, the less text you can fit on a page. As a very rough rule of thumb, you'll want to allow *at least* a half-inch of margin on all four sides—any less and your book will look skimpy and cheap. Also, you need to allow a certain amount of "extra" margin for the printer to trim in production. If your margins are too small, you can lose essential white space, or even worse, text on the page.

Running Ahead

A running head is the book title or chapter title that runs across the top of each page. Some books place the book title at the top of each verso, or left-hand page, and the chapter title at the top of each recto, or right-hand page. Others use only the book title as a running head; still others don't bother with a running head at all.

Some publishers place the folio, or page number, on the same line as the running head, while others put it at the bottom of each page. Where you place yours is entirely up to you. Again, peruse other books whose style you admire and emulate them.

Head of the Chapter

Chapters should always start on a right-hand page. Chapter titles are usually in a larger point size than the text and can be in a different font, which gives them a nice design touch.

Besides your chapter titles, you'll want to break up your text with *major heads* and *subheads*, particularly in nonfiction books. Major heads are headlines that define the topic of a particular section in a chapter. Subheads are mini-headlines that define a sub-topic within the major head area. Place major heads in a larger point size and, if you like, in a different font than your regular text—but not as large as your chapter titles. Subheads are generally the same size as your text, but in a different font or in boldface.

Checklist of Book Design Elements

Design Element	Font	Point size	Graphics (if any)	Dimensions (1-inch margin, etc.)	Placement (top of page, centered, right-hand page, etc.)
Main text					
Top margin					
Bottom					
Left margin					
Right margin					
Leading					
Chapter heads					
Major heads					
Subheads					
Tip boxes					
Sidebars					
Running heads					
Folios					
Quotations					
Pull quotes					

Got It Covered

Bright Idea

Try to get a celebrity— not necessarily Oprah or Tom Cruise, but an expert in your niche market—to write a foreword. Then you can splash, "Foreword by so-and-so" on your front cover.

Your cover is not only protection for your book's pages but also your sales pitch—the only real way you have of attracting that potential reader's attention at the bookstore and guiding him to the checkout counter. As your most important sales tool, its makeup should not be a hit-or-miss affair. Start thinking "cover" early on in your book's planning stages, and don't stop thinking and planning it until the final moments of preproduction.

Front Cover Story

The front cover is your first-line sales pitch. As the element of your book that prospective readers look at first, it has to sell your story in a critical eight seconds. Make sure your cover contains these components:

- *Color*. The human eye is attracted to color—that's why so many packages on the supermarket shelves are splashed with reds and yellows. Your book does not have to have a four-color cover but, if you go for just one or two colors, make sure they fit your theme and have a strong design to pull the eye in. For exam- ple, take a look at the black-and-white photo with orange print that graces the cover of John Berendt's celebrated *Midnight in the Garden of Good and Evil* (Random House Inc.).

- *Design*. Simply stating your book's title and your name doesn't draw readers in. A strong design does. This is why a book cover designer is so important. If you're not a graphic artist, and you don't have a graphic arts-savvy friend or rel- ative who'll design a cover for you, spend the money to hire one.

- *Title*. Print the title in letters large enough to make a statement. Remember, you're selling the book here.

- *Subtitle*. In nonfiction, a subtitle is important; it tells browsers what your book will do for them, and what they can expect inside. *Raising Radishes*, for instance, tells the reader only that it's a gardening book. When we add, "*How to Earn Big Money from Your Own Backyard Garden*," we have a book that people interested in making money will want to read. A book called *Are We There Yet?* doesn't really explain what it's about. If we add, "*How to Vacation with Your Kids without Losing Your Mind, Your Money, or Your Temper*," we've got a book most parents would be interested in.

- *Sales pitch*. Your cover is the ideal place to add anything that makes you an expert on your book's topic, or that makes the book itself stand out from the competition. If you've written a book on how to help kids excel in school, and you're an award-winning teacher, for instance, you could put something like, "California's Teacher of the Year Shares Secrets for Parents." The author of a book on dog obedience might trumpet (tastefully) below his name, "Founder and President of the Dog Can-Do Obedience Academy and American Kennel Association Judge." Your credentials can make a big difference. Testimonials from opinion molders

who've read a pre-publication copy can add a nice punch as well. A book on helping kids excel in school might add a line like, "A must-read for every parent—Dr. Benjamin Spock."

- *Author's name*. Don't forget this on your cover—seeing your name in print is one of the most satisfying aspects of authorship. Once you've got one successful title under your publishing belt, readers will look for more books written by you.

Back Cover Sensation

The back cover is as important as the front—your last, best chance to sell your book to that browser. While the front cover acts as a teaser, the back closes the sale by explaining how your book will solve the reader's problems and/or enhance the reader's life. Use the following elements to press home your point:

- *Bookstore section*. By this stage of your preproduction, you should know what section of the bookstore or library your book fits into (reference, crafts, business, religion, etc.). Print this section in small but legible text at the top left of your back cover. That way the bookstore knows where to put it so readers and store personnel can find it easily.

- *Headline*. Here's your opportunity to reinforce what your book will do for your reader. Instead of, "How to travel with your kids so you all have a good time," nab that bookstore browser with something like, "Make your next family trip a memory instead of a nightmare." Don't use the same text you used for your subtitle—get creative and keep it snappy. Your headline must make your browser want to read on.

- *Features and benefits*. Now write a short, concise description of just what your book will help the reader accomplish and with what tools. Tell people how they will lead better lives after reading your book. Will they learn the secrets to financial success? The secrets of successful gardening? How to live longer or healthier, or enjoy more romantic relationships? This section of your back cover is a sort of mini-outline of each chapter, written as a tempting list of tidbits. If your book has pullout charts, worksheets, illustrations, or other helps, mention them here. Remember that your goal is to whet the reader's appetite so she will thumb through the book and then take it straight to the checkout register.

- *Recommendations.* After your features and benefits, add a few endorsements and/or testimonials from opinion molders in your niche market. Endorsements are glowing words about your book like, "Every paparazzi-hounded Royal should have a copy of *Simply Snubbing* on her nightstand. —Queen Elizabeth." Testimonials are explanations of how your book changed or enhanced a life like, "I couldn't have developed the Theory of Relativity without first having read *Hair-Raising Genius.*—Albert Einstein." Again, these words of praise do not need to come from tabloid-type celebrities, but they should be people recognizable and impressive to your target readers.

- *Author, author.* At the bottom of your back cover, write a short paragraph explaining why you're an expert on this subject. Let browsers know they're in the best possible hands when they pick up your book and take your advice.

- *The big finale.* Finish off the copy on your back cover with a bang—a final hook that turns a looky-loo into a buyer. Tell your reader one more time what your book will do for him: "Buy this book, and you'll never suffer credit woes again."

- *Price tag.* List your book's retail price in tactfully small print at the bottom right, along with the Bookland bar code and ISBN. If you have a hardcover book with a dust jacket, the price goes on the inside front flap at the top right.

Growing a Spine

Yes, even your book's spine deserves design attention. This is usually the only part of your volume bookstore browsers will see on the shelf. There isn't a whole lot you can do with a book's spine, so make sure your title is clearly visible and legible, and that it stands out as much as possible.

This is yet another place where color can make a major difference. Go to the bookstore; stand in the reference, religion, or romance section and look at which book spines leap out at

Smart Tip

Tip...

Don't think books sell based on their covers? Most book sales reps and distributors carry only book covers and dust jackets to show booksellers and other buyers. Buying decisions are based on covers, not on content.

you. You'll find that there aren't many. You don't want to color your background and print chartreuse and magenta simply to make your spine stand out from the crowd, but if you can use color wisely, do it. It also helps to make your print as large and striking as possible. You want your book to boldly proclaim itself, not timidly whisper.

Besides the title, your book's spine should also include your last name and your publishing company's name and logo. People don't generally buy books based on the publisher, as in, "Oh, wow, another book from Arithmetic Press!" But it doesn't hurt either, and, if you plan to enter various publishing industry book design competitions, you can get points knocked off your score if you don't have your logo on your book's spine.

Cover Stock

OK, with all this advice tucked under your hat, it's time to start making publisher/printer decisions. While you're designing your cover, you'll need to decide between hard and soft formats. Softcover is less expensive, which is an obvious advantage for both you as the publisher and for your buyer—but less isn't always more. Readers want some books printed as *case bound*, or hardcover volumes.

Professional and business books are often case bound—doctors, salespeople, CEOs, and other white collar types will more readily buy an expensive hardcover in their field than an inexpensive softcover, believing that a hardcover edition has more merit.

Coffee table and gift books are also generally bound in hardcover—it makes for a more impressive and longer-lasting presentation.

Taking Stock

If you're going with softcover, you'll need to choose a cover stock, or paper. The two standard choices are *10 point C1S* and *12 point C1S*. Translation: C1S is *cover coated on one-side* with untreated stock on the other side. The 12 point stock is slightly heavier than 10 point and, therefore, more expensive.

You'll also need to decide on a cover finish. The standard choices are *gloss lamination* or *matte lamination*. Lamination means the paper cover is treated with a plastic coating that protects against moisture, scuffing, and fingerprints. Gloss lamination provides a shiny finish; matte lamination does not.

Make sure you specify a *lay-flat*, or curl-resistant laminate, or your covers will roll like surf after a storm when any humidity is present. Cost differences in laminates are minimal—about a nickel more per book for matte than for gloss. And although you may pay marginally more for lay-flat, you really only want lay-flat. You'll be sorry, and so will your readers, if you elect not to use it.

▲

In a Bind

Once you make a decision on the hardcover vs. softcover issue and how you want the spine to look, you will need to choose a binding. If you go with hardcover, you will probably want a *Smythe-sewn* (pronounced "Smythe-sewn," with the "y" pronounced as a long "i") binding, in which the signatures are sewn together and then glued into the cover. This is the most durable case-bound binding, and the one most publishers choose.

Your hardcover itself won't look very interesting, so you'll need an eye-catching dust cover or jacket. If your jacket will consist of just a few artistic hues, you'll need to tell the printer what ink colors you want to use by referring to the *Pantone Matching System (PMS)* of ink colors. PMS numbers designate specific ink colors. It is sort of the same thing as the house paint samples you find at the home improvement store. PMS numbers ensure that the "burnt orange sienna" you have your heart set on is the same one the printer is looking at. PMS colors come in swatch books that you can flip through. If your printer is in Michigan and you're in Nebraska, go to a local printer

Ideal Specs

Use this sheet to fill in your ideal specs before you go on to that RFQ (request for quote) you'll send to printers:

Trim size: _____

Hardcover or softcover: _____

Cover stock: _____

Gloss or matte lay-flat laminate: _____

Disk-to-film or camera ready: _____

Four-color/PMS number(s): _____

Binding type: _____

Paper stock (weight and color): _____

Bleeds: _____

Halftones: _____

Color separations: _____

Text ink—black plus any PMS color(s): _____

and ask to look at their PMS colors. Note the numbers you've chosen and let your long-distance printer know.

Fun Fact
Library books that are bound in a standard format, instead of a heavy-duty library binding, last through only about 18 reads before falling apart.

You'll also need to specify how you will provide your jacket art. If you go with a professional book designer, you may send it to the printer *camera ready*, which basically means that you send the original artwork ready to be photographed and then printed. Or you might send your cover as *disk to film*, which means the artwork has been done on a software program and transferred to a CD or zip disc for the printer to use.

Perfectly Bound

For softcover books, you will probably want to stick with the publisher's premier choice, *perfect binding*. This is the type of binding used for virtually every softcover at the bookstore or library. The cover is glued onto a tidy, squared-off spine on which you can print your title and author/publisher information. Perfect bindings can also be Smythe-sewn.

Perfect binding is more expensive than other softcover bindings but has the double advantage of being more durable as well as being the only one most bookstores and libraries will buy.

If you are not concerned with these markets, though, and you're planning to sell via mail order, at seminars and workshops, or to specialty stores only, you've got several less expensive choices:

- *Spiral binding*. Wire is used to bind the pages of a book together in spiral binding. The blank notebooks you find at Wal-Mart or the supermarket are spiral bound.

- *Comb binding*. This type of binding involves the squiggly-plastic stuff you often see on junior league cookbooks to bind pages together.

- *Saddle-stitch binding*. This isn't stitched at all but stapled through the center, like the programs handed out at high school graduations or community theater productions. If your book is 72 pages or less, and you're marketing it as an inexpensive pamphlet or report, this could be the binding to use.

- *Velo binding*. A plastic strip holds the pages (perforated at the left margins) together. Gary S., the military memoirs publisher in Panama City Beach, Florida, uses velo binding for his books.

You might go with spiral or comb binding if you are producing a workbook for a seminar or workshop that will only be used by one reader during a brief period, or for a junior league or chamber of commerce cookbook where buyers do not expect a "fancy" binding job. For everything else, stick to perfect binding. It's the best!

Pricing
and Selling

We've explored the costs to set up shop as a self-publisher and the costs to have a book printed or e-published. But just having your book in hand doesn't mean your fling with financing is over. There are other factors that contribute to the cost of that book, from distributors to storage to shipping. You need a way to get your books from your storage

▲

facility to your readers. You can use wholesalers, distributors, direct mail, specialty stores, and a host of other venues. But nobody is going to beg you to sign on—it's up to you to make the first move. In this chapter, we'll investigate the elements involved in pricing and selling your book.

The Sticker Price

You'll need to decide on a sticker price for your book. You can't forecast profits if you don't know how much you'll charge. An industry rule of thumb is to base your price on your production costs multiplied by 5 or by 8. Note that this rule applies to traditional printing methods only—not print on demand (POD), which we explored in Chapter 6.

In addition to or perhaps in explanation of this rule of thumb, you'll want to consider that book prices are based on two defining elements:

1. *Your production costs*. Obviously, you must charge enough to cover your expenses including not only printing but also editing and artwork.

2. *Comparable retail prices*. If all the other softcover inspirational books on the shelf are priced in the $12.95 to $16.95 range and yours is priced at $30, it's not going to sell. Even if it's a million times better than the competition, people will perceive it as overpriced and give it a thumbs down. This is yet another reason to get out there and do your market research!

Let's take another look at *The Night Garden*, the title Glowworm Press printed at a per-book cost of $1.37, and let's decide that, based on comparable books in the marketplace, we're going to price it at $12.95. That leaves us with a per-book profit of $11.58, right? Well, not exactly. Now we have to take into account the other costs that you will encounter in addition to printing.

Divvying Up Discounts

The traditional method for getting books from your office or garage to your readers is to engage a distributor to sell them to bookstores on your behalf. You can also sell directly to booksellers yourself, but since there are more chains and fewer independents, this is becoming more difficult. Chains generally buy from distributors and wholesalers, and not from publishers. Whichever route you choose (and you should try both), you will need to give a percentage or *discount* off the book's retail price.

Distributor/Wholesaler Dance

Wholesalers and distributors play a big part in the publisher's world. New publishers are often confused about the difference between wholesalers and distributors—and no, they're not the same. A wholesaler is basically a mega-warehouse stacked to the rafters with millions of books. Wholesalers sit back and wait for booksellers to order books; they don't actively sell.

Distributors, on the other hand, act as sales representatives, designing catalogs that showcase their publishers' books, making marketing suggestions to help sales, and visiting booksellers with the sole purpose of convincing them to stock your title (as well as those of their other publishers). They also handle *fulfillment*, or orders from booksellers, including shipping, invoicing, and collecting payments—saving you lots of time.

Distributor Dating Game

Steve C., the independent publisher in Hinesburg, Vermont, says the terms "wholesaler" and "distributor" are often misused. "A distributor handles all your trade [bookstore and library] sales, on an exclusive basis. It will generally take about a 67 percent discount and may even levy added costs that you will have to pay. Distributors obviously give a large part of that big discount to the stores and wholesalers they sell to, and they have to pay a percentage to their sales reps. Some distribution companies are National Book Network, Publishers Group West, and IPG," explains Steve.

Turning Heads

So what will turn a distributor's head and make them want to represent you?

1. *Your book's saleability.* A business book distributor is likely to be far more interested in Bill Gates' sales secrets, as told by his secretary, than in Bill Gates' home décor, related by his housekeeper.

2. *Your book cover and design.* A book with a savvy cover or dust jacket looks like the product of a professional publisher. If everything—including the binding, layout, margins, leading, and the blurb on the back cover—is sharp and skillful, you've passed one of the biggest tests.

3. *Your marketing plan and promotional budget.* Distributors will do their part to sell your book with catalogs, booths at industry shows, and more, but they want to know that you've got a major campaign underway as well.

4. *Your product line.* Distributors prefer seasoned publishers with several titles under their belts. If this is your first title, you can't do too much here except push the sales value of your book. You can also discuss other titles you're working on, if that's the case. If not, don't invent; it won't ring true.

▲

There are many distributors to choose from, and they may require different discounts. Keep in mind that besides a hefty discount, distributors can and often will charge you for a slew of other services, including setup (to set you up in their system), catalog advertising, book fair advertising, and warehousing. After you add all this up, you're looking at as much as another $1,000 or more.

Some distributors are generalists, while others specialize in niches like education, Christian themes, the outdoor-enthusiast market, the health and fitness market, or books for the business-oriented, etc. If your title fits neatly into one specialty, this might be the place to start. If not, investigate the generalists.

Just because you decide on a distributor doesn't mean they'll choose you. It's a distributor dating game. You will have to convince them that your book is worth representing—and more than that, worth making a significant effort for. The trick here is that distributors like exclusive contracts—they do not want to deal with you if you are also working with another distributor. And since you will be tied solely to that distrib-

Interviewing Potential Distributors

These are questions you should ask any potential distributor in order to evaluate whether there is a good fit between your needs and their services.

1. What book genres do you handle? _____

2. How many publishers do you have on board? _____

3. How many trade accounts do you service? _____

4. What other types of accounts do you service, if any (i.e., libraries, specialty stores, airport shops, or convenience stores)? _____

5. What sales volume do you expect for my book this year? _____

6. What percentage do you pay for each sale? _____

7. When do you pay sales? _____

8. How do you handle returns? _____

9. What do you charge for warehousing? _____

10. Will you insure my books? _____

11. Do you pay shipping? _____

12. What extra fees can I expect to incur? _____

13. What is the standard length of your contract? _____

utor, you'll rely on them for the majority of your bookstore sales. If you find you don't like their style, you're stuck for the life of the contract. So carefully choose the one that's best for you.

You'll find a list of distributors in the Appendix at the back of this book, but instead of choosing one sight-unseen, get out there and do some additional research. Visit booksellers in your area and ask the manager or buyer about the distributors who service the books similar to yours. Then visit the distributors online and see how the titles they carry stack up as compared to yours. Get a feel for their services and general attitude. For the ones that look promising, place a call or send an e-mail to the new-accounts reps. These are the folks you want to woo. We've provided a list of the questions you should ask when interviewing potential distributors on page 122.

> **Smart Tip**
> Quality Books, a distributor based in Illinois, deals solely with the weighty library trade and doesn't require an exclusive contract. Quality Books has an excellent reputation for working with small publishers, so try to develop a relationship with them. (See Appendix for contact information.)

Wholesaler Heaven

"The fact that a distributor has sales reps may get you greater distribution, but if you can create demand for your book (through good reviews, radio shows, etc.) you can get very good distribution without these people," Steve C. advises. "You do need

Interviewing Potential Wholesalers

To evaluate potential wholesalers, be sure to ask these questions:

1. What book genres do you handle? _____
2. What percentage do you pay for each sale? _____
3. When do you pay sales? _____
4. How do you handle returns? _____
5. Do you charge for warehousing? _____
6. Will you insure my books? _____
7. Do you pay shipping? _____
8. What extra fees can I expect to incur? _____
9. What is the standard length of your contract? _____

▲

wholesalers—the people who take a 55 percent discount. The big ones are Ingram and Baker & Taylor. There are a number of smaller ones that can help reach certain markets, including a few remaining consignment wholesalers that are very open to small-press books (Bookpeople, New Leaf, and Quality Books are examples). Hardly any librarian or bookstore owner wants to order books one at a time from small presses. Their job is easier if they order hundreds of books at a time from the same place—in other words, a wholesaler."

Even though you may have a distributor that sells your book to wholesalers for you, you'll still need a relationship with a wholesaler yourself. Booksellers and librarians who haven't been approached by your distributor may hear about your book and want to order it, and they generally prefer to order it from a wholesaler, for two reasons:

1. Publishers have a reputation for filling orders in a matter of weeks instead of overnight as wholesalers do.

2. In terms of paperwork, it's far easier to order the works of hundreds of publishers from the wholesaler and receive a single invoice, than to pay a different publisher for each title.

Wholesalers are not quite as picky as distributors, but you will still have to do some courting. The two giants of the wholesaling world are Ingram, which holds the lead position, and Baker & Taylor, which focuses on servicing libraries as well as booksellers. There are also a number of smaller wholesalers who have a far better reputation for dealing with small presses—Bookpeople and New Leaf are two shining examples (see the Appendix for contact information). Like distributors, wholesalers demand a discount, generally 55 percent off the list price.

Decide which wholesaler you want to work with in the same way you would seek out a potential distributor, and then go about courting their business in essentially the same manner. You can use the "Interviewing Potential Wholesalers" form on page 123 to help you with this process.

The Bottom Line Revisited

Now you know that distributor and wholesaler discounts can range from 55 percent up to 67 percent. Gulp! This means that if our hypothetical publisher has *The Night Garden* priced at $12.95, and the distributor or wholesaler demands a 60 percent discount, Glowworm Press is really selling its title at $5.18. They still have to deduct production costs of $1.37 per book, so the per-book profit comes in at $3.81— less than before the discount but still a tidy profit margin.

Ship Shape

Yet another expense to consider is shipping—to and from the distributor's warehouse, to the independent bookseller, from the printer to you. Shipping is another of those costs that can vary dramatically depending on departure sites, destinations, and the number of books being shipped. It is not cheap. All you have to do is think back to the days when you schlepped a bag or backpack filled with books home from high school every day, and you'll remember that books are heavy. What this means for the self-publisher is that, rather than going through FedEx, UPS, or the U.S. Postal Service, you'll need to get bids from freight services.

As a rough example, here are some actual cost estimates for shipping our hypothetical *Raising Radishes* trade paperback (192 pages; 6 inches by 9 inches) from a printer in Kansas to a publisher in northwest Florida, using a freight service:

- 500 books costs $112
- 1,000 books costs $168
- 3,000 books costs $329
- 5,000 books costs $508

Return to Sender

There's yet another variable here, and that's returns and damages. Some self-publishers have a terrific relationship with their distributors and wholesalers; others consider them a necessary evil, with the emphasis on "evil." One reason for this sentiment is that some companies go extremely heavy on the returns. They will order 100 books from you on Tuesday, return them to you on Wednesday morning, and then reorder them on Wednesday afternoon.

This can play havoc with your profits—you not only have to take back the books you thought you'd sold and erase the payments you thought were coming your way, but, to add insult to injury, you have to pay shipping both going and coming (and going again). And if the books are damaged in the return process, you can't resell them.

"Unfortunately, I have not had a good experience," says Anna J. in Temple, Texas. Anna had trouble with a wholesaler for over a year. "I finally got the problem settled; now I don't get orders from them (which is better than receiving damaged, returned books and inaccurate bills for books returned). I'm currently in the Ingram Express program, which is specifically

Tip...

Smart Tip
Printers often include shipping costs in the estimate. Check with your printer to find out if shipping has been included.

125

▲

Cinderella Story

As a neophyte in the book trade, you may discover that, even though your book looks professional and has good sales potential, you can't land a distributor. Like those reviews you may not get, this is a fact of life and not a direct insult. Distributors can be snooty, but you can win them in time. Re-contact them every few months and woo them with your solid sales figures, great reviews, news coverage, and endorsements. Sooner or later, they'll say, "Yes."

PMA (Publishers Marketing Association) has devised a special Trade Distribution Acceptance Program to deal with this difficulty for newcomers to the publishing industry. Each summer and winter, a committee made up of reps from Ingram and Baker & Taylor (the "Big Two" of wholesaling); Borders; Barnes & Noble; independent booksellers; and Independent Publishers Group (IPG), which is a distributor, reviews submissions from PMA members. In a sort of Cinderella story, titles they feel are saleable are picked up for distribution by IPG.

for small publishers, and it is a headache. They order books that I send them; I have to give them a 55 percent discount. Then they send the books back to me even while they're ordering more of the same books! It has been most frustrating."

Steve C. warns that "every publisher hates the Ingram returns, which are a big percentage of its purchases—and usually in damaged condition—and you are expected to pay for their return postage!" But Steve concedes that, "if you want to sell to bookstores, you deal with Ingram."

Not every self-publisher we interviewed has had a bad experience with a wholesaler or distributor. "Wholesalers and distributors are a necessary evil as the chain stores will deal only with them," says June H. in Michigan. "I have a contract with Partners Distributors in Holt, Michigan, and Ingram Books in LaVergne, Tennessee. I've had no problems with either."

Your best bet is to check references with other self-publishers and go with the one that has the best reputation. To some extent, you will have to accept that the process may not always be smooth. In some instances, it may be better to make certain trade-offs, like budgeting for the expense of return postage, in order to achieve the sales goals that you set for yourself. How much should you allow for returns? Industry experts recommend that you pencil in a figure as high as 20 percent.

You do have some small measure of control here. Although your printer, distributor, and wholesaler will insist that you pay shipping to and from them, you in turn can insist that independent booksellers pay shipping on any returns they send back to you.

You'll still have to absorb the cost of the books, but you can let them pick up the transport tab. Just make sure you state your return policy in your book sales contract.

Storage Story

If you print 5,000 books and have them shipped to your home office, you're going to have to decide where to stash them. You could cover them with tablecloths, slipcovers, and bed linens, and use them in place of furniture. But barring this scenario, you'll have a problem.

If you live in an area where dampness and/or humidity are not significant factors, you could warehouse your books in your garage. Otherwise, you'll need to rent a climate-controlled storage facility. You don't want creeping mildew to spot all your pages, or your covers to stick together or curl.

Storage prices will vary with your location and the size space you rent, but as a ballpark figure you can pencil in $70 to $100 per month.

Smart Tip

Tip...

We've talked about shipping big-ticket items—cartons or pallets of books. What about when you ship one, two, or three books at a time to readers who order from your web site or order form? This one's easy. You charge them for shipping by adding the FedEx, UPS, or U.S. mail charge onto your invoice. That's the norm in mail order, and your customers will cheerfully pay to receive your products.

Trade Sales and Alternative Venues

OK, you've got those bound galleys out, bundled up your review packages, along with your finished book, sent them off to everybody who's anybody, and dealt with distributors and wholesalers. Good! But you've still got lots more to tackle. You can't sit back and wait for the sales reps to sell for you, especially if you haven't yet been successful in lining up a distributor.

Besides the traditional trade outlets of bookstores and libraries, there are many alternative venues in which to sell your books. We'll take a look at bookstores and libraries, and then everything from direct mail to premiums to museum shops.

Bookstore Bonanza

When you sell directly to bookstores, you'll need to give them a 40 percent discount. This is the industry norm, and they expect it. If you've lined up a distributor, it's easier to let them make sales to the trade while you concentrate on other venues. But you can sell directly to bookstores whether you've got representation or not. The catch here is that the major chains, from Borders to Books-a-Million, usually can't order directly from you unless you've got a wholesaler—corporate policy won't allow it. But you can ask. Sometimes they'll go around their own rules to carry the titles of local authors and publishers. Some bookstores even have a special section set aside to showcase the works of local talent.

Local talent aside, if you don't have a distributor you'll do better to focus on independent booksellers. These are the mom-and-pop places you can still find in quaint or funky downtown areas and outlying suburban strip malls, if you look. Some bill themselves as "used book" sellers, but they often carry new titles as well.

Because these stores generally do not have the budget for major orders, you won't want to spend months canvassing them door-to-door in

> **Bright Idea**
>
> Talk to sales reps and distributors who specialize in the markets you want to reach. The best way to find them is to ask local merchandisers who their reps are. You can also check with national organizations in those specialties. For instance, if you're selling a cookbook, you could check with the National Specialty Foods Association, which can give you leads to reps and distributors for shops that buy gourmet goodies.

the manner of an itinerant salesperson. But you should definitely approach every independent bookseller in your area. Remember, you're a local author and publisher, which means you're a local celebrity. Independents will be charmed to carry your title, and they'll do their utmost to sell it for you. Expect to give independent booksellers 40 percent off your list price.

Appearance Is Everything

Even when chain superstores stock your book, you won't find it on view in the window or on display at the front of the store. Instead it will be tucked discreetly out of sight on the shelf with all the other business books or romance novels or whatever.

Those snazzy cardboard displays, called *dumps* or *point-of-purchase displays (POPs)*, are generally reserved for the products of the major New York publishing houses and the books that have been on *The New York Times* bestseller list for the tenth week running.

There's not a whole lot you can do about this situation since booksellers only have so much display space. Naturally, they're going to give it to the books they expect to sell the best or those that come with dumps for the display areas.

Your best solution is to either stop worrying about it and trust that your books will sell themselves based on your other marketing and PR efforts, or design and build your own dumps. This will add considerably to your advertising budget, but if market research shows it can really be effective—and your wallet can take it—give it a shot. Interview local booksellers to find out if they can use a dump and where they would

Publicity Freebies

You may think that since you've ordered 3,000 copies of your book from the printer, you've got 3,000 copies to sell. But if you do all the publicity that you should, you'll give away as many as 500 copies—absolutely free—to various book review sources, industry experts in your niche market, TV and radio program producers, and other opinion molders. The numbers add up fast.

And you'll have to add in shipping by postal carrier for each one of those books. As an estimate, you can figure that a 1-pound book shipped Special Standard Mail, or book rate, via the U.S. mail costs $1.59. If you send out a total of 500 books during the course of your publicity campaign, that's $795!

prefer to have it placed. There's no point in springing for a five-foot-high floor model when a small counter display would be more effective.

Libraries and Educational Markets

Colleges and other educational buyers will often accept 20 percent discounts. However, educational markets will only purchase certain types of books. If your niche is romance novels, for instance, you can count them out. However, if your book is a nonfiction title like, *My Hero: How Romantic Fiction Affects the Female Mind*, you might just find a buyer among psychology, sociology, or women's studies professors.

Libraries, which can be sizable buyers, will pay full retail price for books with special (and more expensive) library binding. For most books, they expect a 40 percent discount but will take what they can get. Public librarians can be a terrific buying market and may buy just about anything they think will be good for their patrons—that they can fit into their budgets.

Besides traditional public libraries, you can also sell to the thousands of private libraries all over the country. Many churches; synagogues; genealogy societies; film, art, and sports institutes; professional and social organizations; and hospitals and corporations house their own collections. If your book subject would be of interest to any of these groups, try to make sales! Don't forget to offer a fair discount of up to 40 percent.

Tip...

Smart Tip

The best time to pitch your book to public librarians is during June or December—right around budget appropriation and spending seasons.

Stat Fact

According to *Microsoft Encarta Online Encyclopedia*, there are over 130,000 libraries in the United States. Almost 100,000 of these are school institutions, and nearly another 16,000 are public libraries.

The Amazon of Bookstores

A nifty alternative to brick-and-mortar bookstores is the ace of the virtual booksellers' world—Amazon.com. Amazon caters to independent publishers. They'll provide you with a publisher's web site; scan in your book's photo; set you up with an author interview, a book blurb, your comments about your book, a sample passage of your choice, and space for readers' reviews. Your title appears prominently on the site's search results, and, as another bonus, your book is offered with 24-hour shipping—and Amazon.com handles order fulfillment.

What's the catch for all these goodies? Not much—there's no contract to sign and no exclusive. All they ask is that you keep your titles in stock and give them a 45 percent discount on the list price of your book. What have you got to lose?

Premium Grade

There are lots of creative venues for making sales other than bookstores and libraries. One of these is *custom publishing* or *premiums*, two different names that mean the same thing. You are familiar with premiums—those freebie cookbooks given out as advertising incentives by the local natural gas board, the amortization books handed out by the local bank, and even the oven mitts emblazoned with the name of a nearby supermarket.

Your book just might be the stuff of a terrific premium. Take a look at your subject matter and evaluate it in terms of what companies or organizations might benefit from it. You could pitch a sinful dessert cookbook to a dairy products company to showcase their butters and creams or to a chocolate manufacturer to feature recipes for their product. This is where the term *custom publishing* comes in. You may need to customize your text so that instead of "2 pounds of chocolate," your recipes read "2 pounds of Chocoholic-brand chocolate," or whatever it may be.

Your customization might be as simple as adding the store's name to the title. A home improvement chain might be interested in selling copies of your do-it-yourself remodeling manual to its customers. You would simply add the store name to your existing title: "Handy Hal Superstore's *Home Remodeling for the*

Smart Tip

Tip...

When you sell customized publishing or premiums, give your customer discounts based on volume—perhaps 40 percent for 500 to 1,000 copies, and 50 percent for amounts over that. Have the customer pay for shipping.

Hammer-Impaired." Or you might not change anything—a lingerie manufacturer might like to give each customer who orders over a certain amount from its spring catalog a "free" copy of your romance novel. And hospitals might like to tuck copies of your new-baby inspirational book into the their take-home kits for parents.

> **Bright Idea**
>
> Why not sell your book to nonprofit organizations, either as a customized printing or as is? You can offer a deep discount, feel good about helping a worthy cause, and generate a little money and publicity all at the same time.

Obviously, the more changes you make, the more advance notice you will need. You can't change your cover or your text after your books are already printed. You'll need to approach potential customers very early in the game—before your initial printing or before any reprints.

Your other option is to purchase stickers or rubber stamps to add to your cover or title page, ones that say something like "With Best Wishes from Grace Avenue Maternity Hospital," for example.

The Catalog Game

Another nontraditional venue for selling your book is through mail order catalogs. Don't confuse this arena with your own mail order sales—here we're talking about selling quantities of your books to a third-party mail order retailer. There are thousands of mail order catalogs out there, and each one works hard to find one-of-a-kind merchandise for its pages. Your book could be ideal.

As with premium sales, match your subject matter to the catalog. A book on golf techniques might be the perfect match for a catalog of goods for the novice golfer. An aromatherapy title might be just the thing for a health-products catalog. And an inspirational gift book on fathers and sons could sell well in a general interest catalog, especially around Father's Day.

Sell to catalog merchandisers the way you do to anyone else—sell early, sell assertively, push your book's sales potential, and offer a fair discount for volume sales. You can find catalog merchandisers by doing a search on the internet.

Specialty of the House

Bookstores aren't the only retail shops capable of stocking your book. There are also all sorts of specialty stores and boutiques that can be terrific sales outlets. Use the same criteria we explored above for catalog merchandisers. Think about what kind of match your book can make with what sort of shop. There are hundreds of specialties to choose from including:

• Outdoor activities—camping and hiking gear, or canoe outfitters

- Boating
- Health food and vitamins
- Arts, crafts, and hobby shops
- Toys
- Children's and infants' supplies
- Automotive
- Luggage and travel
- Beauty shops
- Gardening
- Computer and software
- Educational
- Fine furniture and home décor
- Cards, stationery, and gifts

> **Tip...**
>
> ### Smart Tip
> Take a ghostly sheet from June H.'s sales book. "I sell anywhere I can," says the horror writer from Rochester Hills, Michigan. "For the last two years, I have sold books at a Halloween event in Stone Mountain, Georgia, called 'A Tour of Southern Ghosts' and [have] done quite well. Look around at the small stores or local events that tie into the types of stories you produce," offers June.

Museum-Quality

When you think alternative retail, don't forget about museum shops. There are thousands of museums and historic homes all over the country, from the mammoth Metropolitan in New York City to the diminutive Franklin D. Roosevelt vacation-home site in Warm Springs, Georgia. Each one has its own shop crammed with merchandise. Your book could be on display as well.

Once again, think about how your title might match the subjects on display or the general ambiance of the museum or historic home. A book about World War II or the Depression might do well at the Roosevelt home, since he was a fixture during both traumas, but a regional title on travel in Georgia might also be a big seller.

Stepping into the Spotlight
Publicity

As a general rule, books don't sell themselves. Unlike hot dogs at a ball game, or iced confections peddled from a cart on a steamy city afternoon, people don't notice books without prompting. One of your biggest tasks as a self-publisher is to publicize your book as effectively, creatively, and energetically as possible. Start thinking about your book, your

▲

personality, your budget, and your niche market and how you can tie them all into a glittering promotional package. In this chapter, we'll explore the very best ways to get your book noticed by the people who count, from pre-publication reviewers to post-publication venues.

Pre-Publication Pow

After you've written and designed your book and sent it off to the printer, it's time to focus on selling it. Note that we didn't say you have recieved your completed volumes back from the printer—the prime time to start your sales campaign is before your book is ever released. In fact, most major reviewers won't accept a finished product. They only want to see a work-in-progress.

Setting the Date

Once you are active in the publishing industry, you will see the words publication date or pub date bandied about. Most people assume this refers to the date the book comes back from the printer and (hopefully) floods those bookstore shelves. Well, it's not. A book's publication date is entirely fictional.

Its purpose is to give you time to get your product from the printer to the distributor and into stores, well before entering the welcome glare of the limelight you'll generate with your marketing blitz. Set your pub date at six weeks to two months before your book is ready for shipment from the printer. Then swing into pre-publication action! Time pre-publication reviews, media appearances, press releases, and news articles so that prospective readers are primed to snap it up by the time your book actually arrives on bookstore shelves.

Bound for the Galleys

Pre-publication reviews can do as much or more to ensure the success of a book than just about any other marketing technique you can employ. A favorable review in a trade publication can net significant sales and generate terrific additional publicity. But trade reviewers are picky. They won't review every book that comes down the pike, and they won't review anything that looks like a finished product. Their reasoning is that if the book is already printed, it's not new enough to warrant their attention.

Instead of a tidy book with a dust jacket or shiny four-color cover, you put together a bound galley to send to reviewers. This is your book on standard 8.5-by-11 copier-quality paper, regardless of what the actual trim size will be. The pages are perfect bound, but with a plain-Jane cover: nothing but a title page printed in black ink on a white background. This is one place where it's fine to have a general printer copy and bind your book. Or you can check prices with a POD printer. The book printer you use will send you F&Gs, which are the folded and gathered signature pages of your book. These are what you can have quick-copied by a general printer and bound to make your bound galleys.

Since this is an advance copy of your book, it's perfectly acceptable to send it without the table of contents, dedication, acknowledgments, index, or other final round of layout material. It's also OK to send a bound galley without illustrations—unless of course it's a children's picture book or other title that depends on illustrations to tell the story.

If you leave out the table of contents, index, illustrations, or other matter, make sure you note that they'll be included in the finished book. And of course, make sure you've done all your copy editing and proofreading. You want the galley as clean and sharp as possible.

Announcements and Accompaniments

You can't send a bound galley out into the cold review world all alone—it will immediately get lost in the crowd. Fashion a one-page cover letter to accompany it. This should briefly describe the book and explain why you, the expert, are the perfect author for this subject.

If at all possible, give your letter a hook to attract special attention to your topic. For instance, if the headlines are filled with news of a scientific breakthrough on aging and your book is about living longer and healthier, you could tie into the media frenzy. If your sci-fi adventure is about life on Mars, you could tie into current news stories on Mars exploration, for example.

Book Announcement

The Night Garden: How to Enjoy Your Garden After Dark

Author: Peter Moss
Publication date: October 15, 200x
Price: $12.95
ISBN: 0946555-23-X
Vital statistics: Trade paperback, 6 inches by 9 inches, illustrations, and index
Number of Pages: 192

Publisher: Glowworm Press, 1 Firefly Lane, Luminescent, FL 10000
Distributed by: Friendly & Reliable Distributors Inc.
Contact: Sally Luna (850) 555-0000, www.glowwormpress.com

You'll also need to make up an announcement form to glue onto the galley itself. Because of the avalanche of books reviewers often get buried under, your galley can easily get lost from your vital information if you don't use glue. And this information is critical: reviewers can't tell the public your book's ISBN, publication date, or price if your galley has gotten separated from your letter. Take a look at the sample "Book Announcement" on page 135.

The Pre-Pub Revue

Once you have your bound galleys, you'll want to send them out for review—three to four months before your pub date. You should target both book trade and general interest publications.

Trade Reviewers

The major publications for trade buyers—the ones that have the greatest impact—are *Publishers Weekly* and *Library Journal*. Don't neglect the rest, though. The more pre-publication reviews you can garner, the better your book's chance of success.

The following is a list of publications you'll want to include on your mailing list. While most are interested in a wide range of materials, they all have their own guidelines. Some will accept only children's books; some won't review textbooks; and others shy away from mass-market paperbacks and poetry.

Although we've provided you with some tips on who reads what, it's up to you to check with each publication to make sure they review your book's genre. While you're at it, get the name of the editor for your genre (with the correct spelling!). Address your package specifically to him and add his title as well—that way if he's moved onto another publication or gone to Tahiti for two months, his substitute can receive the materials.

- *Publishers Weekly*. This is the penultimate pre-publication review machine. If you get a rave response here, you've just about got it made. The entire trade goes by what *Publishers Weekly* says is good—bookstores, libraries, and wholesalers alike. The main area of interest for Publishers Weekly is just about anything that will appeal to the general public.

- *Library Journal*. Almost as powerful as *Publishers Weekly*, *Library Journal* is the

---

Tip...

Smart Tip

Send a bound galley to Quality Books, based in Illinois, a company that distributes independent publishers' products to libraries. Unlike most wholesalers and distributors, Quality Books wants to see your pre-pub product rather than wait for the finished book.

Molding Opinions

While you're in your bound galley review phase, don't forget to send copies to opinion molders in your niche market. If your book is targeted toward physicians, for instance, send copies to doctors who can give you a favorable review, an endorsement or testimonial, or perhaps even write the foreword. If your book's niche is crafters, send galleys to noted crafters and to crafting publications.

Sending galleys to opinion makers is a good way to generate early interest in your book and get readers looking forward to its appearance on bookstore shelves. You may even make advance sales.

Send as many bound galleys as your budget will allow and get creative about who's an opinion maker. Anna J., the self-publisher in Temple, Texas, sent her book targeted toward siblings of critically ill children to nurses and social workers—people who have the power to suggest it to families in need.

---

reviewer of choice for public librarians all over the country, as well for wholesalers who sell to libraries. An A-plus here can mean sales of 1,000 to 5,000 copies—an entire print run. Not surprisingly, *Library Journal* looks for books that will appeal to the broad readership of a public library.

- *Kirkus Reviews*. Another major trade reviewer, *Kirkus Reviews* is read by booksellers and librarians. *Kirkus Reviews* takes on fiction and nonfiction of just about any genre but poetry, mass-market paperbacks, and picture books for the toddler set.

- *School Library Journal*. The junior version of the venerable *Library Journal*, *School Library Journal* reviews fiction and nonfiction for children and teens, including picture books. Despite the name, *School Library Journal* is read by public librarians, as well as those in school settings.

- *ALA Booklist*. The ALA stands for American Library Association, which tells you that this is another journal targeted toward librarians. *ALA Booklist* reviews fiction, nonfiction, and reference (but not textbooks) for children, teens, and adults.

- *Choice*. This journal also targets librarians, with a focus on those in academic and research settings. *Choice* is the place to go if your book has a technical or scholarly bent. Recent reviews include an encyclopedia of dinosaurs, a documentary history of sports in North America, a volume examining Lewis Caroll's use of earlier childhood literature, as well as the layperson-oriented *Marketing for Dummies* (John Wiley and Sons).

- *ForeWord.* A trade journal targeted toward booksellers, librarians, and publishers, *ForeWord* specializes in the products of independent and university presses. Although they don't want to see textbooks or technical tomes, *ForeWord* is open to just about everything else including e-books and audio books.

General Interest Reviewers

The following is a list of publications that review books for the general public. As with trade journals, it's up to you to double-check all the contact information before sending out your galleys. Life is not static. Reviewers move on or retire; newspapers change their guidelines. Part of effective PR is staying on top of details.

- *New York Times Book Review Section.* This is the *Publishers Weekly* of the general interest world—the supreme review mechanism. If you're a smash in the pages of *The Times*, you can expect the orders to roll in. A bonus to a review here is that it may be syndicated, which means it will appear in other newspapers nationwide. *The Times* is interested in just about everything but technical tomes.

- *Los Angeles Times Book Review Section.* The West Coast *Times* is not as big a draw as the Big Apple version but can do well by you. This *Times* takes on most general interest books.

- *Book reviewers at other major metropolitan newspapers.* Send galleys to other major newspapers such as *The Boston Globe, Chicago Tribune, The Philadelphia Inquirer,* and *San Francisco Chronicle.* If your budget will stretch to it, also send galleys to book review editors at newspapers in Atlanta, Louisville, St. Louis, San Diego, Seattle, and other points around the country. But use common sense. If your book has a strong regional appeal, as in Smoky Mountains Gardening, don't send it to out-of-the-area reviewers.

Significant Others

Steve C., the independent publisher who has produced over 20 books, believes in the power of advance reviews. "There are some important publications that need to receive bound galleys three or four months in advance of the official date of publication—otherwise, they won't review the book," the Vermont resident says. "The most important of these are *Library Journal* and *ALA Booklist*. Without review there, you sell no books to libraries and miss out on the best chance to make back your initial investment quickly.

"Other significant publications that need advance galleys include *Publishers Weekly* and *The New York Times*. A favorable *Publishers Weekly* review will help with bookstore sales and is useful to quote in your publicity to show that you've been reviewed by a prestigious publication. That can open doors for you that might otherwise be closed to a new self-publisher. The *Times* probably won't review your book—certainly not if the editors notice that you are a self-publisher. But it's worth trying anyway because, if they do, a review from The *Times* all by itself may sell 10,000 books and propel the book to continuing publicity elsewhere.

"A great many other publications do not want advance galleys and prefer to receive finished books when they are available," says Steve. When submitting your galleys to publications other than the biggies, it is important to check into their policies—particularly if the publication is subject- or genre-specific. "Making the wrong type of submission can cost a review and can cost many book sales," warns Steve.

> **Tip...**
>
> ## Smart Tip
>
> Sending a bound galley for review doesn't guarantee that your book will be written up in a trade or general interest publication. Most major publications receive thousands upon thousands of galleys each year, more than they could ever read and make room to review in their pages. Don't be deterred by this, and don't feel you've failed or been slighted if you don't get reviewed.

The Post-Pub Revue

Once your book has been printed, you can send out more review copies. But instead of bound galleys, you'll send the finished product, along with a tidy review package (which we'll discuss in the next section). Send your finished book to:

- All the sources to whom you previously sent bound galleys (Often, the receipt of the actual book will prompt a review.)
- Magazines, journals, and other publications in your niche market
- Any opinion makers you didn't catch the first time around, or whom you would like to thank or woo with the finished product
- Local media including newspapers, regional magazines, TV, and radio
- National media (Your chances for success here are far slimmer than with local media, but if you follow up—over and over again—you can get noticed.)
- The major wholesalers: Baker & Taylor and Ingram
- Book review magazines

Reviewing the Package

When you send review copies of your finished book, you'll put together an entire package full of goodies that reviewers, editors, TV and radio producers, and other media types can use to fill in their own blank spaces and promote your book at the same time.

Here are the elements you'll want to include in your review package:

- *Cover letter*. This can be basically the same letter as the one that accompanied your bound galleys. Update it to reflect your finished book and any newsworthy hooks you can devise.

- *Sample review*. Write up your own review of your book—it's not tacky; it's smart. Editors often don't have the time or the person-power to read and review your book, but they'd like to include it in their pages. If you write a review for them, they can use it as is, use snippets with their own comments as a frame, or paraphrase it. And if you have written the review, you know it will be favorable. Read reviews of other books similar to yours to get ideas of how to write your review.

> **Bright Idea**
>
> The best way to get testimonials and endorsements is to ask. It's a two-way street. Opinion makers are helping you, but in return you're giving them an absolutely free opportunity to get their names in the press before their market niche and yours.

- *News release*. This is your review written like a news story. Make it as topical and newsworthy as possible. Publications that don't use reviews will use a news release—it helps them fill space on a page or on the air. As with your sample review, they do not have to write it up unless they choose to because you've done it for them.

- *Copies of other reviews*. Add good-quality copies of other reviews of your book. Remember that the purpose here is to blow your horn, and the more A-plus publicity the better.

- *Testimonials and endorsements*. Print up a page of testimonials and endorsements, and add it to your package. Word-of-mouth—even on a printed page—sells.

- *Interview questions*. Make up a list of ten questions for interviewers to ask you. Radio and TV interviewers especially like this feature, but print media writers also find it a plus. They don't have to take the time to read your book to ask you intelligent questions about it. Design your questions to highlight the important points of your book and to divulge a few tips. Once you whet people's appetites for what they will get if they buy the book, they'll be eager to do so.

- *Demo tape announcement*. If you've allowed for a demo interview videotape in your budget, add a sheet to the packages you send to national TV shows, letting them know that you have a demo available for review. Producers like demos so they can see for themselves that you're personable, presentable, and interesting.

- *Photo*. Add a professional-quality, black-and-white photo of your book or of yourself. Most of the time this won't be used, but it doesn't hurt either.

- *Your shiny new book.* Don't send a copy that has been damaged in transit or splashed with coffee while gracing your coffee table. This is your calling card, so it must look sharp. Order a rubber stamp that says "Review Copy" and stamp the surface formed by the outside edges of the pages when the book is closed. This way nobody can return your review copy to the bookstore—which could result in having it sent back to you for credit.

> **Tip...**
>
> **Smart Tip**
> Some budget-conscious publishers send a press release instead of a cover letter to all but the most important and most likely reviewers. This way, they can ask that the recipient request a book only if interested.

Traveling Man

You'll want to take into account some sort of dollar figure for promotional travel. How much depends on how you plan to promote your book and how much you can afford to spend. Promotion is one of the very most important aspects of self-publishing. If you don't get the word out, you don't sell books.

Are you thinking all out media blitz, flying out to guest on as many TV stations around the country as will have you? Or will you stay more focused on your local market, with a plan to drive to every niche market event (like games, meets, conventions, or shows) within a 400-mile radius? Or do you plan to do the majority of your promotions through the internet and through radio interviews that you can conduct from your home phone? In this case you will not need much of a travel allowance at all.

Sending yourself on an author tour where you stay at the Ritz and get around by limousine is not a must. It's perfectly acceptable to go the Motel 6-and-minivan route. Perhaps you won't even need to budget money for lodging. Do you have friends and relatives with whom you can stay, or an RV to use as a temporary base? If you have a limited budget, there are many ways to keep your travel expenses reasonable.

Guest Spot

Once you've sent out all those review copies, you may start getting requests from the media. There's nothing quite like the thrill of that first phone call from a producer asking if you'd care to guest on a radio or TV show. Of course, you'll say, "Yes!"

▲

But after the initial glow of accomplishment wears off—and as airtime nears—you may find yourself starting to get nervous. What will you wear? What will you say? How will you say it? And what if—the ultimate horror—you absolutely freeze up?

To perform well in the media arena, it's essential that you do your homework and prepare for the task. Here's how:

- *Realize that everybody gets butterflies.* OK, maybe not Jim Carrey, but every other star of stage and screen. This is healthy. It keeps you sharp. And once you get past the first couple of interviews, you'll learn to relax and have fun while you're at it.

Bright Idea

Always follow up an interview with thank you notes to the show's host and producer. This is a nice personal touch that shows your appreciation and leaves the door open for further interviews down the line. Be sure to enclose your business card!

Good Morning World

It's fairly easy to get an interview on local radio and television—depending, of course, on where you live. The producers of "Good Morning Apalachicola" are hungry for stories and will be delighted to have you on. But the producers of "Good Morning Manhattan" may have more than they can handle already. And national shows—the ones that give you the greatest exposure and the greatest endorsements—are extremely difficult to get on.

But this doesn't mean you should give up. It can be done. Be persistent. Send publicity material every month or so and be creative. Producers of these shows are flooded with mail, faxes, and phone calls from interview hopefuls on a daily basis. They can't and won't follow up on anything that doesn't reach out and grab their attention. Think about how you can tie into another media or news event, or how you can hook them with a clever ploy that will make your package stand out from the crowd. If your book is about travel, for instance, you could send your PR kit wrapped up in a road map, tucked into an oversized "passport," or stashed in a cardboard "suitcase."

Although most self-publishers go it alone, hiring a publicist is an option here. It can be an expensive one. The advantage is that the publicist may know more than you do about PR and have more contacts. The disadvantage, aside from the costs, is that you may very well know your market better than anyone else. If you choose to explore this avenue, start by checking in with self-publishing organizations like PMA (Publishers Marketing Association).

- *Realize that you're the expert here.* You have written an entire book about your subject. By this time, you know your material inside and out. You have also written up all sorts of publicity materials from your sample review to your galley cover letter to your news release. You have already got down on paper just about everything any interviewer is likely to ask. You know your stuff.

- *Ask the producer if she'd like to send you a list of ten interview questions before the air-date.* She will probably accept in a second. And by doing this, you appear professional, make her job easier, and give yourself a heads-up on what the questions will be. You also will not have to worry about being hit with something for which you haven't thought out an answer.

- *For radio interviews, keep your phone line free.* You do not want that distracting call-waiting beep in the background with your mom calling from Nebraska to ask what the garage man meant when he said her distributor cap is clogged, or your daughter phoning from the mall to ask if she can get her navel pierced. Tell friends and family who are likely to drop by that you'll be unavailable during airtime. If possible, have the phone company temporarily disable your call waiting, give the radio station a number that doesn't have call waiting (like your fax or internet line), or tell everyone you know not to call at airtime.

- *For TV interviews, dress like you would for a business meeting—professional but not formal.* You want to look polished but not stuffy. Of course, you should dress to match the show's ambiance and your own subject matter. If your book is for golfers and you're being interviewed on the links, you'll look pretty silly standing around in a business suit. In this case, you'd wear your golf duds. If you'll be demonstrating painting techniques from your crafts book, wear something that looks artistic but workable.

- *Practice—but not too much.* Have a friend or family member "interview" you so you can practice what to say and how to say it. But don't overdo it. If you memorize your lines, you will end up sounding wooden during the actual interview. And if the interviewer asks a question that's not on your list, she may throw you for a loop. It's best to feel comfortable with your material but stay loose. It's OK to improvise a little.

- *If your budget allows, hire a professional videographer to make a demo tape.* This serves two purposes: It allows you to "practice" with the real thing—a live

Bright Idea

You may want to spring for a demo tape—a "pretend" videotaped interview about ten minutes in length, which national-caliber TV shows like to see before asking you on as a guest. If you decide to go this route, hire a professional videographer. Expect to pay $200 to $400, depending on prices in your area.

interview—and get all those first-time nerves out of the way in a situation where they can be edited out. It also gives you a professional edge with producers.

- *Most producers will give you an idea of how long the interview will be.* For radio, an interview is usually about ten minutes—unless you're the only guest on an hour-long phone-in show. But some media interviews—especially for TV—are astonishingly short. You've barely been introduced, and it's over. If you know the interview will be brief, state your most important points first so you get them out there before you're gone.

- *Don't be shy.* For TV interviews, look at the camera—which is the viewing audience—as well as at your host.

Adventures in Autographing

One of the most terrifying things in the author's world is the book signing. Unlike interviews, where you have a mission—to answer questions asked by an experienced host—the book signing sets you out on the floor of the bookstore with nothing to do but sit there and try to look interesting.

It's only in the movies, or when you reach Stephen King caliber, that you'll find a line of book buyers snaking across the room to have their copy autographed. The truth is that very few people show up for book signings. If you sell a half dozen volumes in an afternoon, you can consider that you did exceptionally well.

So why bother? Because of the accompanying publicity. Even if few people show up at the bookstore for an autograph, you can use a signing event to garner a write-up in the local newspaper, get a mention on local TV and radio, and convince bookstore management to prominently display your title (at least temporarily).

Since you will need do these autograph sessions, try these tips for book signing success:

- *Make sure you've got all your publicity lined up in a timely fashion.* Supply the bookstore or specialty retailer with a poster and fliers about two weeks before the event. Have local media get the word out no more than a week ahead of time (although earlier is fine if they'll repeat the news within a few days of the event).

- *Set your signing for a time and day when the store will be busy, say on a Saturday afternoon.* One ideal date—especially if your

Bright Idea

More fun with desktop publishing: Make up bookmarks featuring your title and a quote or a few tips from your pages, and hand them out at signings. Give a large supply to booksellers to display and hand out at their checkout counters.

book would make a nice gift—is Black Friday, which is what retailers call the Friday after Thanksgiving, the kick-off of the holiday shopping season.

- *Try tying into the store's own events. Some bookstores, for instance, host a weekly kids' story hour.* Offer to read your tale aloud and then have your book signing directly afterward.

- *Make an effort to greet shoppers, who are often as shy in this setting as you may be.* Smile and say hello as they pass by. Offer a few words of chat about your book if they slow down to look. Be friendly and accessible.

10

Advertising
and Marketing

You may have wondered why we have not talked about advertising yet. The reason is that it doesn't really work for books. As a new publisher with a limited budget, you can spend your money in far more effective ways by concentrating on publicity and promotions rather than by running ads in magazines, newspapers, or other media.

We covered how to publicize your new book in Chapter 9. In this chapter, we'll discuss some additional avenues for promoting and marketing your book including word of mouth, book fairs, direct mail, seminars, and developing your own web site.

The Golden Word

Even though books are a print medium, you can still sell more through word of mouth than just about any other source. Its power is astonishing. One of these terrifically effective techniques is writing articles for magazines, journals, and newspapers—which works much better than any advertising possibly could. People glaze over when it comes to ads, but they do read articles and not only read but heed. Your credibility as an expert soars if you're in a magazine. People reason that you must be a pro, and as your credibility takes wing, so will your book's desirability. And the benefits don't stop with the reader. People won't tear out an ad, but they'll tear out an article and pass it along to friends and relatives, so you get the word-of-mouth effect even in print.

"Word of mouth is a powerful thing," agrees June H., the horror maven in Rochester Hills, Michigan. "Donate a copy of your book to the local library. Get in touch with the chamber of commerce and get some leads on speaking engagements for writers' groups and anyone else who needs a speaker. One can sell an ample amount of books at these events.

"And do not forget the book trade shows—my personal favorite is the Horror Writers Association, which I attend each year and set up a table to house my books for sale. Volunteer for panels at the events and bring along more books to sell."

"Talk to anyone and everyone who will listen," advises June. "Call your local radio and TV stations, and request an interview. Call bookstores and ask for the event coordinator and set up an autographing—that's one good way to get stores to stock your books. Send a copy to Amazon.com and Barnes & Noble online, and ask your friends to write blurbs about how they enjoyed—or didn't enjoy [in the case of a horror title]—the book."

Gary S., the military memoirs publisher, agrees. "We are in the start-up phase of our company, so we haven't done much advertising," says the resident of Panama City Beach, Florida. "We attend veterans' functions. This is how we make our contacts and sell our books—largely

Bright Idea

If you think the topic of your book lends itself to some limited advertising, barter an article or two, or a monthly column, in exchange for a quarter-page or larger ad. This method can work wonders with smaller publications, if they target a specific market suited to your book.

personal contact and word of mouth. Also, my company has appeared on the web page directory of the Association of Personal Historians, and our books are prominently displayed on local booksellers' racks."

Headline Fever

What publications should you submit to? Take a look at your niche market, then go for the trade or professional journals they read, whether it's *Dog World* or *Direct Marketing*. If you're going for a general audience, you can also target general interest publications—the ones you find in the supermarket checkout lines (not tabloids like *The National Enquirer*, but titles like *Woman's Day* or *Self*.) General interest magazines are much more difficult to get into than trade and professional publications, but if your topic and your writing skills are terrific—and if the editor is in the right frame of mind—you can do it.

The best way to approach the issue is to head down to your local public library and sit down with the latest copy of *Writer's Market* (Writer's Digest Books). Thumb through this hefty volume—you'll be amazed at the number of publications in every imaginable specialty. Pick out the ones that might be good targets for your articles.

Back at home, call the magazine or journal to find out which editor to send your piece to. Then send a one-page query letter describing the article and asking the editor to contact you if he's interested.

The most important thing about writing articles, of course, is that you tie them into your book. You want people to recognize not only you as an expert but also your book as an expert source. Try these tips for getting the most from print exposure:

- *Your article does not have to be long.* Magazines usually have plenty of material for their main copy but are always hurting for those fillers—the one-page to one-sidebar length piece to fill in the gaps. Make your story in the form of "Ten Tips for Cooking Lean" or "Ten Ways to Help Your Child Excel," etc. These are the perfect length and are also great for people to snip out and mail to a friend or stick on the fridge.

- *Mention your book in the text so readers understand where to turn for more information.* Have the publication add an endnote that says something like: For more information or for a free tip sheet, call or write to Glowworm Press at Box 17, Luminescent, FL 10000, (850) 555-0000, www.glowwormpress.com.

> **Tip...**
>
> ### Smart Tip
> Despite *The New York Times* and other bestseller lists, a bestseller is just a name. If your book on raising radishes sells better than any radish-raising tome on the market, or better than any of the other titles your company publishes, you can honestly call it a bestseller.

▲

- *Expand your horizons.* Tweak your material so that it fits the subject matter of as many magazines or journals as you can match. If your book is about gardening, for instance, you could devise articles like these:

    For culinary magazines—"Cooking with Your Garden's Bounty"

    For parenting magazines—"Helping Children Learn Science in a Garden"

    For ecology journals—"Gardens as Environmental Lifesavers"

    For business magazines—"Using Gardening to Combat Office Stress"

    For regional magazines—"Gardening in the Wine Country"

My Fair Book Fair

As June H. says, book trade shows (commonly called book fairs) are events not to be missed. The major-league highlights of the season are the annual BEA, or Book Expo America, which is held each spring in a metropolis like Los Angeles or Chicago, and the Frankfurt Book Fair, held each October in Frankfurt, Germany, and conveniently timed to coincide (more or less) with Oktoberfest. There are also dozens of smaller, regional book fairs held all over this country each year. See the Appendix for a listing of contact information for several prominent book fairs.

These events are terrific places to see and be seen. You can schmooze with other independent publishers, pick up tips and industry gossip, look over the competition, make friends and contacts—and also make sales. A major book fair is the place to sell your title to a big publisher and land that legendary five-figure contract, to sell the foreign rights for another hefty sum (more on this in Chapter 12), or to catch the eye of a distributor. The smaller fair is a terrific place to meet your readers and local booksellers, and sell directly to them.

Exhibit space at smaller book fairs will cost you in the range of $200 to $2000. Booth space at the big fairs can go for thousands of dollars a pop, but you can often band together with other small presses and share a booth. Publishers Marketing Association and other independent publisher organizations often sponsor booth spaces.

Take-Along Kit

Book fair organizers will provide you with a cloth-draped table for exhibiting your wares. You'll want to bring:

- *A box of your books (enough to display and sell).* Don't over-pack but don't run short either. Even regional events can attract as many as 18,000 patrons.
- *Brochures.* Make up a brochure that encapsulates your review package. Start with a thumbnail photo of your book cover; then add an enticing overview of

your books, some stellar testimonials or endorsements, snippets of outstanding reviews, and whatever else you think will sell your title. As with your other materials, observe good design sense. Don't clutter your brochure with so much information that it turns readers off.

- *Bookmarks or other give-away goodies.* The book fair is a great place to hand out bookmarks, tip sheets from your text, or other sales freebies that will make readers remember your book and decide to buy it.

Mail Order Magic

Mail order, or *direct mail*, can be magic in terms of sales for the self-publisher. In fact, some self-publishers sell almost exclusively by mail order without worrying their heads with the book trade. Mail order is an art in and of itself and can be very expensive. If you plan to take it on in a big way, read everything you can about it before you take the plunge. You'll find a list of sources in the Appendix at the back of this book.

Winged Success

Direct mail can take the form of sales letters, fliers, brochures, postcards, or any other printed material you send winging into the mailboxes of potential readers. You can use any direct-mail format that works for you, from a letter describing your book to a one-page flier or multi-page brochure.

The Participation Effect

One of the quirky things about direct mail (and human nature) is that people are far more likely to respond to an offer they have to actively do something for than one they do nothing for. In other words, people like direct mail offers in which they're asked, for example, to paste a "yes" or "no" sticker on the reply card. That's why all those Publishers Clearing House packets are full of stickers, reply cards, and tear-offs. They work. Call it the participation effect.

Of course, these gimmicks cost money, but if you can afford them and they fit your style, by all means use them. If not, think how else you might incorporate the same idea into your order form. If you're offering a discount for early ordering, for instance, you might let your customer "flag" the discount by checking a box on your form. Make sure your form is clear, easy to understand, and easy to fill out.

Experimentation, testing and—always, always—market research will give you the best idea of which format is the best for your company. We're going to talk here about sales letters, but you can and should apply these same success secrets and tips to any other direct-mail pieces you design.

Since most people today are flooded with direct mail pieces, yours needs to leap off the desk or table and instantly capture your potential client's attention so that she'll pick it up instead of tossing it aside. Then, when she does pick it up, it must keep her attention so she'll read it through. Besides interest and attention, the main thing to aim for in your letter is the sense that you're writing to her personally with the answer to her gardening or personal finance dreams or problems, for example.

The Hook

If this sounds daunting, try reading all those direct-mail pieces that come to your mailbox. The best ones to study are those that pitch books, but carefully examine all of them, even those selling winter underwear or summer flea sprays.

What do they have in common? For one thing, they start off with something that immediately hooks your attention. Maybe it's a description of the book, enticing you to read on with tidbits of the information you'll harness when you buy the book. Maybe it's a description of the benefits of having read the book, like a healthier financial picture, a healthier mind and body, or a garden that's the showplace of the neighborhood. Try the same approaches with your sales letter. Experiment until you hit on something that sounds good to you and matches your particular niche.

Then go to work on the body of the letter. Again, analyze the ones you've received. What makes them work? Notice that they spend a lot of time describing the benefits of the book. You'll want to do the same thing. Emphasize the benefits of your book throughout your body copy, repeating them as often as you can, using different descriptions so they stick in your customer's mind. If you've got testimonials, use them too. They lend credibility to your book and your company, and they add another dimension to your copy by showing that it's not just you who thinks your products are great—it's real people just like your prospect.

After the main body of your letter, tell your customer what she needs to do to buy your book. Put in a convenient order form that she can send back, or make your phone number easy to spot so she can call and order if she'd prefer. If you've designed a discount with a time element or a freebie, this is the place to mention it.

Bright Idea

Join any organizations that match your target market. Volunteer for things that will get your book and your publishing company recognized and thought well of. Most people respect volunteers within an organization and consider them experts in the organization's area of interest.

Prospecting for Attention

Be sure to check out the sample sales letter we have provided on page 154 and look over the following sales tips:

- *Grab that reader's attention.* Remember to relate it directly to your book and how it will benefit your customer.
- *Use time-proven winning words like "secret" and "free."* Everybody wants to know a secret, and everybody wants something for free! Like what? How about something like: "Learn the secrets of financial security for life!" Or you might say: "Receive a free gardening calendar when you buy *The Night Garden!*"
- *Where you have space, try for headlines of ten or more words.* Generally speaking, longer sells better than shorter when it comes to headlines.
- *Don't write for thousands of prospective readers.* Write to just one reader, as though you're speaking to him or her personally.
- *Save the flowery prose for a poetry contest.* Instead, use everyday language that the average person can relate to.
- *Don't focus only on the features of your books.* Spend time highlighting the benefits, too.
- *Try indented paragraphs, underlined words, and two colors.* These pack more of a punch and outpull plain text. But use elements like boldface type, underlining, and italics sparingly. If you use them for no particular reason, or too often, they become annoying instead of intriguing.
- *Keep your materials clean and free of grammar and style errors.* Have someone you trust as a spelling, punctuation, and grammar star check your work before you commit to a print run.
- *Relax and enjoy yourself.* Have fun! It will come across in the marketing materials you produce.

Winning Ways

OK, we've seen what direct mail looks like and how to design your own for optimum effect. Now let's review some sure-fire techniques for winning customers:

- *Give away freebies with prompt purchase.* Remember that everybody likes to have something for free. Everybody likes a gift. Depending on your style, budget, and target market, you can give away something substantial (but still relatively inexpensive) or a mere trinket. If your books focus on home décor, for

Smart Tip *Tip...*
Accept credit cards and toll-free calls. It's much easier for your customer to fill in a credit card number on a form, or call and give it to you over the phone than to sit down and write out a check.

153

Sales Letter

Glowworm Press

Hello Charlie Gardener!

I'd like to offer you a very special invitation—*and a free gift*.

I've chosen you to receive this offer because I know you love gardening, just as I do. You treasure the fragrance of roses after a rain and the fresh scent of moist, rich earth under your fingers. Now you can enjoy a brand-new book just for gardeners. **The Night Garden** is the only book you'll find that reveals the secrets of tending to your garden after dark. You'll learn:

- *How to plant and grow organic vegetables after dark. Even if you work all day, you can have a bounty of fresh vegetables on the table for supper.*

- *How to grow night-blooming flowers that fill your home and garden with thera-peutic scent. You'll sleep better than you have in years.*

- *How you and your family can use your garden as a source of rejuvenation and renewal. Instead of watching TV on warm summer evenings, you'll be out enjoy-ing your own private sanctuary.*

- *How to attract nocturnal wildlife into your garden, while you and your family gaze on in wonder.*

The Night Garden is the perfect book to read alone or to share with family and friends. With all the tips and tricks you'll learn, you'll find yourself referring to it again and again. I'm so sure you'll be delighted with **The Night Garden** that I'm offering you a special publisher's edition printed on luxurious cream stock, with illustrations by noted garden artist Lel Lorin, for only $14.95—that's 10 percent off the retail price!

Free Gift!

As an added bonus, I'm also offering you a free gift: a special gardener's calendar that helps you plan your hours in your private backyard getaway. Packed with full-color photos and handy gardening tips, you'll treasure the garden calendar almost as much as **The Night Garden.**

I hope you'll take advantage of this offer. *I can't offer it for long.* Just fill out the enclosed reply form and pop it in the mail to me. If you're not pleased for any reason, just send it back in its original condition, and I'll cheerfully refund your money. Don't take too long! Because of demand, my offer must end June 1st.

Best regards,

Peter Moss

Author and Independent Publisher

P.S. I'm so positive you and your family will love **The Night Garden** that I'm also going to send you a hand-crafted cricket house for your own garden! It's absolutely free, along with the garden calendar. All you have to do is circle the cricket on the reply form when you send it back.

1 Firefly Lane • Luminescent, Florida 10000 • (850) 555-0000 • www.glowwormpress.com

instance, you could include a color chart, a measuring guide, or designer's notebook.

- *Time-date your offer*. Say something like: "If you respond within the next 30 days, you'll receive a free _____." You might also try: "This offer is good only through _____." This encourages readers to buy now instead of at some nebulous time in the future.

- *Write a riveting headline*. Your letter must compete with scads of others crammed in your customers' mailboxes. Penning your headline before your copy will help you focus on the basic need or desire your product satisfies and the appeal your copy should make.

- *Offer testimonials from satisfied customers*. Use real first and last names, and real hometowns. Remember that you must notify testimonial-givers that their names and hometowns will be used and get their permission.

- *Remember the participation effect*. Give your customers plenty to look at, lots to read, and, if possible, something to stick, paste, or tear off.

The List

A mailing list can make or break a direct-mail campaign, and a good list can be worth more than double your ad budget. You can target your audience more effectively with a mailing list than with any other medium.

Say you decide to go with an alternative and advertise on television. We don't recommend it, but for the sake of making a point, let's look at the following example. You might choose "I Love Lucy" reruns or "The X-Files" or the "Tonight Show." Although each will have its demographic profile, you'll get a fairly indiscriminate selection of viewers. You have no way of knowing if they're junior teens whose main reading passion is *Goosebumps* (Scholastic Inc.), homemakers who like to do arts and crafts, sailing enthusiasts, or maximum security prison inmates whose mail is carefully monitored.

When you rent a mailing list, however, you can target your audience to a tee. For a health and fitness book, you can choose Midwestern women who have bought health and fitness magazines; or you might target Northeastern men who buy marine equipment and earn over $50,000 per year for your book on sailing adventures in Maine.

The Response, Please

In the mailing list world, there are two types of lists: the *compiled list* and the *buyer* or *response list*. A compiled list is made up of people with the common thread of a group or organization—for example, members of alumnae organizations or car clubs; members of professional organizations from doctors to contractors; or even people who have attended different types of vacations, tours, seminars, or workshops. A compiled list can also be made up of people with certain demographic characteristics in common such as: people who live in Manhattan and make more than $30,000 a year, and who are between 45 and 70 years old.

The main point to remember with compiled lists is that unless you rent a list comprised of people who have previously bought books similar to yours, you can't know that those doctors or contractors or car aficionados have ever bought a book by mail in their lives.

Now, the other type of list—the buyer list—is the one you want to shoot for. Why? The people on it are already known to order books through the mail. They might be buyers of gourmet cookbooks, or books on vegetable gardening, or Disney collectibles editions, but the main idea here is that since they've already bought books similar to yours, they're likely to buy yours as well. This may not be the case with people on compiled lists. This doesn't mean you should never use compiled lists. It does mean, though, that you should use them carefully. List brokers are experienced at this sort of thing, so let them advise you on what's best for your particular situation.

Going for Broke

Where exactly do you get mailing lists?

- Rent them from any number of list brokers, which you'll find in your local Yellow Pages under "Advertising—Direct Mail," or within the pages of direct-marketing magazines like *Catalog Age* and *Target Marketing*. We've provided the names of a few list brokers in the Appendix to get you started.

- Rent or swap lists directly from your competition—other publishers engaged in selling books to similar target markets. Yes, they'll often share!

- Rent directly from associations whose members fit your target market.

- Buy lists from a competitor who has gone out of business. This doesn't happen too often but is worth keeping an eye out for.

- Build up your own list and use it often.

The Rules

As a direct mail merchandiser, you must follow the rules—specifically, the Federal Trade Commission's *Mail or Telephone Order Rule*, which regulates direct-marketing businesses (and that includes you). These rules also apply to orders placed via fax, e-mail, and the internet. You can find yourself flailing in rough seas if you ignore the guidelines set forth in the *Mail or Telephone Order Rule*, so we have laid them out for you below. Unlike a lot of government legalese, the guidelines actually make sense and are easy to follow:

- *You must send ordered merchandise within the time period specified in your ad or, if you don't specify a shipping time, within 30 days.* The clock starts ticking on this time requirement when you receive the completed order. An order is complete when you have a) received your customer's cash, check, or money order, or b) charged the person's credit card account, and c) have all the information you need to process and ship the order. If the customer doesn't specify essential information, such as size or color preferences, the order is considered incomplete.

> **Smart Tip**
> Get your own complete copy of the *Mail or Telephone Order Rule* from the Federal Trade Commission at www.ftc.gov. The complete text is available online and can be downloaded as a PDF.

- *If you do not specify a shipping time and your customer is applying for credit to pay for the purchase, you have 50 days to ship after receiving the order.* This is the one exception to the 30-day shipping rule.

- *If you can't meet the shipping deadline, you must notify your customer and offer an alternative option.* The customer can either receive a prompt refund or agree to a delay. Your notice must include a new shipping date, instructions on how to cancel the order, and a postage-paid way to reply.

- *If your customer agrees to a new shipping date and you can't meet it again, you must send a second notice as soon as possible.* Unless the customer signs and returns this second postage-paid notice, you must automatically cancel the order and refund the person's money.

- *What happens if you don't ship the merchandise on time and don't notify your customer as required by law?* You must count the order as canceled and send a refund.

- *If your customer cancels an order, you must refund his or her money.* If the customer paid for the order by cash, check, or money order, you must return the money within seven business days. If the order was paid for by credit card, you must credit the customer's credit card account within one billing cycle.

The *Mail or Telephone Order Rule* applies to almost everything ordered through direct-marketing sources. The exceptions are photofinishing services, magazine subscriptions (after the first issue), COD orders, seeds, and plants.

Seminar Time

As we explained at the beginning of this book, self-publishing and seminars go hand in hand. Many, many self-published authors use their books as a springboard for paid seminar success. This can be a lucrative enterprise that can tidily augment your book's income. It can also be extremely helpful in spreading the word about your subject matter. If you're a crusader for saving the planet or teaching kids self-esteem, for example, your books and your seminars can be the best platform for your work.

Order Form/Reply Card

Yes! Send my copy of *The Night Garden* today!

Just fill in the following information to send your copy winging its way to you:

Quantity	Item	Cost
_____	*The Night Garden* ($14.95 per book)	$ _____
_____	Garden calendar ($10.00 value, free with this offer)	FREE
_____	Cricket house ($20.00 value, free if you circle the cricket on this card)	FREE
	Florida residents add 6% sales tax	$ _____
	Shipping and handling ($3.95 per book/gift set)	$ _____
	Total Cost	$ _____

Name _____

Address _____

City _____ State _____ Zip _____

Phone _____

☐ Check   ☐ Visa   ☐ MasterCard

Card number _____ Expiration _____/____

Signature _____

Glowworm Press • 1 Firefly Lane • Luminescent, Florida 10000
(850) 555-0000 • www.glowwormpress.com

Like the world of mail order and the world of self-publishing, however, there's much to learn about seminar production. Before you dive into this arm of your career, read everything you can on the subject. You'll find a few useful books listed in the Appendix to get you started.

Net-Etiquette

A company web site is another terrific promotional tool—and it can be on call 24/7, offering articles and excerpts that whet readers' appetites for your actual book, and taking orders while you're out on the road doing media appearances and book signings.

Web Relations

As another bonus, web customers, by virtue of the fact that they're shopping online, tend to be more adventurous, more willing to try something new, and more interested in forging a relationship with the site (which is you).

What can you do to take advantage of these tendencies? Interact with readers. Give them something new and exciting. Foster that relationship by giving them the sense that they're getting value from the information posted on your site. They'll want to order your book to get even more of the same.

This is also a stellar spot to give web readers your credentials. You might include your 25-year history as an Audubon birder, teaching credentials, or your insider knowledge of your hometown.

No Shouting, Please

People who shop for books—or anything else—the e-commerce way don't like hype. They expect to be informed and entertained, but they don't want to be electronically shouted at, patronized, or pandered to. Sending requested e-mail updates is good business, but "spamming," or sending junk e-mail, is definitely poor Netiquette. This approach will not win friends and influence customers.

What will? Show your web customers they're important to you by treating them considerately. Offer a web site with information that is both current and correct. Offer discounts, freebies, and any other perks you can think up.

Try these tips for winning and keeping internet mail order customers:

- *Give your customers easy access to important information.* Do not force them to wade through page after page of your web site before finding your e-mail address and phone number.

- *Check and answer your e-mail on a daily basis.* Don't let virtual customers languish.

- *Add new information frequently.* This helps you market new products as soon as you have them available, and also keeps readers coming back for more. If your web site stagnates with the same material week after week and month after month, people will get bored and stop visiting.

- *Don't frustrate customers with a site that's slow or difficult to figure out.* You will quickly lose people this way. Keep your site user-friendly and easy to navigate.

- *Offer customers information and entertainment, elements that will draw them in, hold their attention, and make them feel you're a part of their world and they're a part of yours*. Post an article on the best golf vacation spots for the season, or ten tips for teaching kids to golf (or whatever suits your subject matter).

- *Go easy on the graphics*. Pictures add impact to your web site, but if readers have to wait seemingly endless minutes for your page to become viewable because it's graphics-heavy, you're going to lose them. Make sure any photos you use are small enough to load quickly.

- *Check out competitors' web sites, just as you check out printed materials put out by your competitors*. Borrow the best of what they're doing, then do it better.

11

Controlling
Your Finances

Whether you're a chronic number cruncher or one of the finance-phobic, you'll want to give your company periodic financial checkups. You may feel that you have already done all the math stuff several chapters back—which is true. But that was for the purpose of figuring out how much it would cost to get started and whether your book would

▲

earn enough potential profit to make it worthwhile. Once your publishing company and your first book(s) are a reality, you'll want to do periodic checks to make sure you're still on the right page. If there's a problem, you'll want to find out before it becomes critical.

In this chapter, we will discuss the monthly operating expenses that you will encounter in running your business, and we'll walk you through determining your projected annual net income. You will also learn about financial statements and tips for being prepared when tax time rolls around.

Operating Expenses

Besides your company setup costs, book production and promotion costs, your new company will also have the various and sundry monthly expenses that make up the backbone of every business. We will assume that you'll be homebased when you first start out in this business, so we won't worry about the expenses for office rent, utilities, or employees. As a homebased self-publisher, you will need to consider the following monthly operating expenses:

- Phone
- Postage
- ISP (internet service provider)
- Web hosting (so your web site, if you choose to have one, has a server to keep it up and running)
- Electronic card processing
- Stationery and office supplies
- Ongoing legal or accounting services
- Loan repayment
- Promotions/marketing (covered in Chapter 10)

Phone Facts

You will definitely rely on phone service for many aspects of running your business. Start with a base rate of $25 per line per month—one for your business, which is separate from your home phone, and one for your fax machine and e-mail. Then add in estimated long-distance charges based on the locations of your customers, your printer, your distributor and wholesaler, and anyone else you will do business with on an on-going basis. Also figure in what sort of rate you've negotiated with your long-distance carrier.

If you plan to sell books by direct mail or do seminars in various regions around the country, you may want to invest in a toll-free number so customers can call at your

> **Beware!**
> Though the lure of free web hosting is attractive, do your homework first. Someone's got to pay for your hosting, and it's often advertisers whose banners pop up all over your site. Know what you're getting into before you commit to a free host.

cost instead of theirs. There are many good deals to be had on toll-free plans, so shop around. In many instances, you pay a small monthly fee and the incoming calls are charged at your normal long-distance rate. This can be pricey as you receive more calls, but if the number of customers you'll nab increases exponentially as a result, it's probably worth it.

Access to the Net

ISPs or internet service providers generally charge a flat rate of $20 to $25 for unlimited monthly service, which gives you access to the World Wide Web and to e-mail. Check with your cable TV provider. Many local cable services now also offer internet service—this can save you the cost of an extra phone line—and the broadband modem speed is much faster than conventional telephone modems.

Web Host

If you've decided to have a web site, your potential costs don't end with the fee you pay for having one designed by a professional. You'll also need a web host, which is not a dapper chap in a tuxedo standing at the door with a tray of champagne cocktails. It's the computer or computers that handle all your customer traffic. A web host can be likened to an internet service provider such as America Online or CompuServe. While you can manipulate your web site all you want from your home/office computer, it takes a much larger server to handle the complexities and size of web traffic. That's why you need a host. How much can you expect to pay? Expect to pay in the range of $5 to $75 per month depending on the services they offer.

Getting Carded

If you decide to have an electronic credit card terminal so that you can accept orders by internet or direct mail, you'll have operating expenses associated with this. To keep your merchant card service humming along, you will pay a monthly statement fee of $5 to $15. And if you've decided to lease your terminal instead of purchasing it, you'll have that fee of $19 to $72 per month to account for as well.

Paper Tiger

Once you've made your initial outlay for office supplies and stationery, your fixed expenses in this category should be fairly low. Staples last a long time, you can reuse paper clips, and you shouldn't have to replace office items like a letter opener and scissors for quite some time after your initial purchase. Your main expense will be paper: lots of paper for your printer and fax machine, fine-quality paper for stationery, and envelopes.

Paying the Piper

We've set aside a fixed expense called loan repayment. If you do not borrow money to start your business, you won't need to bother with this one. If, however, you finance your start-up costs through any means, you'll need to repay the piper. Here's where you pencil in whatever your monthly fee is.

Dollar Stretcher

Be environmentally and economically smart. Reuse that printer paper. Instead of practicing hoop shots into the trash with all those versions of letters, evaluation sheets, and other printed materials that you decided you didn't like, set the pages aside. When you've compiled a tidy stack, load them back into your printer and print on the blank side. Save your "good" paper for the final draft that goes out in the mail.

You may have many more expenses than the ones discussed here, such as employees and the worker's compensation and payroll costs that go with them; auto expenses; and subscription fees for professional publications. We have not included the costs associated with rent, utilities, and employees on our worksheet, but they are common features of financial projections. If they will not apply to your homebased company, of course, you won't need to worry about them. But when you start publishing more books, you may find your business is successful enough to start considering them! Use the worksheet called "Your Projected Annual Income/Expenses Statement" on page 168 and pencil in your estimated operating expenses over the course of your first year.

Making a Statement

Financial checkups don't have to be negative. They can give you a rosy glow by demonstrating how well you're doing—possibly even better than you expected. If you've been saving for a new printer or software upgrade, or if you're hoping to take on an employee, you can judge how close you are to achieving that goal. And if there are problems, you can catch them early by doing regular financial checkups—and then you can make any changes you need to. For instance, if you discover that your income barely covers your promotional or operating expenses, you can change gears along with the number of direct-mail pieces you send out.

An important tool for keeping your finances on track is the income and expenses statement, also called a profit-and-loss statement. This type of financial statement charts the revenues and operating costs of your business over a specific period of time, usually monthly or annually. Check out the annual income statements on page 167 for our two hypothetical publishers, Glowworm Press and Bell & Candle Publishing. Glowworm projects an annual income of $7,991, while Bell & Candle projects it yearly earnings at $27,235.

Smart Tip

As your company grows, your postage expenses will bloom, too, but for your first year of operation you should be able to keep it to a minimum. If you figure on an average of two pieces of mail per day at the first-class rate, you can pencil in about $20 per month.

Adding It All Up

And now, the moment we've all been waiting for: the grand total for how much it will cost to get to the end of publishing your first book and what profits you can expect. As we have said repeatedly, these figures will be different for every publisher. You need to do your own careful homework to determine what your expenses and your bottom line will be.

Let's go back to the "Your Projected Annual Income/Expenses Statement" worksheet on page 168. You should already have filled in the operating expenses you project, but you're not finished yet. Next, you need to determine your projected income, taking into account both retail and wholesale revenue (use the worksheet on page 167 to arrive at a projection for profits from your first book). After you have an idea of what your projected gross income will be, then you need to subtract your expenses from this figure to arrive at a net income figure. Your expenses will include not only the operating expenses that you have already listed, but also the "cost of sales," which includes:

- The total for your projected company start-up costs, from the worksheet on page 71.
- Your projected production costs for your first book, from the worksheet on page 91.
- The additional costs of distributor fees, returns, a travel budget, shipping and postage, which were discussed in Chapter 8. Use the worksheet on page 168 to help you calculate these additional costs.

Add all of these elements to arrive at a figure for the cost of sales. Once you subtract both your operating expenses and the cost of sales from your projected gross income, you will arrive at the projected net income for your company's first year.

To give you a few typical scenarios, we have once again used our two hypothetical publishers, Glowworm Press and Bell & Candle Publishing, to show you how to arrive at a projected annual net income. Look at the calculation of gross income and cost of sales for these companies in the "Annual Book Profits" chart on page 169. Yes, they do make a profit! Also take a look at the "Annual Income/Expenses Statement" for the companies on page 167.

see page 167

Getting a Grip

The whole point of doing financial checkups is to get an overview of your profits—or losses—and then get a grip on them. If you discover, after inking in your expenses, that you're not going to be able to afford that trip to the book fair in London (much less the price of a London broil at the supermarket), don't panic. Get a grip!

Smart Tip

Tip...

To draw up a monthly income statement, you'll need to prorate items that are paid annually, such as business licenses and tax-time accounting fees, and pop those figures into your monthly statement. For example, if you pay annual insurance premiums of $600, divide this figure by 12 and add the resulting $50 to your insurance expense.

First, realize that the first year in the life of your company is generally the most expensive. You've had all those setup costs, from buying equipment to software to registering your business name. Those are one-time fees that you won't incur again unless, or until, you splurge for a hardware or software upgrade, for example.

Second, your book won't cost as much the next time around. When you go back to the printer for another run, those reprints will have far fewer production costs. You won't need to pay for copy editing or proofreading because those are already done. You won't have cover design or illustration costs—those are already done. And you won't have to pay for the printer to put the book on film because that's already done.

Raising Cain

You've got other options for raising your income as well. One way is to bump up your book's list price. You may think this is akin to raising Cain, but it's not. If you increase your retail price from, say, $12.95 to $14.95, readers are not likely to see an appreciable difference. It is not the same as jumping from $12.95 to $20.95. Before you do raise your price, however, engage in some last-minute market research. In most cases a raise of a dollar or two doesn't make a huge difference, but there are ceilings for most products beyond which most consumers won't budge, and your book may already be there.

Another way is to shoot for those alternative sales outlets, the ones where your discount is not as high. Try for more library sales, more specialty store sales, and more direct sales garnered through your web site and by writing articles for publication. Use more of the same creative energy that goes into getting your book written and designed to boost your profit potential. That's a big part of being a self-publisher.

Annual Income/Expenses Statement

INCOME/EXPENSES STATEMENT
For the Year Ended December 31, 200x

	Glowworm	Bell & Candle
Projected Income		
Retail sales	$16,835	$49,900
Wholesale sales	$7,965	$24,950
Gross Income	**$24,800**	**$74,850**
Projected Cost of Sales		
Company start-up expenses *(total from worksheet on page 71)*	$3,561	$10,764
Production costs *(total from worksheet on page 91)*	$7,542	$19,226
Other costs of doing business *(distributor fees, returns, travel budget, shipping, and postage)*	$3,519	$12,080
Gross Cost of Sales	**(−$14,622)**	**(−$42,070)**
Operating Expenses		
Phone	$900	$900
Toll-free line	$0	$1,200
Electronic credit card processing	$300	$300
Postage	$240	$300
Legal services (beyond start-up)	$360	$400
Insurance (remaining six months)	$850	$1,150
Accounting services (beyond start-up)	$300	$350
Office supplies	$120	$150
Internet service provider (remaining six months)	$120	$120
Web hosting (remaining six months)	$180	$300
Loan repayment	$0	$2,000
Miscellaneous	$300	$500
Total Operating Expenses	**(−$3,670)**	**(−$7,670)**
Projected Net Annual Income	**$6,508**	**$25,110**

Your Projected Annual Income/Expenses Statement

For the Year Ending _____

Projected Income

Retail sales $ _____

Wholesale sales   _____

Gross Income $ _____

Projected Cost of Sales

Company start-up expenses
(total from worksheet on page 71) $ _____

Production costs
(total from worksheet on page 91)   _____

Other costs of doing business
*(distributor fees, returns, travel
budget, shipping, and postage)*   _____

Gross Cost of Sales   (−$ _____)

Operating Expenses

Phone $ _____

Electronic credit card processing   _____

Postage   _____

Legal services (beyond start-up)   _____

Insurance (remaining six months)   _____

Accounting services (beyond start-up)   _____

Office supplies   _____

Internet service provider (remaining six months)   _____

Web hosting (remaining six months)   _____

Loan repayment   _____

Taxes   _____

Miscellaneous   _____

Commercial office only:

Rent   _____

Utilities   _____

Employee payroll & benefits   _____

Total Operating Expenses   (−$ _____)

Projected Net Annual Income $ _____

Annual Book Profits

		Glowworm Press	Bell & Candle Publishing
Projected Income			
	Retail price	$12.95 per book x 1,300 copies sold = $16,835	$24.95 per book x 2,000 copies sold = $49,900
	Distributor wholesaler price (at 60% discount)	$5.31 x 1,500 copies sold = $7,965	$9.98 x 2,500 copies sold = 24,950
	Gross Income	**$24,800**	**$74,850**
Cost of Sales			
	Company set-up expenses	(–$3,561)	(–$10,764)
	Production costs	(–$7,542)	(–$19,226)
	Distributor fees (set-up, warehousing, etc.)	(–$500)	(–$1,000)
	Returns	20% of $7,965 = (–$1,593)	20% of $24,950 = (–$4,990)
	Free copies for publicity	200 copies (included in production costs) (–$0)	500 copies (included in production costs) (–$0)
	Travel budget	(–$1,000)	(–$5,000)
	Shipping to distributor	(–$200)	(–$300)
	Postage (to send publicity copies to reviewers)	$1.13 x 200 copies = (–$226)	$1.58 x 500 copies = (–$790)
	Gross Cost of Sales	**(–$14,622)**	**(–$42,070)**
Operating Expenses			
	Total Operating Expenses	**(–$3,670)**	**(–$7,670)**
Net Income			
	Net Income after all Expenses	**$6,508**	**$25,110**

▲

Your Bottom Line

Use this worksheet to calculate your annual projected income and expenses. Make copies and work up several different scenarios, then go with the one that works best.

Annual Book Profits for _____

(Your company name)

Projected Income		
	Retail price	$ _____ per book x _____ copies sold = $ _____
	Distributor/wholesaler price (at 60% discount)	$ _____ per book x _____ copies sold = $ _____
	Gross Income	$ _____
Cost of Sales		
	Company start-up Expenses (total from worksheet on page 71)	(–$ _____)
	Production costs (total from worksheet on page 91)	(–$ _____)
	Distributor fees (set-up, warehousing, etc.)	(–$ _____)
	Returns	20% of $ _____ profit from sales to distributor/wholesaler = (–$ _____)
	Free copies for publicity	_____ copies (included in production costs) (–$0)
	Travel budget	(–$ _____)
	Shipping to distributor	(–$ _____)
	Postage (to send publicity copies to reviewers)	$ _____ x _____ copies = (–$ _____)
	Gross Cost of Sales	(–$ _____)
Operating Expenses		
	Total Operating Expenses	(–$ _____)
Net Income		
	Net Income after all Expenses	$ _____

Smart Tip

Tip...

Use your book's second printing as a promotional tool. A reprint is proof that readers are buying it and it's in demand. Spread the word!

Uncle Sam Speaks

When you earn money from your book, someone will be queuing up for a piece of the action: Uncle Sam. If your budget allows, you should engage an accountant. You probably won't need her for your daily or monthly concerns, but it's well worth the expense to have someone in the know at the reins when it comes to April 15, or for those questions that come up now and again.

Your tax deductions should be about the same as those for any other small or homebased business. You can deduct a percentage of your home office, so long as you're using it solely as an office. These deductions include all normal office expenses plus interest, taxes, insurance, and depreciation (this is where the accountant comes in handy). The IRS has added in all sorts of permutations such as: The total amount of the deduction is limited by the gross income you derive from the business activity minus all your other business expenses, apart from those related to the home office. And you thought that interactive software game was complicated! Basically, the IRS does not want you to come up with so many home office deductions that you end up paying no tax at all.

Driving Yourself Crazy

What else can you deduct? Acceptable deductions include business-related phone calls; the cost of business equipment and supplies (again, so long as you're truly using them solely for your business); subscriptions to professional and trade journals; and auto expenses. Your auto expenses accrue when you drive your vehicle in the course of doing business or seeking business. In other words, you're chalking up deductible mileage every time you motor out to conduct research, do a book fair, give a seminar or a guest spot on TV or radio, visit your printer, or take a cross-country spin on an author tour.

To keep from driving yourself crazy, keep a log of your business miles. You can buy one of several varieties at your local office supply or stationers, or you can make one yourself. Keep track as you go. It's no fun having to recreate a year's worth of driving adventures at tax time to

Smart Tip

Tip...

Tax questions? Beard the lion in its den and call the IRS. First go online at www.irs.gov to find the toll-free number for your region. You may have to go through voice mail or the on-hold forever period, but once you get a live being on the line, they're surprisingly friendly.

guesstimate how many miles you drove to how many places and for what purpose during the year.

Let Me Entertain You

You can deduct entertainment expenses like a book launch party or a dinner to wine and dine a distributor. Keep a diary of all these expenses as well, especially if they come to under $75 a pop (you do not technically need to keep receipts for these). And if you're entertaining at home, have your customers sign a guest book.

Remember that you must have a business-related purpose for entertaining, like a sales presentation. General goodwill toward potential customers or sales reps doesn't make it, so be sure your diary contains the reason for the festivities.

Tip...

Smart Tip

The IRS loves documentation. The more receipts and logs you accumulate and carefully organize, the happier you will be if that horrid "A" word (audit) rears its ugly head.

Planes, Trains, and Automobiles

When you travel for business purposes, you can deduct airfares, train tickets, rental car mileage, and the like. You can also deduct hotels and meals. And you can even—under certain circumstances—deduct recreational side trips you take with your family while you're traveling on business. Since the IRS allows deductions for any such trip you take to expand your awareness and expertise in your field of business, it makes sense to also take advantage of any conferences or seminars that you can attend. You can stay abreast of events in your target market or see how the competition's doing.

Looking Ahead
Small Press to Publishing Giant

OK, you've successfully written your book, have it stocked in bookstores and other outlets, and launched an ongoing promotional campaign. Is that all there is? Well, no, not by a long shot.

For the savvy self-publisher, there are many avenues left to explore—other outlets for your talents and your message, and other ways to augment your income. In this chapter, we will investigate these other avenues, from making a deal with a mega-publisher to selling subsidiary and foreign rights, and more.

Let's Make a Deal

The publishing industry is rife with stories of writers who became self-publishers because no traditional house would buy their work. They later sold that same "unsaleable" property for hundreds of thousands of dollars. This doesn't happen to every independent publisher, of course, and not every self-publisher wants it to happen—some would rather keep all the control and profits for themselves—but it's definitely worth considering.

Selling Out

In Cinderella scenarios, a big publishing house sees your book at a book expo, or picks up on all your terrific publicity, and approaches you with an offer. In other cases, it's up to you to make the first move, going after a traditional publisher the same way you go after reviews from trade magazines and opinion makers.

Why would you want to sell out after you've done all the work of grooming your book for success all by yourself? The simple answer is money. In the Cinderella scenario, it's hard to say no to a mega-publisher that courts you with a staggering sum for your book. And in the you-court-them scenario, you can land significant earnings upfront by selling out and then using those earnings to bankroll your next successful book.

The Acquisition

The Cinderella scenario is not as uncommon as you might imagine. It's unlikely that you will be wooed with a million-dollar contract, but it's perfectly likely that you'll be courted with a reasonable offer. Traditional publishers send talent scouts called *acquisition editors* to book fairs, like the yearly colossal Book Expo America, to seek out likely titles and snap them up.

And why not? You've done the hard part. Besides writing your book, you've designed it and laid it out in a format that sells. You've conducted all the market research—you've found a niche market, written for that market, and promoted to it. You've done the testing that proved the market is viable and lucrative. So what publisher wouldn't like to have a piece of the pie?

It's flattering to have a New York publisher take interest in your book. It's validation from the most cliquish sector of the industry—sort of like being the wallflower at

The Sadie Hawkins Approach

If major publishers do not single you out for attention, you can take the Sadie Hawkins approach and tackle them. Use the same campaign techniques you will use to garner media attention during your pre-publication and early release phases.

Put together a package that includes a cover letter detailing:

○ Why your book would be the perfect purchase

○ Every great review you've ever received

○ A compilation of sterling testimonials and endorsements

○ Magazine reprints and news articles about your book—not written by you

○ A blurb about any subsidiary rights you've sold and any particularly large orders you've filled

You'll have to do your homework here, too. You won't send a children's picture book to a publisher of technical tomes, or a cookbook to an aviation publisher. Do your research. You'll find hundreds of publishers listed in the pages of *Literary Marketplace* (R.R. Bowker) and *Writer's Market* (Writer's Digest Books). Once you've identified potential candidates, ship your query package off to all of them. Note in your cover letter that you're sending multiple queries (i.e., you're sending your query to other publishers)—it's considered courteous if you do and irreparably rude if you don't.

the senior prom and suddenly having the homecoming queen or football star ask you to dance.

It can also be dangerous. Self-publishers often are so thrilled by this coveted attention that they give away their books. And the big houses—no dummies—take full advantage. They'll usually offer a 10 percent royalty, or even less.

Demanding More

As the publisher, you deserve a lot more. Remember, you have done all the work up to this point: you've burned the midnight oil to create the product; taken all the financial risk to make it a reality; and put in countless hours to make it a promotional success. Don't take the first offer—instead do some heavy negotiating and be sure to include the following:

• *Cost plus.* Your contract should give you a fee of two to three times your book's production costs, plus 10 percent of the projected sales.

- *Royalty inclusive*. Make sure the contract reads royalty inclusive. This means you get the projected royalties immediately—a major perk compared to the traditional method where you wait for months at a time until the publisher tallies up its quarterly earnings and then divvies up your share.

Dollar Stretcher

One week after Stephen King offered the first installment of his e-serial, *The Plant*, in July 2000, he had already sold more than 152,000 downloads.

- *Easy on the rights*. Don't give away all rights to your book—you don't have to. Give the buyer North American rights only, which is permission to sell the book in the United States and Canada. You still retain the foreign rights, which can be considerable.

- *To the trade only*. Specify that the buyer gets the rights to sell only to the book trade—libraries and bookstores. This gives you the option to continue selling to nontraditional outlets and also lets you continue to sell by direct mail.

- *Electronic egress*. Do not give away e-book and e-publishing or electronic rights. Either retain them for yourself or give the buyer a short-term option to purchase those rights separately.

- *Audio outlet*. Don't give the buyer audio book rights unless they normally release audio books along with the print version.

- *Out of print*. Make sure all rights revert to you once the book is out of print. If and when the buyer decides not to publish it anymore, you can pick up right where you left off if you so choose.

- *Release date*. Insist on a specific release date so that the buyer is forced to actually print and sell your books. Occasionally publishers buy books for the sole purpose of removing the competition; they have no intention of actually entering into distribution. When you insist on a specific release date, you nip this strategy in the bud.

Selling Subsidiary

Smart Tip

When you sell condensations, it is up to the magazine to condense your material—they pay for it, not you.

Subsidiary rights are the rights to morph your book into different forms, including movies and television (imagine your own miniseries!), magazine condensations or reprints, book club editions, and foreign language editions.

Handled wisely, subsidiary sales can be extremely lucrative. In fact, this—rather than book sales—is where the major New York publishers make the most money. As a self-publisher, you may not find vast fortune with subsidiary sales, but you'll certainly augment your income. You may negotiate a deal that nets you millions of dollars, but it's far more likely that you'll get in the neighborhood of a few thousand dollars.

Even if you only land $300 to $600 for that first magazine reprint right, you stand to make thousands more over the long haul from the

Smart Tip

With foreign translations, it is up to the buyer to have his version of your book translated, printed, and bound. All you have to do is deliver a few copies of your original title and the rights to go with it.

additional exposure. Each time readers see your book in any form, it's free advertising and promotion. And the more subsidiary rights you can claim, the hotter property your book becomes.

Hot Serial

You can sell to magazines or periodicals in several ways—as excerpts, serializations, and condensations. A *serial* is a book divided into installments that run in successive issues of newspapers, magazines, or other periodicals. A *condensation* is a book that's condensed or abridged, primarily as a space-saving measure, and then printed in a periodical or anthology.

Whether you sell the rights to excerpts, serializations, or condensations before your publication date, you sell the *first serial rights*. When you sell the rights after the publication date, you sell the *second serial rights*. First serial rights are generally considered more of a scoop than second, for the obvious reason that before your publication date nobody (more or less) has yet laid eyes on your story; it's so hot it hasn't even rolled off the press.

When you sell excerpts, choose sections that relate to the subject matter of the publication. If your gardening book has a chapter on cooking with your bounty, use that chapter (or a piece from it) to sell to a vegetarian cooking magazine. Sell the section on garden furniture to a home décor magazine. Send bound galleys to the magazines you think are the most important and review copies to the rest.

Whichever route you take, make sure the periodical prints something like this at the end of the article:

Reprinted with permission from *The Night Garden*, by Peter Moss ©2007. Available for $14.95 + $3 shipping/handling from Glowworm Press, Box 17, Luminescent, FL 10000, (850) 555-0000, www.glowwormpress.com.

Join the Club

You know book clubs—those mail order houses that send blurbs urging you to buy the first five books for $1 and receive a free tote bag if you join. As a casual browser you may have tossed the catalogs, or added them to an ever-growing stack of mail on the kitchen counter.

But as a publisher, these book clubs should have a whole new dimension to you. If they buy your book, you'll have great advance sales and you can use the fact that your title is a Book of the Month Club pick, for example, as a terrific promotional blurb. Send bound galleys to the major clubs like BOMC and Literary Guild, along with any that specialize in your market niche. Then follow up with review copies if you didn't get a response the first time around. You'll find lists of book clubs and their contact information within the pages of *Literary Marketplace* (R.R. Bowker).

Foreign Affairs

You can sell your book to foreign markets in two different ways, as *foreign rights* and as *translation rights*. As you can probably guess, foreign rights give publishers in English-language countries a license to reprint your book, while *translation rights* give foreign publishers the license to reproduce the book in their own language.

Not all books lend themselves to foreign sales. If your title is *The Truth about Social Security*, a foreign audience will not be interested—it's a country-specific topic. But if your title is *Reversing the Aging Process*, you've got something of interest to almost any human on the planet.

For foreign rights, you can sell the British, Australian, or other publisher F&Gs (folded and gathered signatures) from your print run so that all they have to do is bind the books with their own covers. Or you can offer them the camera-ready copy or print-ready film that they can print as is.

Foreign publishers usually get hooked on books at book expos. The mega-event of the year internationally is the annual Frankfurt Book Fair, which takes place in Germany every October (see the Appendix for contact information).

The Reel Story

You can also go after movie and TV companies and sell the *film rights* to your book. These are far more difficult to land than other types of subsidiaries. Hollywood types are notoriously fickle and are unlikely to look at anything

Fun Fact

Clark Gable initially turned down the role of Rhett Butler in MGM's movie version of *Gone with the Wind* (1939), fearing he wouldn't measure up to the Rhett millions of American women had envisioned while reading the book.

unless it's already a hot property in print. Nevertheless, it does happen. Even nonfiction occasionally hits the silver screen.

The trick with film companies is that they frequently purchase the rights to your book and then—because of their own funding woes—fail to actually produce the movie. This can be extremely disappointing. In an effort to save themselves the full expense of buying film rights, movie and television companies often purchase options to the film rights, which gives them a period of time (typically from six months to two years) to find the funding and buy the full rights.

Movie-making is astonishingly expensive and many movies never make a substantial profit. So if and when you do sell your film rights, make sure you negotiate a percentage of the *gross* profits and not the net.

Because this particular market is so complex, you may want to have an agent—or even better, an attorney—who specializes in publishing and entertainment to walk you through negotiations. Choose your mentor with care. Agents especially can sometimes put their percentage of your profits ahead of your best interests. Start your search for an agent or attorney by asking for referrals from publishing industry associations. Then make sure you check references thoroughly and interview any potential candidates to make sure their vision (and their values) match yours.

The Adventure Continues

Once you are a publishing pro, you will want to take advantage of all your hard-earned expertise with another exciting project. With the greater part of your learning curve behind you, as well as a growing professional reputation, you can launch another book of your own or publish the works of another author.

Launch Pad

A new book is a natural. Hopefully you have located a niche market, established yourself as an expert, found readers eager to hear what you have to say, and found promotional opportunities and outlets to sell your books through. Take advantage of those eager readers by giving them another product to purchase. Your book doesn't have to be on exactly the same topic, so long as it caters to the same market. If your last cookbook was on desserts, make this one on main dishes, cooking for campers or boaters, or culinary skills for kids.

Your new project can take the form of a full-length trade paperback or hardcover, a series of reports on short topics related to your previous book, an audio book, a video primer to complement your existing title, an e-book or POD adventure, or any combination of the above. Do your research, keep promoting and selling your existing book, and have fun!

Be aware that there is always the possibility that your market, production costs, promotional opportunities, and sales outlets may change. So it's up to you to stay in touch with your niche and with new developments in the publishing industry.

Somebody Else's Baby

Once the word gets out in the industry that you're a publisher, you'll find there's no shortage of authors eager to have you publish their baby. It's a kick to be on the other side of the fence as the final word on accepting or rejecting manuscripts, instead of being the one on the receiving end of all those rejection letters.

Tip...

Smart Tip

If your publishing niche is very narrow, you'll want to publish similar titles. Take advantage of the niche market and promotional contacts you've already established. If you go with a different genre title entirely, you may want to establish an imprint, which is a different company with its own name under the umbrella of your main firm. Consult your attorney on just how to proceed.

The first rule, of course, is to be nice. Don't trample on someone else's feelings, but don't accept a project that you don't feel you can put your own heart and soul into either.

Keep in mind that even though somebody else writes the text, you will still be responsible for the book layout and design. You'll have to make sure it's properly edited, which can mean requesting that sensitive authors make sometimes heart-wrenching changes. You'll be in charge of all the promotional work including writing sales copy, back cover blurbs, and sample reviews.

You'll have to consider advances, royalties, subsidiary rights, what happens if you decide to let the book go out of print, and other financial issues. It can be a lot of work. So if you don't believe in a project, chances are you won't be very happy putting so much effort into it—and it may show in the final product.

When you do find a project and an author you believe in, the experience can be almost as magical as seeing your own book to fruition. Helping someone else to success is more satisfying than you might imagine.

Bestseller or
Bomb

Success in the self-publishing industry is achieved by following the tried-and-true business methods of persistence and plain, old-fashioned hard work—along with a healthy dose of optimism. If we've illustrated anything in this book, we hope it's that becoming a successful self-publisher involves a lot of work. It is rewarding and sometimes exhilarating work, but hard work nonetheless.

We also hope we have managed to convey that becoming a self-publisher is not the same as becoming an overnight success. It takes diligent market research, loads of planning, and abundant creativity to achieve bestseller status.

Words of Wisdom

When we interviewed the self-publishing entrepreneurs included in this book, we asked them to give us some words of wisdom for neophytes—and we got them! Following are stories of success and failure from these entrepreneurs. We hope their hard-won lessons and advice will help you as you start-up your own self-publishing business.

Helping Thousands

"Read, read, read, and research, research, research *before* you get started," advises Anna J. in Temple, Texas. "I just decided to do this because I knew my book was needed. I jumped in without really looking. Of course, then I think that if I had researched too much, I might have been too intimidated to start, and that would have been a pity. I have now helped thousands of people who heretofore had nothing to help them through one of the most difficult passages of their lives. I have a binder full of thank you letters and cards from people who have been touched by my books. I know I've made a difference in this world....

"So maybe instead, the best advice I can give is to decide why you want to publish. Is it to make money? Is it to develop a new line of books never thought of before and thus too risky for the big publishers? Is it to make a difference? Decide now what you will consider 'success' and write it down.

"For my husband and me, we felt we would be successful if we helped even only one family," Anna says. "We have done that. We consider our publishing company a great success. For us, the bottom line is that we know we're providing useful resources that are helping people all over the world, and that is more valuable than money. If you are publishing for altruistic reasons, you have a different perspective on business."

Ever Erratic

"In retrospect, my wife and I made a mistake by quitting our nice day jobs before starting the company," says Steve C. in Hinesburg, Vermont. "Small publishing provides too erratic an income (at least until you have a collection of steady-selling backlist) to count on as your only source of income while raising a family. Therefore we took on some side ventures—the book fulfillment and the software—to provide a steadier income.

"I'm terribly proud of what we accomplished with those aspects of the business, but they diverted a lot of effort away from publishing, the main thing I wanted to do. I now think it makes a lot more sense to keep your day job while you write and publish your first book, or maybe your first several books. Or at least, if you're married, one of the two of you should keep the day job until the books are providing enough steady income to support the family.

"I think I'd have a lot more books in print today if I had done it that way—my regular job was a more reliable way of supporting the family than the new ventures I took on all at once," the veteran publisher says. "Again, I can't regret what was accomplished. The software program in particular is very successful, and I take great pride in it. But we'd be farther along in book publishing if we had phased into it directly from our regular jobs, rather than taking on the side ventures."

Swing Low

Gary S. in Panama City Beach, Florida, who has kept his day job while moonlighting in self-publishing, concurs with Steve. "Keep overhead low at first," the environmental protection agent advises. "Book production and storage is a big expense. Try out the print-on-demand option first until you see how well the books will sell."

"One thing I wish I had done was visit with some other publishers face-to-face," Anna J. says. "I think this might have helped me. I've been reading lately where some publishers form co-ops, and that seems like something worth investigating. Perhaps I could have found a mentor. There were so many things that I learned the hard way. It would have been nice to have someone to hold my hand through the beginning stages of my business.

"The one thing I neglected to do which I really think would have made a difference for my business was creating a real business plan. I have since hired a lawyer who is helping me prepare to become a nonprofit organization, and the time I have spent brainstorming with her and developing a solid business plan has been invaluable. That should be part of everyone's start-up expense—and it will cost a couple of thousand dollars, but it will give you a solid foundation. I think that if I had done that, I would have distributed a lot more books by now," shares Anna.

> **Fun Fact**
> Many authors have gone from writing books to screenplays or vice-versa, including F. Scott Fitzgerald, Sidney Sheldon, and Nora Ephron, who penned the ever-popular *Sleepless in Seattle* (1993).

Love What You Do

"Love what you do," Anna also advises. "This is a tough business, but if you love what you do then you will be successful. Don't let others define success for you. You will know in your heart if you are successful or not. Success is not measured in dollar signs but in the way you feel about your business. Love what you do, and maybe your books will make a difference in someone's life—then you will be successful."

June H. in Rochester Hills, Michigan, agrees. "Any privately-owned business overtakes your life from time to time and so, therefore, you must truly love it," June says. "And if you truly love it, don't let anyone say it can't be done—because it can. Be passionate about it and believe in yourself."

The Happiness Factor

If you're the type of person who can handle the ups and downs of entrepreneurship in general, and the yin and yang of creativity and number crunching that makes up the self-publisher's world, you'll probably thrive. If not, you may discover during your company's first year of life, or beyond, that the business isn't for you. You may feel that instead of a bestseller, you're dealing with a bomb.

Ten Tips for Self-Publishing Success

1. *Read.* Read everything you can find about the business of self-publishing.
2. *Read even more!* Soak up everything available about running a small business.
3. *Join in.* Join groups, take classes, ask questions, and do market research.
4. *Write from the heart.* Be passionate and let your readers share your sentiments.
5. *Produce the best book you possibly can.* Don't skimp on your cover, copy editing or proofreading. Cross every "t," dot every "i," and check every fact.
6. *Send pre-publication materials to every industry source and opinion molder.* Then follow up where appropriate to start collecting endorsements and testimonials.
7. *Maintain a steady post-publication publicity campaign.* Track down every possible PR opportunity and then follow it up.
8. *Don't be afraid to blow your own horn.* Your book's future depends on it!
9. *Send thank-you notes after all reviews, interviews, speaking engagements, articles, and other PR opportunities.* It's common courtesy and also leaves the door open for further opportunities.
10. *Have fun.* After all, isn't that at least half the point?

Whether or not you're earning money, the success of your business is contingent on a happiness factor. Because it involves a good deal of work and responsibility, you may discover that you'd be just as happy—or more so—working for someone else. And that's OK. With everything you will have learned, you'll be a great job candidate.

None of the people interviewed for this book, from a newbie to a veteran with 15 years' experience, seem to have any intention of packing it in. Rather, they seem to have a sense of delight at doing what they enjoy, helping others with the same interests, and being a part of the larger world.

Success and Failure

But is it all sunshine and roses? Surely, we hear you asking, even the most successful self-publishing professionals hit some bumps on the road to achievement. So we asked our interviewees about their worst—and best—experiences in the business.

Stress!

"My worst experience has been with my most recent printer," says Anna J. "The books were not done as well as I thought they should have been done, and I had a terrible time getting any satisfaction from the printer. Then they went bankrupt! It wasn't hard to see why, but it was a very stressful and costly experience."

Steve C. counts a different sort of trauma as his stress memory. "The worst was a book that didn't get any library reviews, and that we'd counted on selling to college professors as texts or recommended reading for their courses; but we weren't successful in that form of marketing," the Vermont resident recalls. "I won't tell you the title of the book, because it's a great book, and it's still actively in print; but we've spent a lot of money on promotion that didn't work and, after several years, we still have half the first printing of 5,000 copies."

June H., the horror writer, also went through a publisher's horror scenario. "My worst experience was when I assigned the same ISBN to two different books," she says. "Ultimately, I retired the first book—which wasn't a big seller anyway—and notified the distributors and bookstores of the error. I still get backlash from that mistake, but it's improving."

Bright Idea

Joining a writer's group can be a wonderful way to keep yourself motivated, pick up tips from other writers, and talk shop to your heart's content. Most groups allow members to share their work once a month (or whenever they meet) and receive free friendly and constructive critiques. Plus, you'll be surprised how much you can learn about your own writing by critiquing someone else's!

Springboard to Success

"My best experience came from last year's anthology," June says. "Two of the contributors were beginners, and since then one has published two e-books, and the other has sold more than a dozen short stories since their work first appeared in my book. I hope that, in some small way, the success of that book was a springboard to their other projects."

Gary S. in Florida feels his books help others, too, garnering long-awaited acknowledgment for men who laid their lives on the line for their homes and families. "It's been a very gratifying experience writing and publishing books for veterans," the Panama City Beach resident explains. "Really, I would say that it was an honor to be involved in it. I can't say that I've had a bad experience thus far. It's all been positive." What more could anyone ask?

Steve C.'s books make a difference in the quality of people's lives as well. "The best experience has been my wife's books on caring for the dead," Steve says. "Her latest is a 640-page book that sells for $30, and we're quickly going through a printing of 10,000 copies. She gets a lot of publicity. Any time a newspaper, magazine, or television program covers abuses by the funeral industry, she gets interviewed, and that helps to create a continuous market for her books."

Goose Bumps!

"My best experience?" Anna J. says. "There have been so many! There was the time I was first introduced as an 'author'—what a thrill! There was that first letter I got from a stranger thanking me for my book. I will never forget the time a woman called me from a Chicago library. She told me she had read the review of my book in *Library Journal* and wanted to know how to order my book. I didn't know about the review (I got a letter from them later), and I got goose bumps while she talked to me.

"I think that the best experiences come when you least expect them... I was just recently at the 'Meet the Author' session of an international parenting conference. It felt so good to attend the sessions with a little green 'Author' ribbon attached to my nametag—somehow it seemed to validate so much of what I have done, but it was during lunch one day that I felt most honored. I could not find any parents I knew to eat with on the last day of the conference, so I just decided to eat at the first available table. I asked a woman sitting alone at a table if I could eat with her, introduced myself, and put my things down.

> ## Smart Tip
> Tip...
>
> Don't get so busy that you don't take the time to give back to your community. When you're asked to speak for free at a local writer's group or a school, say, "Yes!" It's an honor—and it's free publicity as well.

"When I came back from the buffet line," Anna recalls, "the lady said, 'I didn't realize who you were!' She then proceeded to tell me that her son had the same heart defect my son did, and that she had bought my book from a social worker in Boston. She told me that my book had helped her. There were over 1,000 people at that conference, and it catered to parents of children with mental retardation, autism, Down syndrome, and a host of other special problems. There were only a handful of us 'heart' parents there, so having this happen was quite extraordinary."

Honors

"Recently I was asked to attend some parenting conferences as a vendor," says Anna, the mother of two. "This was an honor to me because the doctors didn't charge me to attend their conferences—they let me set up a table free of charge and were very supportive. Perhaps the greatest honors to come from the medical field for me recently have been: 1) to write a chapter for a medical textbook (a chapter from a parent's perspective), and 2) to be a guest speaker at a major children's hospital for their first parenting conference. Not only was I asked to be a speaker, but I was also asked my opinion on topics to be addressed during the conference. When others value your opinion and want to hear what you have to say, that makes everything else worthwhile."

A Job Well-Done

This seems to be the attitude of all the self-publishers who so generously helped with this book—the joy in a job well-done and the desire to make a difference for others. If you go into this business with the right stuff—a willingness to work hard, to learn everything you can, the confidence to promote yourself and your business, and the drive to succeed—chances are you will.

Appendix A
One Day at a Time: Basics of the Publishing Process

So you've got a great idea for a book. You know in your heart you've got a winner. Now, you just need to realize the dream. But where do you start? No matter how much time you spend deciphering the ins and outs of book publishing, you can expect essentially the same basic steps to apply to the process:

- *Market research*. Take the time to make sure you have a saleable product. After all, the book business is a BUSINESS, which means you need to make money to survive. Spend time both online and in the bookstore researching similar, competitive titles. If you choose to shell out the money for it, this is the right time in your process to access Nielsen Bookscan and find out the most detailed sales information on your competitors.

- *Create a P&L.* A profit/loss statement is an essential tool in figuring your production and printing costs in relation to estimated income for the book.

- *Hire an author.* Most of the time, you will already have an author in mind (particularly if the book concept is one being shopped TO you), but this is the point at which you solidify your potential scribes so that you may prepare to extend an offer.

- *Extend a verbal offer and negotiate author's contract.* At this point, you will not only be negotiating money, but other essential elements of the author contract like due dates, payment dates, marketing responsibilities, author copies and discount, and subsidiary rights (like audio, script, etc.).

- *Execute contract.* All parties involved should receive an electronic or paper draft of the contract for final review. Many authors (and rightfully so) will want to have an agent or lawyer look over the legalese before signing their skills away, so be prepared to wait a few days and possibly to make edits to the document. Once everyone is in agreement, have them sign and date the final document, send copies for their records, and file the originals in your office. If an initial payment is due to the author, send it now.

- *Wait, wait, wait.* This is the hardest part for some publishers—to wait for the final manuscript. The writing process usually (hopefully) lasts only a few months, so be patient. It can be a good idea to arrange some interim due dates with your author to keep him on track and to be sure you are getting the manuscript you want, being mindful not to micromanage. If you do find that your author is not performing up to professional standards, you have options like extending the due date or termination of the contract. You DID specify non-performance options in the contract, right?

- *Request ISBN, LCCN, and CIP.* Log onto www.isbn.org and www.loc.gov to find out more about the process. Note that obtaining CIP information from the Library of Congress can take up to two weeks, so be sure to send in the appropriate information with enough lead time. Keep in mind that the Library of Congress does not typically provide CIP for single, self-published works, so make sure your book is eligible.

- *Premarketing.* What? I have to sell my book before it's actually book? You bet— and in the book trade, advanced marketing is truly the key to your sales success. For example, if you want your book reviewed by industry publications like Publishers Weekly, you must send pages about three months prior to the book's publication. This is the time to create and send advance press releases, send manuscript pages to publications for review, start doing the legwork for setting up author interviews, planning author appearances, and requesting advanced praise for the back cover copy. You will find that the time goes quickly, so don't burn daylight—get marketing!

- *Check availability of freelancers.* While the author (or you, if you're the one with your fingers on the laptop keys) is writing, now is the time to assemble your design team. You will need an editor (again, you, if you've got the skills), a cover designer, an interior designer, copyeditor or proofreader, and indexer. Many book designers offer multiple services, so shop around. If you are planning to hire freelancers you haven't worked with yet, be sure to check references and get plenty of samples of their work. And always use a contract that allows you to get your money back if you are not satisfied with the work or if important deadlines are missed.

- *Acceptance of manuscript.* If someone else is writing the manuscript, your contract should specify that you, as publisher, have a specific amount of time to either accept the manuscript as-is or request changes if the end product is far from your expectations. Thirty days is a typical amount of time for most publishers to accept a manuscript. This is typically the point where a publisher will make final payment to the author.

- *Manuscript edit.* This is your chance, as publisher, to mold the original manuscript into your ideal book. Ideally, there should be three rounds of editing: a substantive edit in which you consider the "big picture" and move chunks of text around and arrange chapters; a line edit in which you fix grammar, spelling, and clarity; and a copyedit in which you dot all the "i"s and cross all the "t"s.

- *Interior design.* Once the text is the way you want it, it's time for the interior designer to get to work. Trust your designer to create a look and feel of design elements that will complement your text. You will want to try out two to three different designs before deciding on one. Most designers will create some examples and allow one to two rounds of changes prior to your final decision.

- *Cover design.* Like interior designers, your cover designer will create examples based on the concept of the book for you to peruse and will allow a certain number of "rounds" in your selection process.

- *Author review.* Once the interior is designed, allow your author to view the pages and make any necessary editorial changes. The key word here is "necessary." Some authors have a nasty habit of trying to do an editor's or designer's job (or, better yet, thinking they know more than the pros), so be sure your author knows what you expect of him. Your author should be looking for factual errors and any major boo-boos that stand out or were missed by the copyeditor. We are, after all, human.

- *Indexing.* When all editorial and design changes have been made and you are absolutely sure the pages are complete, it's time to send them off to the indexer. This is a job that you should not attempt yourself unless you are trained to do so. Indexing is time-consuming, to say the least, so it pays to pay a professional. Turnaround time is usually about one to two weeks.

- *Send to printer.* The pages are designed and indexed, the cover is gorgeous, and you've backed up all files. Now, send your baby to "bed."

- *Digital prints/proofs.* A few weeks after you send files to the printer, you will receive digital prints, what used to be referred to as "bluelines," or "blues." These are unbound, uncut proofs of what your pages and cover will look like. This is your absolute, final chance to make any changes. At this point, you should only change items that MUST be fixed, like typos, incorrect page numbers, etc. Before you mark up your digital prints, though, know what your printer charges for changes. Some printers charge per page changed, and the cost can be as high as $100 per change. Other printers include a set amount of changes in your printing price. Be sure to ask. Most printers request that you turn around digital proofs in 1-2 days in order to keep your book in the printing queue.

- *BBD.* The bound book date, or BBD, is the date you have books in hand, available to sell.

Appendix B
The Grass Is Greener: Tips and Tricks for Great Grassroots Marketing

Most small and self-publishers don't have million dollar marketing budgets. Most publishers regardless of size, in fact, are on a fairly tight budget when it comes to spreading the word about their books. There are only so many hours a day and inches of copy that media outlets can devote to shameless self-promotion, which makes the competition tighter than Scrooge's wallet. Here are some tips to help you develop a strong grassroots marketing network.

- *Think locally.* For now, at least, put your dreams of the New York Times Bestseller List aside and work on making your book a hit on the local scene. Think of the process as a ripple effect. Success in your town breeds success in the neighboring town, then the next town, then the state, and so on. Focus on making lasting (i.e. for more than the release of your first book) relationships with the local media. In other words, do

▲

more than send out a press release. Get to know reporters, radio and TV personalities, and local bookstore owners on a personal level. Join a local organization like Rotary or Lions Club—you'll be surprised how the power of networking can spread the word about your book.

- *Make your book a component of a bigger news story.* It's all fine and dandy to send out a press release announcing the release of your latest book, but . . . zzzzzzz. Bo-ring! News people want NEWS, so give it to them. Focus your release on a timely event or current issue, then quote the author or yourself (as publisher) as an expert, citing the recently released book. For example, say you have a new book about the history of women's colleges. You do your homework and find a newly-released report that proves graduates of women's colleges earn more money and secure higher-ranking jobs. There's your release! Lead with the report and include quotes from the author about the importance of women's colleges. You've practically done the reporter's job for him.

- *Put your holiday greeting card list on steroids.* Beef it up! Create a database of everyone—and we mean EVERYONE—you know, from relatives to passing acquaintances to the people who work at your favorite coffee joint. Then, use the list for good. Send postcard announcements of a book's release, host a book reception, invite them to events. Most people will find they know more people than they think. And those people know people . . . and so it goes.

- *Get yourself some loyal fans, because they get results.* It pays to have friends and relatives beat the drums on your book's behalf by hounding their local booksellers to stock the book. Some discretion is necessary on their part, though. They don't need to explain that they are your third cousin on your mom's side twice-removed and they're just trying to help you out. They simply need to go in and ask about the book and tell the fine folks at the bookstore that they are looking forward to its release, as are their 100 best friends.

- *Think outside the bookstore and consider unconventional sales venues.* Most local businesses will agree to put a few copies of your book near the cash registers, even if books aren't their main source of revenue. Does your town have a local farmers' market or flea market? Look into scoring some booth space. What about any conventions or festivals nearby? Find out how you can get in the door. And bring that trusty friend database back into play by calling in some favors with local business people. Local libraries and places of worship often offer seminars and workshops, so find out how you can help out and do some cross-promotion at the same time.

- *Speaking of seminars, start offering them to your adoring public.* If you are a professional with a new book, you have at minimum ten different seminars in you. Create a brochure or prospectus-style booklet that details all of the workshops you offer. Distribute them to churches, colleges and universities, libraries, local civic clubs, the YMCA and YWCA . . . anyplace you can get a room filled with people. Many colleges and universities offer non-credit classes and are actively looking for people to teach them. All of these events offer ample opportunity to sell your books at the back of the room.

These are just a few ideas to kick-start your grassroots marketing efforts. Spend some time having your own personal "blue sky" meeting and brainstorm every crazy marketing idea you can conjure. Even if you walk away with ten feasible ideas out of the 100 you started with, that's ten great ideas you didn't have before!

Appendix C
Self-Publishing
Business Resources

The ultimate jackpot for the savvy, successful self-publisher is a wealth of resources—a publisher's clearinghouse of places to go and people to contact for information on everything from book fairs to wholesalers. We've compiled a list of resources to help get you started on your own personal information blitz.

These resources are a starting place. They are by no means the only sources out there, and they should not be taken as the "Ultimate Answer." We've done our research, but businesses—like people—do tend to move, change, fold, and expand. So as we've repeatedly stressed, do your homework. Get out and start investigating. Don't be afraid to ask questions. You'll be amazed at how much you'll learn!

As an additional tidbit to get you going, we strongly suggest the following: If you haven't yet joined the Internet Age, do it! Surfing

▲

the net is like waltzing through a vast library, with a breathtaking array of resources literally at your fingertips.

ABI Forms

R.R. Bowker, 630 Central Ave., New Providence, NJ 07974, (888) 269-5372, www.bowkerlink.com (Click on the "Books In Print" link on the left side of the web page.)

Associations

Association for Postal Commerce (Post Com), 1901 N. Fort Meyer Dr., #401, Arlington, VA 22209-1609, (703) 524-0096, www.postcom.org

American Booksellers Association, 200 White Plains Rd., Tarrytown, NY 10591, (800) 637-0037, (914) 591-2665, e-mail: info@bookweb.org, www.bookweb.org

American Library Association, 50 E. Huron St., Chicago, IL 60611, (800) 545-2433, www.ala.org

Association of Science Fiction and Fantasy Artists, P.O. Box 65011, Phoenix, AZ 85082-5011, www.asfa-art.org

The Direct Marketing Association (DMA), 1120 Avenue of the Americas, New York, NY 10036, (212) 768-7277, www.the-dma.org

Graphic Artists Guild, 32 Broadway, Suite 1114, New York, NY, (212) 791-3400, www.gag.org

National Association of Independent Publishers (NAIP), P.O. Box 430, Highland City, FL 33846-0430, (863) 648-4420

National Mail Order Association, 2807 Polk St. NE, Minneapolis, MN 55418-2954, (888) 496-7337 (for ordering books and reports only), (612) 788-1673, www.nmoa.org

National Speakers Association, 1500 S. Priest Dr., Tempe, AZ 85281, (480) 968-2552, www.nsaspeaker.org (This is the place to go if you're planning on doing paid seminars.)

Publishers Marketing Association (PMA), 627 Aviation Wy., Manhattan Beach, CA 90266, (310) 372-2732, www.pma-online.org

Small Publishers Association of North America (SPAN), 1618 W. Colorado Ave., Colorado Springs, CO 80904, (719) 475-1726, e-mail: span@SPANnet.org, www.spannet.org

Small Publishers, Artists and Writers Network (SPAWN), PMB 123, 323 E. Matilija St., Suite 110, Ojai, CA, 93023, (818) 886-4281, www.spawn.org

Society of Children's Book Writers and Illustrators, 8271 Beverly Blvd., Los Angeles, CA

Bookland Bar Codes

Bar Code Graphics Inc., 444 N. Michigan Ave. #3500, Chicago, IL 60611, (312) 595-0600, www.barcode-graphics.com

General Graphics, P.O. Box 3192, Arnold, PA 15068-0092, (800) 887-5894, www.ggbarcode.com

Book Clubs

Book of the Month Club, c/o Bookspan, 15 East 26th, 4th Floor, New York, NY 10010, www.bomc.com

The Literary Guild, www.literaryguild.com

Note: There are hundreds of book clubs to choose from—some are imprints of venerable Bookspan, while others are stand-alones. Check them all out via the Literary Market Place at www.literarymarketplace.com.

Book Designers and Cover Artists

Dunn + Associates Design, Kathi Dunn, P.O. Box 870, Hayward, WI 54843-0870, (715) 634-4857, www.dunn-design.com

Knockout Design, Peri Poloni-Gabriel, 5304 Velvet Bent Ct., Naperville, IL 60564, (630) 718-0861, www.knockoutbooks.com

Opus 1 Design, Pam Terry, Owner/Senior Designer, P.O. Box 3653, Beverly Hills, CA 90035, (800) 590-7778, (323) 935-6666, www.opus1design.com

Book Expos and Fairs

Book Expo America (BEA), www.bookexpoamerica.com

The Center for The Book (book fairs and other literary events), Library of Congress, http://lcweb.loc.gov/loc/cfbook/bookfair.html (Go to this terrific site for information on book fairs across America.)

Frankfurt (Germany) Book Fair, www.frankfurt-book-fair.com

Reed Exhibition Companies (handles four foreign book fairs as well as Book Expo America), www.reedexpo.com

Book Printers

Bang Printing, 3323 Oak Street, Brainerd, MN 56401, (800) 328-0450, (218) 829-2877, www.bangprinting.com

Central Plains Book Manufacturing, 22234 C St., Strother Field, Winfield, KS 67156, (877) 278-2726, www.centralplainsbook.com

Data Reproductions Corporation, 4545 Glenmeade Ln., Auburn Hills, MI 48326, (800) 242-3114, (248) 371-3700, www.datarepro.com

Hignell Book Printing, 488 Burnell St., Winnipeg, MB R3G 2B4, CAN, (800) 304-5553, (204) 784-1030, www.hignell.mb.ca

McNaughton & Gunn, 960 Woodland Dr., Saline, MI 48176, (734) 429-5411, www.bookprinters.com

Thomson-Shore Inc., 7300 W. Joy Rd., Dexter, MI 48130, (734) 426-3939, www.tshore.com

Books

The Complete Guide to Self-Publishing, by Tom and Marilyn Ross, F&W Publications Inc.

The Entrepreneur Next Door, by Bill Wagner, Entrepreneur Press

The Fine Print of Self-Publishing: The Contracts & Services of 48 Self-Publishing Companies—Analyzed, Ranked, and Exposed, by Mark Levine, Bascom Hill Publishing Group

Guerilla Marketing for Writers: 100 Weapons to Help Sell Your Work, by Jay Conrad Levinson, Writer's Digest Books

Jump-Start Your Book Sales: A Money-Making Guide for Authors, Independent Publishers and Small Presses, by Marilyn and Tom Ross, Writer's Digest Books

Kirsch's Handbook of Publishing Law: For Authors, Publishers, Editors and Agents, by Jonathan Kirsch, Silman-James Press

Literary Market Place, R.R. Bowker, www.literarymarketplace.com

Print-on-Demand Book Publishing: A New Approach to Printing and Marketing Books for Publishers and Self-Publishing Authors, by Morris Rosenthal, Foner Books

The Self-Publishing Manual: How to Write, Print and Sell Your Own Book, by Dan Poynter, Para Publishing

Ultimate Guide to Direct Marketing, by Al Lautenslager, Entrepreneur Press

Consultants

About Books Inc., 1618 W. Colorado Ave., Colorado Springs, CO, 80904, (719) 632-8226, www.about-books.com

Mary Embree, (805) 643-6279, e-mail: embreebooks@earthlink.net

Para Publishing, Dan Poynter, Box 8206-240, Santa Barbara, CA 93118-8206, (805) 968-7277, www.parapublishing.com

Copy Editors and Proofreaders

Archer Editorial Services, Laura Poole, Senior Editor, 112 Blue Ridge Ct., Durham, NC 27703, (919) 596-7047, www.archereditorial.com

Bibliotechnica, 119 Middle St., Hadley, MA 01035, (413) 586-4267, bibliotechnica.com

Quinn's Word for Word Editorial Services, 10573 W. Pico Blvd., #345, Los Angeles, CA 90064, (310) 838-7098, e-mail: quinnrobin@aol.com

Distributors

BookWorld Services Inc., 1941 Whitfield Park Loop, Sarasota, FL 34243, (941) 758-8094, www.bookworld.com

Consortium Book Sales & Distribution, 1045 Westgate Dr., #90, St. Paul, MN 55114, (800) 283-3572, (651) 221-9035, www.cbsd. com

Independent Publishers Group (IPG), 814 N. Franklin St., Chicago, IL 60610, (312) 337-0747 (trade or publisher inquiries), www.ipgbook.com

Partners, 2325 Jarco Drive, P.O. Box 580, Holt, MI 48842, (517) 694-3205, (800) 336-3137

Publishers Group West, 1700 Fourth St., Berkeley, CA 94710, (800) 788-3123, (510) 528-1444, www.pgw.com

Quality Books, 1003 W. Pines Rd., Oregon, IL 61061, (800) 323-4241, www.quality-books.com

Unique Books, 5010 Kemper Ave, St. Louis, MO 63139, (800) 533-5446, www.unique booksinc.com

e-Publishers

Booklocker, www.booklocker.com

eBook Shoppe, www.ebookshoppe.com

Bookface Technologies, www.bookface.com

Helpful Government Agencies

Bureau of the Census, www.census.gov

Federal Trade Commission, www.ftc.gov

Library of Congress, www.loc.gov (For ISSNs, LCCNs, CIP data blocks and other Library of Congress services, click on "Resources for Publishers.")

Patent and Trademark Office, (800) 786-9199, (571) 272-1000, www.uspto.gov

U.S. Copyright Office, (202) 707-3000, www.copyright.gov

U.S. Postal Service, (800) 843-8777, www.usps.com

ISBN and SAN Provider

R.R. Bowker, www.bowker.com (Click on "Bowker Publisher Services.") or www.isbn.org

Magazines and Publications

ALA Booklist, 50 E. Huron St., Chicago, IL 60611, (800) 545-2433 www.ala.org

BookWire (an e-zine from R.R. Bowker, the people who bring you Books in Print, ISBNs, and other publishers' tools), www.bookwire.com

Choice, 100 Riverview Center, Suite 298, Middletown, CT 06457, (860) 347-6933, www.ala. org/acrl/choice/home.html

ForeWord Magazine, 129-1/2 E. Front St., Traverse City, MI 49684, (231) 933-3699, www.forewordmagazine.com

Library Journal, 360 Park Ave. South, New York, NY 10010, (646) 746-6819, www.libraryjournal.com

Publishers Weekly, 360 Park Ave. South, New York, NY, 10010, (646) 746-6758, www.publishersweekly.com

Sharing Ideas, Walters International Speakers Bureau, P.O. Box 398, Glendora, CA 91740-0398, (626) 335-8069, www.walters-intl.com

Speaker, National Speakers Association, 1500 S. Priest Dr., Tempe, AZ 85281, (480) 968-2552, www.nsaspeaker.org

Target Marketing, North American Publishing Company, 1500 Spring Garden Street, 12th Floor, Philadelphia, PA 19130, (215) 238-5300, www.targetonline.com or www.napco.com

Writer's Digest, 4700 E. Galbraith Road, Cincinnati, OH 45236, (513) 531-2690, www.writersdigest.com

Note: Most magazines will send a sample issue free of charge if you call and ask. So do it!

Mailing Lists

Allmedia Inc., 6900 Dallas Parkway, Suite 750, Plano, TX 75024, (800) 466-4061, (469) 467-9100, www.allmediainc.com

American List Counsel, 4300 Route 1, CN-5219, Princeton, NJ 08543, (800) ALC-LIST, (609) 580-2800, www.alc.com

Info USA, (800) 321-0869, www.infousa.com

Note: Check into any issue of magazines like *Catalog Age* or *Target Marketing*—advertisements for list brokers, managers, and owners abound.

Merchant Card Services

1st American Card Service.com, www.1stamericancardservice.com

Merchant Express, 20 Trafalgar Square, Suite 466, Nashua, NH, 03063, (888) 845-9457, www.merchantexpress.com

Print On Demand

iUniverse.com, www.iuniverse.com

Lightning Source, 1246 Heil Quaker Blvd., La Vergne, TN 37086, (615) 213-5815, www.lightningsource.com

Trafford Publishing, 6E-2333 Government St., Victoria, BC V8T 4P4, CAN, (888) 232-4444, (250) 383-6864, www.trafford.com

Xlibris, International Plaza II, Suite 340, Philadelphia, PA 19113-1513, (888) 795-4274, www.xlibris.com

Shipping Supplies

Anchor Box Co., 5889 S. Gessner Rd., Houston, TX 77036, (800) 522-8820, (713) 977-3100, www.anchorbox.com

Associated Bag Company, 400 W. Boden St., Milwaukee, WI 53207-0120, (800) 926-6100, www.associatedbag.com

▲

Software for Publishers

Adobe PageMaker and Adobe InDesign, Adobe Systems Inc., www.adobe.com

Quark Xpress, Quark, www.quark.com

Publishers' Assistant, 41 Lawrence Heights, Jericho, VT 05465, (800) 310-8716, www.pubassist.com

Publishing Manager, Trilogy Group, www.trilogypublishing.com

Publishing Solutions, Quality Solutions, Inc., 44 Merrimac St., Newburyport, MA 01950, (800) 779-7345, www.qsolution.com

PUB123, Adams-Blake Publishing, 8041 Sierra St., #102, Fair Oaks, CA 95628, (916) 962-9296, www.adams-blake.com

Note: Most small software vendors will send you a free or nominally priced demo if you ask. This doesn't apply to the big-ticket goodies like Adobe PageMaker. For these, you might do better in terms of price and returnability to purchase from a local office supply warehouse or software center.

Successful Self-Publishers

Steve Carlson, Upper Access Inc., 87 Upper Access Road, Hinesburg, VT 05461, (800) 310-8320, (802) 482-2988, www.upperaccess.com

Anna Jaworski, Baby Hearts Press, 3910 Sierra Blanca, Temple, TX 76502, (888) 222-4649, (254) 778-4770, www.babyheartspress.com

Wholesalers

Baker & Taylor, 2550 West Tyvola Road, Suite 300, Charlotte, NC 28217, (800) 775-1800, (704) 998-3100, www.btol.com

Bookpeople, 7900 Edgewater Dr., Oakland, CA 94621, (510) 632-4700, www.bponline.com

National Book Network, 4501 Forbes Blvd., Suite 200, Lanham, MD 20706, (301) 459-3366, www.nbnbooks.com

New Leaf, 401 Thornton Rd., Lithia Springs, GA 30122 (770) 948-7845, www.newleaf-dist.com

Workshops and Seminars

Publishers Marketing Association, 627 Aviation Wy., Manhattan Beach, CA 90266, (310) 372-2732; www.pma-online.org

Santa Barbara Publishing Workshops, Dan Poynter, P.O. Box 8206-240, Santa Barbara, CA 93118-8206, (805) 968-7277, www.parapublishing.com

Small Publishers Association of North America (SPAN), 1618 West Colorado Ave., Colorado Springs, CO 80904, (719) 475-1726, www.spannet.org

Small Publishers, Artists and Writers Network (SPAWN), 323 E. Matilija St., Suite 110, Ojai, CA 93023, (818) 886-4281, www.spawn.org

Glossary

ABA: American Booksellers Association.

Acquisition editor: a publishing company editor who scouts out potential new acquisitions.

Back matter: all pages in a book after the main body of text.

Back-of-the-room sales: see BOR.

Bleed: the area of a page that will be lost when a book is bound.

Bluelines: page proofs printed on white paper with blue ink.

Bookland EAN: bar code for books.

BOR: back-of-the-room sales; books and/or other merchandise that are sold by seminar professionals at a seminar or workshop.

Bound galley: a perfect-bound set of galleys.

C1S: cover coated on one side; a type of paper stock used for soft-cover books.

Camera ready: ready to be photographed and printed.

Case bound: hardcover.

Cataloging in Publication record: see CIP.

▲

CIP: Cataloging in Publication record; a block of information helpful to librarians that includes a book's shelf category and catalog numbers.

Color separation: printing technique in which color artwork is photographed and separated into four different-colored layers of film.

Comb binding: a type of plastic binding.

Content editor: see copy editor.

Copy: text; written material in a manuscript.

Copy editor: editor who evaluates manuscripts in terms of content, style, and continuity.

Custom publishing: tailoring a book for a specific customer.

Dead tree book: slang term meaning conventionally printed book as opposed to an e-published book.

Direct mail: mail order.

Disk to film: book material sent to the printer on a CD or zip disc and ready to be transferred to film.

Dump: a cardboard display stand.

e-Book reader: hardware device for reading downloadable books.

F&Gs: folded and gathered signature pages of a book.

Fiction: a tale invented for the purpose of entertainment.

First serial rights: serial rights sold before the publication date.

Folio: page number.

Font: typestyle.

Foreign rights: the rights to publish a book in a foreign English-speaking country.

Four-color: printing process that utilizes black, yellow, blue, and red to produce all the colors in the spectrum.

Front matter: all pages before the main body of text.

Fulfillment: filling orders for books or merchandise and shipping them to customers.

Galleys: page proofs from the printer—the final copy before a print run.

Ghostwriter: writer who pens a book for someone else to put his name to as author.

Gloss lamination: a glossy cover stock laminated for protection from fingerprints, smudges, and moisture.

Half title page: the first standard page in a book; contains the title and subtitle.

Halftone: a printing technique in which artwork is photographed through a fine screen to increase sharpness and clarity.

HTML: hypertext markup language; a language used to put up and edit web site content.

Imprint: the identifying name of a publishing company under a parent company.

Independent publisher: a small publisher who may produce his own work and/or those of other authors.

International Standard Book Number: see ISBN.

International Standard Serial Number: see ISSN.

ISBN: International Standard Book Number; assigned by publishers and used to identify a book by edition, binding, and publisher.

ISSN: International Standard Serial Number; assigned by the Library of Congress to identify serials.

Lay-flat laminate: a type of laminated cover stock that won't curl up when exposed to humidity.

LCCN: Library of Congress Catalog Card Number; used by librarians to identify and order books.

Leading: the space between lines of text, measured from the bottom of one line to the bottom of the next.

Library binding: a heavy-duty binding designed for repeated readings.

Library of Congress Catalog Card Number: see LCCN.

Listserv: e-mail message-sharing group.

Major head: headline that defines the topic of a section in a book.

Mass market paperback: a paperback book with a trim size of 4.5 inches by 6.75 inches; the size of paperbacks commonly found in supermarket and drug store racks.

Match print: color-copy page proofs.

Matte lamination: a non-glossy cover stock laminated for protection from fingerprints, smudges, and moisture.

NAIP: National Association of Independent Publishers.

Nonfiction: fact-based book.

North American rights: the rights to sell a book in the United States and Canada.

OEB: open e-book language; used to produce some e-book content.

Overs and unders: a 10 percent margin over or under the number of books a printer has been commissioned to print.

Overruns: extra copies of a book's cover.

Page proofs: final before-printing copy of a book provided by a printer for error-checking.

Pantone Matching System: see PMS.

P-book: conventionally printed book as opposed to an e-published book.

P-CIP: CIP made up by a publisher or its agent instead of by the Library of Congress.

PCN: Pre-assigned Card Number; what the Library of Congress calls an LCCN until the book is printed.

PDF: Portable Document Format.

Perfect binding: softcover bookbinding in which the cover is glued onto the page ends.

Periodical: magazine or journal.

PMA: Publisher's Marketing Association.

PMS: Pantone Matching System; a standard set of ink colors used by printers.

POD: print on demand; the process of printing a book one page at a time instead of by 16- or 32-page signatures.

Point-of-purchase display: see dump.

POP: see point-of-purchase display.

Pre-assigned Card Number: see PCN.

Premium: a book or other merchandise given away by a company or organization for promotional purposes.

Print on demand: see POD.

Proofreader: evaluates a manuscript for correct spelling, punctuation, and grammar.

Publication date: a hypothetical book premiere date set by a publisher, generally six weeks to two months after the book is delivered by the printer; also called "pub date."

Pull quote: an interesting phrase or sentence from your text that is "pulled" and reprinted elsewhere on the page.

Request for quote: see RFQ.

Recto: right-hand page.

Reprint: another printing of a book.

Revised edition: another printing of a book in which significant changes have been made.

RFQ: request for quote or bid from a printer.

Running head: book or title chapter that runs across the top of each page of a book.

Saddle-stitch binding: bookbinding achieved by stapling through the center of the pages of a book.

SAN: Standard Address Number; used to identify industry entities and give billing and shipping information.

Second serial rights: rights sold after the publication date.

Serial: ongoing or frequently revised publication such as a magazine, newspaper, annual, or directory.

Sidebar: mini-articles that are one-quarter page to one-half page in length; inserted on the page to complement the text.

Signature: a huge sheet of paper used by book printers on which 16 or 32 pages are laid out and run through the press at once.

Small press: see independent publisher.

SPAN: Small Publishers Association of North America.

SPAWN: Small Publishers, Artists, and Writers Network.

Special Standard Mail: book rate postage; less expensive than regular postage.

Spiral binding: a type of wire binding.

Standard Address Number: see SAN.

Stock: paper.

Subhead: headline smaller than a major head that defines a sub-topic within a book section.

Subsidiary rights: the rights to publish a book in various other forms.

▲

Subsidy publisher: a company that charges money to publish an author's book; also called "vanity publisher."

Tip box: one-sentence to one-paragraph factoids that can be scattered throughout your text to add information or interest.

Trade paperback: larger or "quality" format softcover book, generally 6 inches by 9 inches to 5.5 inches by 8.5 inches.

Translation rights: the rights to translate a book into a foreign language.

Trim size: outside dimensions of a book.

Vanity publisher: see subsidy publisher.

Velo binding: a type of plastic binding.

Verso: left-hand page.

Work for hire: a method of payment for writing; the writer is paid a flat fee instead of royalties.

Index

A

Accountant, hiring an, 47, 171
Acquisition of self-published
    books by major publishers, 7,
    174–176
Advance, author, 6
Advanced Book Information (ABI)
    form, 79–80
Advertising and marketing,
    147–160
Advice
    expert, 46–47
    from successful self-publishing
        entrepreneurs, 182–187
Amazon.com, selling through,
    130
Anthologies or collections, 27–28
Appendix A, basics of the publish-
    ing process, 189–192
Appendix B, tips and tricks for
    great grassroots marketing,
    193–195

Appendix C, self-publishing busi-
    ness resources, 197–205
Attorney, hiring an, 46–47
Audiobooks, 93–94
    production costs, 95
Author tours, 141
Autobiography, perils of, 23

B

Back list, 20
Back-of-the-room (BOR) sales at
    seminars/workshops/lectures,
    21
    and product merchandising, 96
    audiobooks, 93
    video productions, 95–96
Backgrounds of self-publishers,
    11–13
Bank financing, 72
Bar code system, book, 78, 79
Bestseller, anatomy of a, 21–22
Blockbusters, emphasis on, 5

Blurbs, book, 103
Book announcement, sample, 135
Book club sales, 178
Book fairs (trade shows) as invaluable promotional and networking tool, 150–151
Book limbo, 4
Book proposal as business plan, 15, 16
Book signings, 144–145
Bookland EAN number with price code, 79
Books sales, projected growth of, 4
Bookstore
    research, 39
    sales, billion dollar, 12
    sales, direct, 127–128
Bound galleys with announcement to reviewers, 135–138, 140
Business cards, company, 45
Business structure, establishing your publishing house, 41–47

C

Career jump-starter, self-published books as, 6–7
Cataloging in Publication (CIP)/(P-CIP) records, 81–82
Children's picture book, 27
Cinderella scenario, 126, 174–176
Clarity sells, 34
Co-authors, 101
Commercial office, 50–51
    outfitting your, 51
    worksheet, 50
Competition, researching your, 38–39
Computer system, 54–59
Consultant career jump-starter, self-published books as, 6–7
Cookbooks, 24
Copier, 61
Copy editors, 76–77
Copyrights, 57, 97
Cover
    as sales pitch, 112
    back, 113–114

    binding, 116–117
    book, 74–75
    design, 112–117
    front, 112–113
    specs, 116
    spine, 114–115
    stock, 115
Creative control, benefits of maintaining, 4, 5–6
Creativity, 11
Credit card
    electronic sales terminal, 61–62
    financing, 72
Customized publishing or premiums, 130–131

D

Definition of self-publisher, 2–3, 5
Demographic research, 36, 38
Design elements, checklist of, 111
Designers, book cover, 75, 79
Digital camera, 57
Direct mail
    advertising, 151–157
    book sales, 20–21
Distributors
    and wholesalers, how it works, 120–126
    bypassing, 21
    interviewing potential, 122
    PMA special "Trade Distribution Acceptance Program" to help newcomers, 126
    what will make them want to represent you?, 121, 126
Drawbacks to self-publishing, 5

E

e-publishing, 15, 17, 26, 96–98
    book readers, 98
    downloadable format from your web site, 97
    going with an established provider, 98
    the potential of, 28–30

Earnings
    over expenses, 6
potential, 8–9, 166 (*See also* Finances)
Editors as minions of marketing depart-
    ments, 5
Electronic credit card terminal, 61
    fees, 62, 163
Embree, Mary, 14, 16
Equipment expenses checklist, 69
Exhilaration and panic, 100–101
Expertise, self-publishing as a vehicle to
    establish your, 9

F

Famous self-published authors, 2, 20
Fax machines, 59
Fiction
    commercially viable, 25–26
    formats, 26–27
    specialized, 26
Film rights, 178–179
Finances
    annual book profits, sample, 169
    annual income/expense statement, sam-
        ple, 167
    bottom line (calculating annual pro-
        jected income/expenses) worksheet,
        170
    controlling your, 161–172
    income and expense statement (profit
        and loss), 164–166
    loan repayment, 164
    operating expenses, 162–164
    projected annual income/expense state-
        ment, sample, 168
    raising your income, 166
    start-up, 53–72
Focus, narrowing your book's, 32, 34
Follow-through, 11
Foreign markets, rights or translations,
    178
ForeWord, 68
Friends and family financing, 72

Front list, 20
Fry, Patricia, 14–17
Future of self-publishing industry, 17

G

Ghostwriters, 101
Glossary, 207–212
Good writing, 12
Graphic artists, hiring, 75, 79
Growth
    of self-publishing industry, 1–2, 8
    of your company, 28, 179–180
Guest spots, media, 141–144

H

Happiness factor, 184–185
Heart defects, books inspired by and
    related to child's, 7–8, 13
Home office, 47–50
    insurance, 68
    organizing your, 48–50
    tax deductions and your, 48
    worksheet, 49
Horror story niche, 12–13
How-to books, 24

I

Illustrator, hiring an, 75–76
Image
    creating a company, 42–45
    software, 57–58
Incorporating, 45
    inspirational/motivational books, 15, 24
Insurance
    agent, 47
    coverage, 68
International Standard Book Numbers
    (ISBNs), 58, 77–78, 79
    anatomy of a, 90
*International Standard Serial Numbers
    (ISSNs)*, 78–79
Internet
    as leveling the writer's playing field, 26
    publishing, the potential of, 28–30

▲

sales and promotion, 158–160
service provider, 56, 163
Interview with SPAWN's Patricia Fry,
    14–17

J
Juvenile books, 15

L
Laying your foundation, 45–47
Layout and design decisions
    back matter, 106–107
    bleeds, 109
    body, the, 106
    book design elements, checklist of, 111
    chapters titles, heads and sub-heads,
        110
    cover, 112–117
    front matter, 103–104
    ink color, 108
    inside pages, 103–110
    layout checklist, 105
    leading, 110
    margins, 110
    page count, 102–103
    paper stock, 108
    points, 109
    running heads, 110
    signatures, 102–103
    trim size, 107–108
Leading, 110
Lectures, 21
Letterhead, company, 44–45
Libraries and educational markets, 129,
    130
*Library of Congress Catalog Card Number
    (LCCN)*, 80–81, 82
Licenses/permits, business, 45, 46
Listservs, 35–36, 65
Logo, creating a distinctive company,
    44–45
Love, doing it for, 8
Loving what you do, 184

M
Mail order
    catalogs, 131
    promotion, 151–157
    sales, 20–21
Mailing lists, 155–156
Making a difference, 7–8
Market research, 15–16, 31–39
    guidelines, 32
    survey, sample of, 37
Marketing, tips for great grassroots,
    193–195
Media interviews, 141–144
Memoir, 14–15, 23
Merchandising, book tie-in product, 96
Mission statement, 46
More bang for your book, 93–96
Moxie, your, 5
Muse, answering the call of the creative, 8
Museum shop sales, 132

N
Naming your business, 42–44
    brainstorming worksheet, 43
    choosing and registering your internet
        domain name, 43, 44
    registering your fictitious "doing busi-
        ness as" (DBA) name, 42–43
Net etiquette, 158–160
Networking
    organizations, 16
    through professional organizations,
        64–65
Niche
    expanding your, 179–180
    finding your, 33–34
    markets, focusing on, 2–3
    publishers, moving from self-published
        to, 9
Nielsen Bookscan, 33, 38
Non-fiction
    as bigger seller than fiction, 15

as constant seller, 24
definition of, 22
edge, 22–25
format, 24–25
improving quality of life niche, 12
male *vs.* female readership of, 22
Non-profit
corporation, 45
organizations, 131
Novel, 26
Novella, 26
Novice, travails of a, 3–4

O
Office
establishing your publishing house,
41–51
furnishings, 61, 63
supplies mini-shopping list, 65
Office equipment checklist, self-pub-
lisher's, 66
Order form/publisher contact information,
107
Order form/reply card, sample, 158
Other writers' books, 28, 179–18
Out-of-copyright books, 27
Outsourcing options, 27–28

P
Paper, 63, 108, 163–164
Partnership, 45
Penny dreadfuls, 25
Permissions, 101
Personality traits for succeeding in self-
publishing, 10–11
Phone system and voice mail, 59–60,
162–163
Poetry, 28
Points, type, 109
Positioning yourself as an expert in your
field through a self-published book, 9
Postage, 63
Pre-assigned Card Number (PCN), 81

Pre-production basics, 74–77
Pricing and selling, 119–132
Amazon.com, 130
bottom line, 124
considering shipping costs, 125
customized publishing or premiums,
130–131
discounts, divvying up, 120–126
dumps/point-of-purchase (POP) displays, 128–129
freebies, promotional, 129
libraries and educational markets, 129
mail order catalogs, 131
museum shops, 132
returns and damages, 125–127
specialty stores and boutiques, 131–132
sticker price, 120
trade sales and alternative venues, 127–132
Print runs, 6
Print-on-demand (POD) self publishing
services, 15
Printers, computer, 58–59
Printing your book, 82–93
advice on selecting the right printer,
84–85, 88
alternative formats, 93–96
color illustrations, 84
determining format, 88–89
determining vital statistics, 83–84
price quote from a printer, sample,
86–87
price quotes, 82–84, 91
print on demand (POD), 90–93
print runs, costs for, 89–90
print runs, overruns and underpins, 90
printer contract, 88
proofing printer pages, 89
shrink-wrapping, 90
typesetting, 88–89
Production costs, 73–98
sample of two hypothetical small
presses, 85

worksheet, 91

Professional organizations, membership in, 64–65, 67

Professional speaking career jump-starter, self-published books as, 6–7

Profit potential, 8–9

Profits, author's, 6

Promotion, 133–145

and sales, taking control of your own through self-publishing, 4, 11

Promotional
budgets, first time author's lack of in major publishing houses, 3–4

chutzpah, 11

Proofreaders, 77

Pub date and promotional activity, 134

Publicist, hiring a, 142

Publicity, 133–145

Publishers Marketing Association (PMA), 67

"Trade Distribution Acceptance Program" to help newcomers, 126

Publishers Weekly, 68

Publishing process, basics of, 189–192

Publishing somebody else's book, 180

Q

Quick quote, sample of, 83

R

Reader base, researching your, 34–35

Reasons to self-publish, 5–8

Regional books, 24

Religious/spiritual topics, 15

Reprints, 81

Request for quote (RFQ), 82–84, 90, 91

quick quote, 83, 91

Returns and damages, 125–127

Reviews
general interest, 138

post-publication promotional package, 139–141

pre-publication/advance, 134–139

trade, 136–138

Revised editions, 81

Risk factors, 10

Royalties, author, 6

S

Sales letter, 153–155

sample, 154

Sales tax license/permit, 46

Self-help books, 24

Self-publishing *101*, 19–30

Selling a product you truly believe in, your own books, 11

Selling other goods and services, positioning yourself to, 9

Selling out, journey from self-publishing to acquisition of your book by a traditional houses, 7, 174–176

Seminar, workshop or lecture
back-of-the-room (BOR) sales, 21, 157

promotions, 20–21, 157–158

Serials, 26–27

International Standard Serial Numbers (ISSNs), 78–79

selling rights, 177

Shipping
costs, 125, 127

supplies, 63

Short story format, 26

Small Publishers Association of North America (SPAN), 65, 67

Software, 12, 55–56, 57–58, 106

Sole proprietorship, 45

SPAWN (Small Publishers, Artists and Writers Network), 14, 16, 64

Speaker career jump-starter, self-published books as, 6–7

Specialty stores and boutiques, selling to, 131–132

Standard Address Numbers (SANs), 58

Start-up
expenses checklist, 70

finances, 53–72
Start-up costs, 9–10
    worksheet, 71
Statistics, citing sources, 101
Storage space, 50–51, 127
Subsidiary rights, 176–179
Subsidy publishers *vs.* self-publishing, 20
Success
    advice from self-publishing entrepre-
        neurs for achieving, 182–185
    and failure, tales of, 185–187
    creating your own definition of, 4
    tips for self-publishing, 184
Successful self-publishers, professional
    backgrounds of, 11–13
Surge protector, 61
Surveys, direct-mail and telephone, 34–36

T
Talent, 11
Tapping into writing talent large publish-
    ers won't take a chance on, 13
Target market, 11–15, 33–34
Tax deductions, 48, 171–172
Tip boxes, 106
Trade magazines, subscriptions to, 67–68
Trends in small publishing industry, 14

U
Uninterruptible power supply (UPS),
    60–61
Unsolicited manuscripts, 13

V
Vanity publishing *vs.* self-publishing, 20
Video productions, 95–96

W
Web site
    design and hosting, 56–57, 163
    your company, 158–160
Wholesalers
    and distributors, how it works, 120–126
    interviewing potential, 123

Word-of-mouth advertising, 148–149
Workers' compensation insurance, 46
Workshops, 21
World War II veterans, biographies of, 13,
    34
Writer's Digest, 68
Writing
    and designing your book, 99–117
    articles for magazines as promotional
        tool, 149–150
    101, 100–101

Y
Young adult books, 15

Z
Zoning regulations, 48

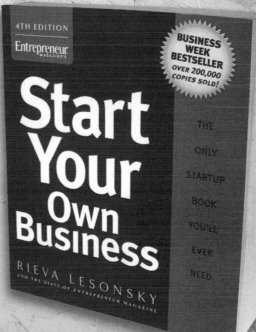